To John Smith

A good friend — one who
has helped one in so
many ways

Wishing you excellent
salads and great wines

Cheers

Bob [illegible]

ROBERT E. LINNEMAN
TEMPLE UNIVERSITY

SHIRT-SLEEVE APPROACH TO LONG-RANGE PLANNING FOR THE SMALLER, GROWING CORPORATION

PRENTICE-HALL, INC.
Englewood Cliffs, New Jersey 07632

Library of Congress Cataloging in Publication Data

LINNEMAN, ROBERT E

Shirt-sleeve approach to long-range planning for the smaller, growing corporation.

Includes bibliographical references and index.

1. Corporate planning. I. Title.

HD30.28.L55 658.4'01 79-9091

ISBN 0-13-808972-8

Editorial/production supervision and interior design by Alice Erdman.
Cover design by James M. Wall, Inc.
Manufacturing buyer: Harry Baisley.

Printed in the United States of America

10 9 8 7 6 5 4 3 2 1

PRENTICE-HALL INTERNATIONAL, INC., *London*
PRENTICE-HALL OF AUSTRALIA PTY. LIMITED, *Sydney*
PRENTICE-HALL OF CANADA, LTD., *Toronto*
PRENTICE-HALL OF INDIA PRIVATE LIMITED, *New Delhi*
PRENTICE-HALL OF JAPAN, INC., *Tokyo*
PRENTICE-HALL OF SOUTHEAST ASIA PTE. LTD., *Singapore*
WHITEHALL BOOKS LIMITED, *Wellington, New Zealand*

To the many seminar participants
who contributed so much,
and, of course, to Annabelle

Contents

Preface

Some claim that man knows 2,000,000 times more about the universe today than he did in Galileo's times. Furthermore, our knowledge is said to double every fifteen years. The effects of this extraordinary increase are both traumatic and far-reaching. As the economist Kenneth Boulding has said: "The world today... is as different from the world in which I was born as that world was from Julius Caesar's. I was born in the middle of human history.... Almost as much has happened since I was born as before."[1]

One consequence of this frenetic rate of change is that age-old methods of forecasting using trend lines seem less valid today than in previous generations. Indeed, the awareness of rapid change and its effects is reflected in the virtual "canonization" of Peter Drucker's *The Age of Discontinuities* and Alvin Tofler's *Future Shock.*

Rapid change has also altered the life cycle of many goods and services. A few hundred years ago a manufacturer could count on the need for his products throughout his lifetime, his children's lifetime, and his grandchildren's lifetime as well. This time period has telescoped —gradually at first, but at an ever-accelerating rate.

As a result, many executives now realize that if their companies are to grow, or even survive, they must adapt to change—rapidly.

And they also realize that readiness for change must be planned for. Consequently, executives who would never have considered long-range strategic planning a few years ago are now seeking effective ways to implement such planning in their companies.

The purpose of this book is to present general procedures for adapting strategic planning into the corporate structure. And as a consequence, most of the emphasis in this book is on long-range strategic planning. Yet there are chapters which suggest how shorter-range planning, implementation, and control can be carried out within the corporation and, of course, be meshed with the longer-range plan.

This book is designed especially for the smaller, growing business; for the company which is centrally organized and has annual sales ranging from 2 to 75 million dollars. Although the procedures are geared for planning at the corporate level, and particularly for the smaller, growing business, they apply to virtually any situation which requires planning.

Intended as a "how-to-do-it" manual for the practitioner, the book fills something of a void. There are many theoretical studies on planning, but few which really explain how to go about it. The idea for the book arose from seminars on corporate planning which I have given over the past several years. As I talked with presidents and managers interested in developing a comprehensive system of corporate planning—and who wanted some practical help in doing so—the need for such a book became apparent.

Unfortunately, too much of planning as it now exists is mechanical, a sort of fill-in-the-square approach. And that is too bad, because the real value in planning lies in the thinking it generates by the people who must carry out the plans. When management is involved, plans are more likely to be realistic. Furthermore, the plans will be more likely to succeed because—since management has been part of the development—they will be more likely to roll up their shirt sleeves and make the plan work under constantly changing conditions.

This book encourages a "shirt-sleeve" approach to planning. The point is to get management involved, and in a way that doesn't sap the time management needs for operating duties. The approach also shows how to deal with the uncertain business future in a positive and creative way. The procedures stem from the experiences of practitioners. Consequently, the recommendations are not "ivory tower": they have met the test of reality.

Although there were many people who helped me with the preparation of this book, I'd like to give special thanks to John D. Kennell, who helped steer me toward the shirt-sleeve approach; Alpha G. Witt and Professor Paul Dauten who taught me much about management; Professors Lloyd DeBoer, and Harvey "Hix" Huegy, who were so instructive in so many ways; Felix Braendel, who contributed so much with his deft editing of the many drafts; and Naomi Elliott, who spent many hours on the typewriter.

1

Benefits of Comprehensive Corporate Planning

Why consider formal comprehensive planning?

There are two overwhelming reasons: Businesses that do generally (1) grow faster and (2) make more money. It's easy to see why. The end results of formal planning—explicit, written-out specific objectives, plans, control points, and backup contingency plans—give you a clear understanding of your company and a firmer control over its future.

But by itself a formal plan is not enough. Consider an incident that occurred several years ago. The director of marketing of a medium-sized bank, with the help of a consultant, developed a formal procedure for locating branch banks. The director of marketing presented the finished "model" to the bank's president, who was excited about the procedure: "This is the most creative piece of work I've seen since I've been with this bank. Implement it." The director of marketing then explained the procedure to other divisions (real estate, branch banking, and so forth). Everybody understood their roles. But one year later the model was junked, its very title a dirty word. Actually, the model was a good one. It failed because most of the bank's executives really didn't care whether or not it succeeded. In fact, because of existing rivalries, some were more interested in seeing it fail. When something went wrong, they wouldn't put forth extra effort to correct it. It wasn't *their* plan, after all.

This dismal case points to a significant truth: Only people who are involved in drafting plans are going to try their best to make the plans succeed. The key is managerial involvement. Nothing flatters people more than being taken seriously, and there is no better way to take managers seriously than to bring them into the planning process. The sense of a shared challenge and real responsibility helps generate a climate that encourages extra effort—as well as stimulating creativity and fostering a positive attitude toward change.

Moreover, the very process of involving management in formal planning improves communications, thereby pulling management together. The assembling of information from all vital areas enlarges managers' understanding of overall company operations. This increased knowledge makes it easier not only to spot problems but to see possible solutions. Beyond that, it makes it easier to see new opportunities—opportunities that might never occur to managers who remain isolated (comparatively) in their own domains.

Since planning and reviews will be scheduled at regular intervals, a formal approach also assures continuity. Of course, merely granting an adequate amount of time and effort to the process does not guarantee thoroughness, but it makes it possible. Because planning occurs on a regular basis, managers gradually become better planners.

Finally, planning *is* managing. Formal planning is one of the best ways to develop managerial skills. And having good managerial depth is one of the best ways to ensure the success of your firm.

THE HIERARCHY OF PLANS

To achieve maximum benefits, planning must be comprehensive. Comprehensive plans involve setting objectives, developing strategic and operational plans, and control. Figure 1-1 illustrates the hierarchy of the process. Note that the strategic plan outlines the general means for achieving the objectives. The operating plan, which derives from the strategic plan, tells you what to do today. The chart also indicates the flexibility that must be built into the planning process: "Control" and the looping lines show the need for continual checks and adjustments.

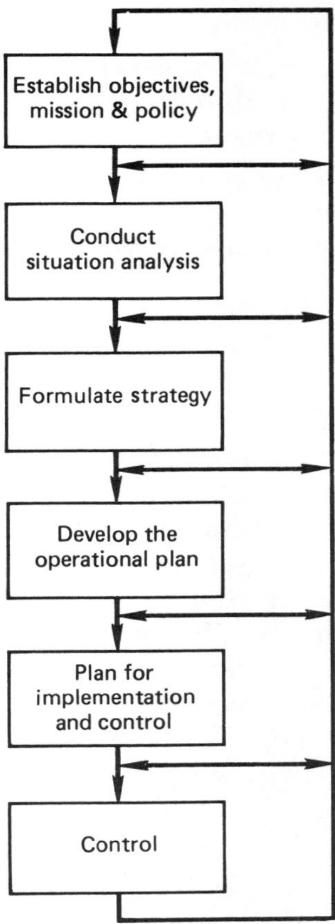

Figure 1-1. The Planning Process

OPERATIONAL PLANNING

Most firms, and certainly those of any size, have a written annual plan—an operational plan—which guides day-to-day company activities. An operational plan is a recipe for action. It specifies what gets done, who does it, and when. Since practically all firms require time—usually several years or more—to change the overall direction of their business, operational planning by itself is tactical in nature. It is almost solely restricted to fine-tuning what the company is already doing.

Strategic planning, on the other hand, involves looking into the future and deciding what the basic thrust of your business ought to be. It may result in a strategy that, over time, brings about fundamental changes in your business. The point of strategic planning is to decide a course today that will get the company where it wants to be tomorrow.

Benefits of Strategic Planning

No one disputes the benefits of formal operational planning. But for a long time managers had to accept the value of formal strategic planning (if they accepted it at all) as an article of faith. Only recently have studies provided hard evidence of its worth.

Using matched pairs—planners versus nonplanners—in the same industries, Thune and House compared the effects of planning in thirty-six firms from six different industries. One-half of these firms were long-range planners; that is, they formally established goals for three years ahead or more, and determined plans and procedures for achieving them. The other half were non-long-range planners. The results were conclusive: Planners outachieved nonplanners, especially in growth. Moreover, after they had introduced strategic planning, planners significantly outstripped their own performance.[1] Studies by Ansoff and others have come up with essentially the same conclusions.[2] Of course, this does not imply that by implementing strategic planning you'll be guaranteed success. Nothing does that. But, in general, strategic planning does pay.

Why is this so? One reason is that firms that do not engage in strategic planning tend to concentrate on what they're already doing. They try to improve present operations by lowering manufacturing costs, increasing sales force efficiency, beefing up advertising, and the like. Sometimes this works. But often the "try-harder" approach fails because external conditions have changed so that their present strategies—indeed, those that may have served them so well in the past—are no longer suitable. The results of such buggy-whip strategies are legend.

In contrast, strategic planning concentrates attention on what you should be doing now to prepare for, say, five years from now. This perspective encourages consideration of nontraditional approaches.

And, it is more energizing in the sense that it forces you to think about where you want to be in contrast to where you will be.

You'll have to make many tough choices in long-range planning. For example, you must decide between: improving your competitive position or taking short-term profits; concentrating on existing markets or developing new ones; high-risk strategies or "riskless" activity; growth in one industry or diversification; growth by acquisition or internal growth; maximizing profits or considering social responsibilities. Of course, whether you engage in formal strategic planning or not, you still have to make these choices. In the final analysis, it's not a question of whether you want to do strategic planning or not. You cannot escape the futurity of your actions. You either build a plant or you don't. You enter a new market area or you don't. You invest in R&D or you don't. And all of these decisions will have long-range implications. So the question is: Do you do strategic planning informally (intuitively) or formally? Formal strategic planning provides you with a framework for determining the best balance.

You may say, "Things are going fine. Why should I go through all the bother?" Let's approach that answer indirectly, with an example of the rapid impact of exponential growth. To begin, a pond has one lily pad growing on it. But every succeeding day the number of lily pads doubles. On the second day, then, there are two pads, on the third day four, and so on. Sixty days later, if growth continues, the pond will be entirely full. It's relatively easy to understand that only half of the pond is free of lily pads on the next-to-last day, the fifty-ninth. But it's usually harder to grasp that on the fifty-third day, just a week before the end, the pads cover less than 1 percent of the surface.

Unfortunately, complications that stem from faulty strategies often grow at close to an exponential rate. To make matters worse, strategic decisions are not self-regenerative like operating decisions. Operating decisions you are forced to make every so often, but, unless you have a formal review process, this is not so with strategies. At first, faults in strategy are hardly detectable, but towards the end they close in with remorseless swiftness. And it takes time to devise adjustments to your strategy, put them to work, and then turn things around. In fact, by the time it's obvious to everyone that your strategy is beginning to flounder, it may be too late to do anything about it.

So consider yourself fortunate (or skillful) if you're satisfied with your firm's current performance. And start strategic planning now. Close scrutiny of your company and its operating environment may uncover concealed threats. If so, you can make gradual changes now that can solve problems before they get out of hand. And the earlier you implement a change, the less disruptive it will be. For example, in 1978 Amcord was aggressively seeking to increase its diversification from the cement business—because of gloomy long-term growth prospects—even though in 1977 Amcord's cement sales had increased 27 percent and profits soared 54 percent. And this followed a good year in 1976. Yet the president claimed that 1978 was the right time for Amcord to put its money to work in other areas.[3]

Perhaps the outcome of strategic planning is that you decide to continue to do what you've been doing in the past. In such a case, was your planning a waste of time? Not at all. As a result of formal strategic planning, you will have systematically examined where your present strategy will lead, and you will have considered the possibility of changing the thrust of your business. You are at least more aware of the risks and advantages in the course you have decided to follow.

Prerequisites for Successful Strategic Planning

Experiences of hundreds of companies have shown that the following points, all of which are basic to successful strategic planning, need to be fully understood—and carried out.

- Include functional area managers in the planning process. Company managers, the people who run the firm on a day-to-day basis, generally understand their divisions better than anyone else. This practical knowledge is critical for the long-range planning process. It keeps planning down to earth. In addition, these are the people who will carry out the strategy, and its success depends on their cooperation. They are far more likely to be enthusiastic over a strategy they've had a hand in making.
- The involvement of the president (or chief executive officer) is essential. Mere support is not enough. After all, strategic planning, by definition, may change the thrust of the organization. Unless the president is involved—deeply involved—in making such plans, he or she is not likely to approve them. Besides, deciding the future directions of the firm is the president's job. Anything less than

full participation by the president will lead to disappointment for everybody.

- Make time for strategic planning. You can't wait until you have time available—job pressures are not likely to diminish. The time must be made. The time requirements are another reason why the president must actively lead the planning efforts. For if this responsibility is delegated to someone else, it soon becomes evident to everyone how the president rates its importance. Other top managers won't put their efforts into strategic planning either. They'll work on something which they think the president views as more important.
- Strategic planning must be integrated with operational planning. For the vast number of firms, the transition from short-range plans must be gradual; few firms can operate with one orientation today and an entirely different one tomorrow. In addition, some short-range commitments simply must be met. If they are not, you may lose your power to act (in plainer words, you may lose your job). On the other hand, you must think of the future. Consequently, it's usually best to develop operational and strategic plans concurrently. Short-range requirements may force you to modify your strategic plans, and vice versa. In any case, it's a hammering and fitting process.
- The strategy must be flexible. Strategy can be described as a company's reaction to the economic, social, and political environment, both as it is at present and as the company expects it to be in the future. There is very little the company can do to affect the environment; on the other hand, it does have control over its own response. The trick is to determine what the future will be like and devise a strategy that enables the company to operate successfully within it. Unfortunately, our forecasting skills leave much to be desired. It's necessary to develop strategy that has sufficient flexibility to succeed in a number of plausible future environments.
- Strategic plans must be continually reassessed. Don't expect to develop a strategic plan and then be done with planning. Thanks to the unpredictability of the environment, plans must be checked and updated. Most firms engaged in long-range planning examine their strategies once a year as part of the regular planning cycle—and on an ad hoc basis should critical elements of the environment

turn out radically different from the forecasts. As a military strategist once remarked, "Planning is indispensable, but plans are useless." Robert G. Page, chief executive officer of Leesona Corporation, put it this way, "We're not slaves to our plan. It's a guide."[4]

- Don't look for the universally ideal method of planning. No single method of planning applies to all companies; what works best for a given firm depends on several basic factors:

  - Is management more comfortable, for example, with "by-the-numbers" procedures or a shirt-sleeve approach? A radical shift from one to the other usually must be made gradually. Then, management with experience in planning is more likely to use sophisticated techniques than management that is fairly new to the process.

  - Size may also determine the method you choose. Large companies can usually afford the staff both to accumulate information and to help coordinate the planning effort. In smaller companies, these tasks must usually be carried out by the operating managers.

  - The length of the planning horizon will vary with the firm's product. For example, a fashion goods manufacturer would find the fifty-year planning horizons of some petroleum firms totally unsuitable. In addition, planning would be highly decentralized in a conglomerate but centralized in a company with a homogeneous product line.

  - Data, time, and staff availability obviously determine how sophisticated the planning will be. In some industries, data may be hard to come by. Then, sometimes staff may be limited in even the largest of corporations.

  - Finally, even for a given company, the ideal method of planning changes through time as management gains more experience in planning, as attitudes change, and so on.

This book presents a step-by-step procedure for planning. Although it is generally suitable for most firms just starting comprehensive planning, keep in mind you may have to make some changes to adapt to the "culture" of your firm.

Probably one of the greatest pitfalls for companies just starting strategic planning is trying to do everything "right" the first time through. As a consequence, they get bogged down on one or several steps. They never get through the planning cycle in time. Sometimes they give up in disgust.

Accept the fact that your first time through will produce only a rudimentary guide to action. Experience has shown that it usually takes about five years to develop "sophisticated" plans. But the benefits from even a rudimentary plan can be great. Remember that you can carry on planning at any level of sophistication you like. Just take care to follow all the steps described in the following chapters.

When should you start the planning process? Right now. Perhaps you think, "It's too late in the year. We're almost ready to make our next year's budgets." If so, why not run through the steps in a very general way taking only a few days? By doing this, you'll have a better feel for your strategic direction, thus improving the focus of your short-range plans. And you'll have gained practice, making the next planning cycle more productive. Then too, you'll have made the commitment, making it less likely that comprehensive planning will be put off until it's too late.

2

The Planning Process

Let's take a look at the steps in the planning process:

Step 1. Establish objectives, mission, and policies.
Step 2. Conduct situation analysis.
Step 3. Formulate strategy.
Step 4. Develop the operational plan.
Step 5. Plan for implementation and control.

Briefly, here's what each of these steps involve.

Step 1. Establish Objectives, Mission, and Policies. First, determine the objectives you want the company to achieve. (Some people differentiate between goals and objectives; here the two are used interchangeably.) Then define your mission and policies. A company's mission states in a general way the broad business(es) in which the firm will engage; it describes the acceptable "playing field." Policies are the rules by which the game is played. They do for the company what manners and social custom do for society at large: They provide guidelines for action. Objectives, mission, and policies will help to promote a mutual understanding of purpose and parameters of action among those involved in the planning process.

Step 2. Conduct Situation Analysis. The situation analysis highlights the firm's points of leverage and vulnerability. It provides knowledge about the company and its competition, furnishes a common understanding of where the company is, and serves as a basic reference for future strategic and operational planning. Normally, every functional area—production, marketing, finance, personnel, and so forth—undertakes a formal situation analysis. These are then consolidated.

Step 3. Formulate Strategy. Given the objectives, mission, policies, and strengths and weaknesses of the firm, next decide what are the plausible environments in which your firm may be operating. In light of these possible futures, what should be the basic thrust of the company? This decision underlies the strategic plan of the firm.

Step 4. Develop the Operational Plan. The short-range plan (the annual plan) must meet short-term objectives and conform to the firm's strategy. It's a recipe for action. It details what the functional areas will be doing during the year.

Step 5. Plan for Implementation and Control. Before plans are put into action, however, responsibilities are documented. "Tolerance points" (or bands) should be specified for minimum/maximum levels of sales, maximum level of expenditures, and the like for designated periods throughout the one-year plan. These are spelled out in responsibility charts. Activity schedules are also prepared. Of course, planning assumptions may prove wrong, or the environment itself may change in a wholly unexpected manner. So plans need to be monitored. If results do not reach—or conform to tolerance points or bands—the plans will have to be revised.

In actual practice, the planning process seldom moves neatly from Step 1 through Step 5. As Figure 1-1 indicates, backtracking may be required at any point. The strategic plan, for instance, although it seemed initially promising, may turn out to be unworkable. If so, you'll have to go back to Step 3 and develop a more satisfactory strategy. Or perhaps it turns out that no strategy whatever is capable of attaining your desired objectives. In that case, you'll have to return to Step 1 and develop more realistic objectives. Finally, after the plans have been put into action, monitoring may reveal they will not meet operational objectives. If the plans have sufficient flexibility, they can be modified in light of the "real" situation. If not, it's time to either make new plans or scale down your objectives.

It's evident that members of your planning team should know your company well. Perhaps this is most obvious in operational planning—we've all heard horror tales of trying to implement unrealistic plans. Extensive knowledge of the company, however, is equally important for strategic planning, and it's one of the major reasons for including executives who head functional areas. These people know their particular areas better than anyone else, and their input during the planning process will help ensure realistic plans.

Determining the correct strategy, however, is not a simple matter of adding up strengths and subtracting weaknesses. The feasibility of a plan, for example, may depend on its ability to attract financing; conversely, its ability to attract financing might depend on the attractiveness of the plan—or how attractively it is presented to a prospective financier. Planning is ringed by such contingencies, and a good planning team will be adept at balancing the concrete with the potential.

Of course, following a planning model does not ensure success (again, nothing *ensures* success). Such a model, for instance, is no substitute for managerial judgment. Its value is that it offers a systematic way of approaching problems. Where management's judgment is poor, a planning model only enables bad decisions to be made in a more orderly fashion.

CASE EXAMPLE

Here's a highly abstract example of how a company with one major product line might apply the six-step planning procedure.

The XYZ Corporation, formed seven years ago, produces electronic components for major manufacturers. Last year sales reached $4,000,000 with profits of $250,000. Although the company has been successful, the president decided that his firm should have a more formal approach to planning. First he put together a planning team consisting of himself and the functional area vice-presidents (marketing, manufacturing, etc.). The planning team then developed a five-year strategic plan as well as an operational plan for the first year.

Step 1. After much discussion, the team emerged with the following goals:

	First-Year Goals	Five-Year Goals
Sales	4,600,000	10,000,000
Profits	290,000	600,000
Return on assets	10%	14%

These objectives were considered absolute minimums. Of course, the team hoped for greater performance, but they believed that this minimum would satisfy stockholders and still maintain the high employee morale necessary for success.

They decided to restrict the firm's activities to the manufacture of electronic items requiring sophistication in design and engineering. This, then, became its mission. They also set two basic policies: The firm would not engage in any activity that might be construed as deceptive or unethical, and the firm would limit its activities to those which provided stable employment for its personnel.

Note that the objectives, mission, and policies served to channel the strategic and operational plans that followed.

Step 2. Functional vice-presidents were charged with making detailed analyses of the strengths and weaknesses of their own areas. On the basis of the completed analyses, the planning team prepared a composite list of the firm's strengths and weaknesses. They agreed that its major strengths lay in its design, engineering, and high-technology manufacturing abilities. Its major weakness lay in its lack of a consumer franchise. The firm received over 95 percent of its sales volume from three major electronic firms that used XYZ component parts in their products. Although XYZ had good cost advantage and was extremely competitive, what would happen if one or two or all three of these customers canceled even part of their orders? Moreover, the company's ability to turn a profit would be alarmingly vulnerable to a technological breakthrough by one of its competitors.

Step 3. The planning team developed several plausible futures and then extended the firm's present strategy into these futures. Even allowing for good luck, the prognoses were gloomy. Although XYZ was extremely competitive in the industry, its overdependence on a few customers and its vulnerability to new technological developments seriously threatened its five-year objectives. With a run of bad luck, XYZ might even fold.

A new strategy had to be developed. But the search was aided by the fact that direction as well as boundaries had been predetermined. The team knew the specific long- and short-range goals they were trying to reach, what general types of strategies would be acceptable (mission), and what rules would have to be followed (policies). There was common agreement as to the current strengths and weaknesses of the company. Finally, the forecasts alerted the team to the faults of their present strategy. Armed with this information, they knew what kinds of plans to avoid. More important, the team realized which aspects of their present operations needed to be changed.

After studying all the possibilities, they decided to greatly expand the firm's sales of an electronic part sold to the automotive aftermarket (which presently accounted for 5 percent of XYZ's sales). In addition, the company intended to develop new high-technology electronic products for this market. Plans were for automotive parts to constitute 35 percent of sales in five years. Sales to electronic manufacturers would comprise the balance.

Step 4. Having decided on their basic strategy, the planning team then formulated a one-year plan. First they put together a "rough-cut" plan. Then the functional area vice-presidents prepared detailed operational plans for their areas. For example, manufacturing plans included the development of new automotive products. Part of marketing's plans was to increase dealer and consumer franchises. Next, these plans were brought together, through the process of replanning and negotiations, to form the company's operational plan. A pro forma P. & L. showed that the plan was on target, providing, of course, that the assumptions were correct.

Step 5. Responsibilities for each of the functional areas were documented. Responsibility charts were prepared. Before the plans were put into action, however, tolerance points were specified for designated periods throughout the one-year plan.

Audits at predetermined points measured how well the plan was working. Adjustments, when necessary, kept its performance satisfactory.

Of course, the process does not move this smoothly in practice. As we've seen, it requires hammering and fitting, backtracking and negotiating throughout. These will be discussed later on.

PLANNING IN A SINGLE-INDUSTRY COMPANY

A single-industry company, generally speaking, is a firm whose products require similar manufacturing technologies and marketing skills and channels. The XYZ Corporation was an example of a single-industry company. The planning process in such a company is outlined in Figure 2-1. For clarity, this chart (and Fig. 2-3) have been simplified. Four of the major steps—conducting the situation analysis (Step 2), formulating the strategy (Step 3), developing the operational plan (Step 4), and planning for implementation and control (Step 5)—have been telescoped into "develop plans."

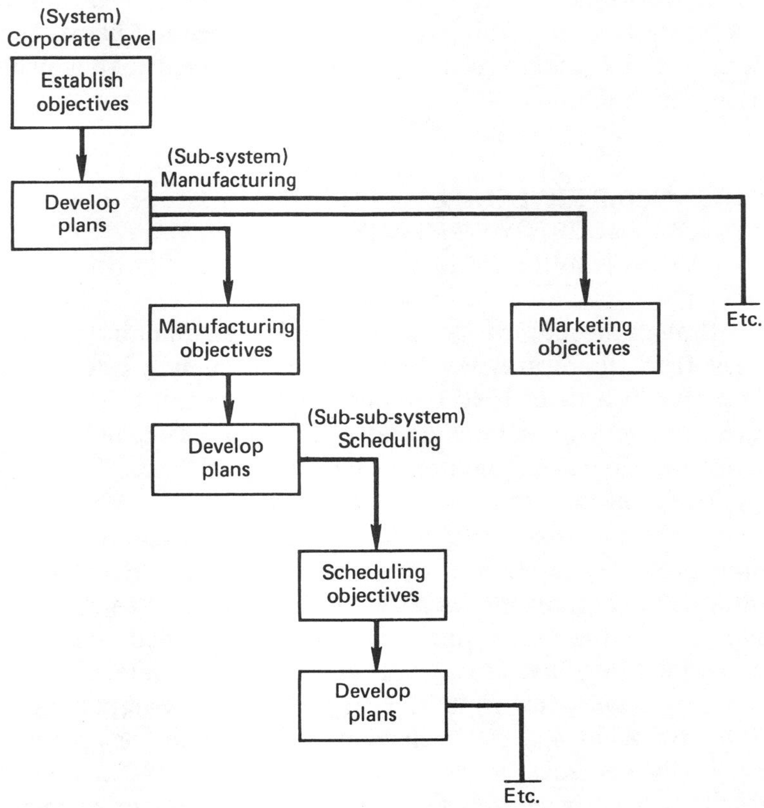

Figure 2-1. The Planning Process in a Single-Industry Firm

Note that the objectives of the functional areas (such as personnel and manufacturing) are derived from the corporate plan, and so on down the line. The manufacturing plan, for instance, dictates the objectives for the manager of scheduling as well as other manufacturing personnel—such as the quality control manager—who report to the director of manufacturing.

In this sense planning operates from the top down, which is the way it should be. When the people at the top fail to dictate the direction of the company, the wrong people are at the top. Of course, there is a certain amount of bottom up input as well, because functional area executives help form the corporate plan which determines their own objectives. Hopefully, these functional area managers consult with managers who report to them, who in turn seek inputs from *their* subordinates concerning their own objectives and plans. If done properly, the end result is realistic plans, commitment to their achievement, and high morale.

DIFFERENCES BETWEEN PLANNING IN A SINGLE-INDUSTRY COMPANY AND IN A DIVERSIFIED COMPANY

Although the major focus of this book is on planning in a single-industry firm, there are two reasons for discussing how planning might differ in a diversified company. For one thing, even though you are a smaller company, you may find it more efficient to organize your product/market structure along divisional lines. For another thing, your firm may someday be acquired.

Figure 2-2 indicates the major differences in characteristics of planning processes between single industry and diversified companies. Essentially, the organizational structure in a single-industry company usually follows functional lines, while in a diversified company the structure falls into divisions according to product category. This is because top management in the single-industry company usually understands the industry better than anyone else within the organization and logically becomes very involved in planning the strategy and tactics of the firm. In a highly diversified company, however, members of top management may have had extensive experience in one or two industries yet, in general, will probably know less than subordinates about the intricacies of each industry in which their divisions operate.

	Single Industry	*Diversified*
Organizational Structure	*Function*	*Product*
Top executives' expertise in industries which company operates	Greater than that of functional subordinates	Less than that of divisional subordinates
Scope of objectives	For functional groups —Market share —Sales —Production	For divisions —Earnings —Return on assets —Cash flow

Source: Adapted from Peter Lorange and Richard F. Vancil, "How to Design a Strategic Planning System," *Harvard Business Review,* 54 (September-October, 1976), 75–81, with permission of the publisher.

Figure 2-2. Contrasts between Single-Industry and Diversified Companies

Then, too, often the sheer number of businesses in which the company operates precludes top management from extensive involvement in strategy development for each of the businesses. Consequently, a highly diversified company is usually organized by divisions. Top management sets objectives for each division, but does not get involved in the development of strategies for these divisions. (Of course, division plans are subject to top management approval.) Objectives for the divisions in a diversified company are usually similar to those for the entire corporation in a single-industry firm (such as return on assets and earnings).

Figure 2-3 illustrates the general planning process in a diversified company (understand there are many variations). Although it's basically the same process as in a single-industry firm, there are some important differences.

Corporate objectives, like those of a single-industry company, are customarily expressed in terms of return on equity, return on assets, and so forth. The corporate planning team also determines the mission and policies of the corporation.

The results of the corporate situation analysis gives the strengths and weaknesses of the corporation as a whole, which means the relative health of the individual subsidiaries and their synergistic "fit." This includes growth, cash requirement for investment, cash flow, and the like. Next, the corporate planning team forms corporate plans, which in effect are allocations of resources. Some divisions receive more, some less. These resulting plans serve as projection of expected earnings, growth, cash flow, and return on assets from each

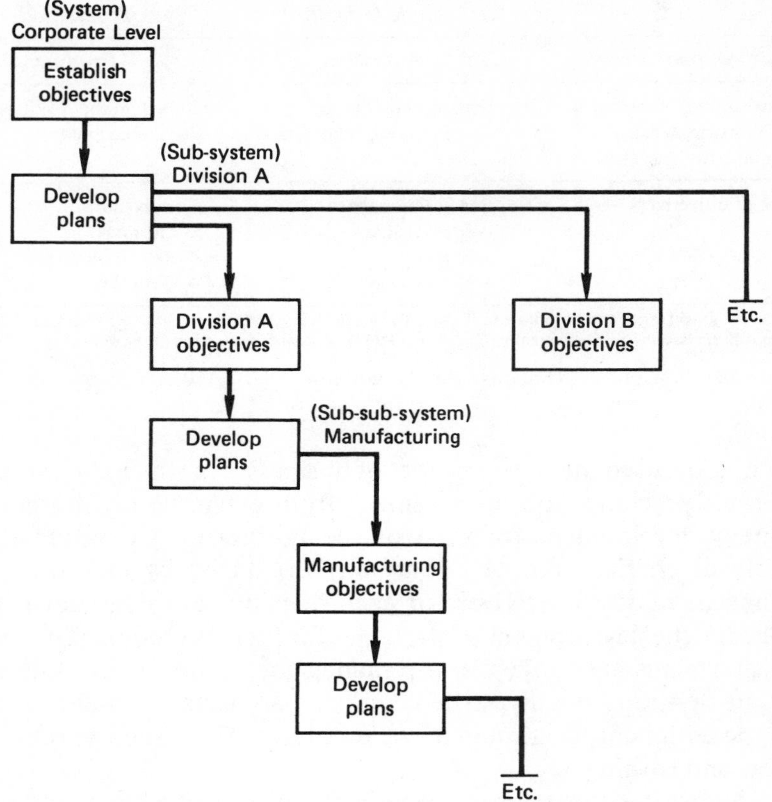

Figure 2-3. The Planning Process in a Diversified Company

of the subsidiaries. The corporate planning team also draws up divisional charters (missions) and establishes a planning format and timetable.

At this point the divisions develop their individual plans and submit them to the committee for review. The committee allocates resources to divisions whose plans it approves, or the committee may suggest modifications or even reject the plans entirely. The committee also authorizes divisions to explore the possibility of diversification beyond the limits of divisional charters.

Note that planning within the divisions is quite similar to that in a single-industry company, except that objectives, mission, policies, planning format, and broad timetables have been specified by an "external" force. The divisional planning team sets a planning timetable (within boundaries set by the corporate planning committee), conducts a situation analysis, develops strategies and an operating plan, and, upon approval by the corporate planning committee, implements the plans and maintains control.

HOW SHOULD YOUR FIRM BE STRUCTURED: CENTRALLY OR BY DIVISIONS?

Generally speaking, if across your product lines the production facilities and marketing personnel are shared, the same make-or-break forces affect the firm's products, and top management has a keen knowledge of production and marketing processes, your firm should be centrally organized. If not, then perhaps you should consider organizing by divisions.

There are exceptions, of course. For example, one manufacturer in the top 25 of the Fortune 1,000 has remained essentially centrally organized even though it operates businesses in several distinctly different areas. The reason for this is simple: 95 percent of its business lies in one area. So the company uses a sort of composite type of planning organization. It is centrally organized for its major business; that is, top management is directly involved in devising action strategies as well as objectives and policies. But it's like a decentralized company for the remaining 5 percent of the business. For minor businesses top management specifies objectives, missions, and policies. Within these boundaries division managers work out their strategies—subject, of course, to top management's approval. Actually, this sort of composite organization is quite common.

If you're still uncertain how your company should be organized, don't worry about it now. Read through the following chapters. By the time you finish, you'll have a better idea what structure suits your firm.

3

Organizing for Planning

ORGANIZING FOR PLANNING IN A CENTRALIZED COMPANY

The Planning Team

The planning team should consist of the firm's top management. In a centralized company this usually includes the president and the functional area managers (see Fig. 3-1). If the chairman of the board plays an active role, he or she should be on the planning team as well. Keep the team to, say, eight members or fewer, however. More will make the committee unwieldy, hindering participation and generally making it harder to get things done.

In some companies it is obvious who should be on the committee. In others, where the situation is more fuzzy, the membership must be worked out with great care. It is important to keep in mind that, since the planning team is one of the most important committees within the corporation, some people may take it badly if they're not included. Here are three broad guidelines:

- Normally the team consists of top management—those officers who report directly to the president. If more than seven people

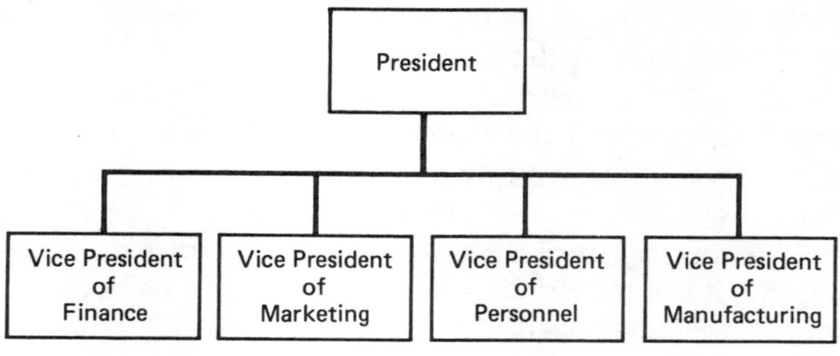

Figure 3-1

are reporting to the president, perhaps there are too many people reporting to him, thereby cutting down his efficiency. Why not consider reorganizing *before* you set up the planning team?

- Is there someone who could make a valuable contribution but is not a member of top management? If you discover that your firm has a number of such people, two things are possible: Either the wrong people are in top management, or management needs to be restructured.

- If you dip below top management, can you afford to include everybody on the next management level? If not, who's going to feel hurt if he or she is left out? Do you really want to keep such people in the firm? And you should ask the same questions about someone with high rank whom you'd prefer to leave off the committee.

The president (assuming the president is the chief executive officer) should chair the planning committee; this will help underscore the importance of the planning team. If someone else serves as chairman, he or she should be unusually important to the firm, perhaps the heir apparent to the president.

The main advantage of the planning team is that it provides an orderly forum for members of top management to "have their day in court." As mentioned in Chapter 1, this boosts morale. People appreciate the chance to present their own ideas; at the very least it makes them more receptive to those of other people. Also, the interchange of ideas usually stimulates creativity, while the company-wide experience of the committee members keeps the plans realistic. Finally, people who participate in the decision-making process feel they have a greater stake in making the final plan work.

The final decisions are ultimately made by the president (again assuming the president is the chief executive officer). He or she must be careful, however, to encourage creative dissent during the meetings. The value of the discussions diminishes drastically if people feel it is pointless (or unwise) to present ideas the president may disapprove of. Similarly, it is up to the chairman to make sure that a clique or an overly aggressive individual doesn't push everybody else to the sidelines.

The major drawback to the planning team is readily apparent: Committee meetings seem to be nonproductive. And it's dismaying to see a collection of the firm's most highly paid officers tied up in committee meetings when so much needs to be done out in the plant. Yet despite this shortcoming, committee meetings are usually the quickest way to a satisfactory result. Consider what happened to President Carter's energy program. In 1977, James Schlesinger and his aides drew it up in a speedy two months, whereupon criticism from interested parties on all sides stopped it almost dead in its tracks. Even President Carter admitted that the program would have moved along faster had he involved Congress, oil companies, and consumer groups in drafting the plans.

To avoid tying up executives when it's really not necessary, sometimes companies use subcommittees made up of planning team members, whose functions might be to evaluate acquisitions, new plants, and so forth. These ad hoc task forces usually include only those members needed to gather information or make analysis.

How much do planning team members need to know? This is a question that has been raised at many seminars—by presidents of closely held businesses. In such firms figures of the business are not known to the outside, or even to some of the key employees who might be on the planning team. The presidents are usually concerned about releasing such figures for several very good reasons: If key employees know how profitable the business is, they may start up competing businesses of their own. If too many people really know the business, it's more likely that competitors will find out important information. If hourly employees find out the profitability of the firm (and the more people who know the profitability of the firm, the more likely it is that they will find out), they're more likely to demand higher wages.

The answer that comes out of these discussions is that there are no rights or wrongs about what should be revealed to key employees. It's a personal choice. The decision boils down to weighing the benefits of involving others versus the loss of secrecy and the costs of doing all planning by yourself. There's a general agreement that if you want others to be on the planning team, these people have to know the firm's objectives, financial strengths and weaknesses, and past successes and failures. Otherwise, they won't be competent to make any meaningful systematic contributions.

Use of Staff

Functional area managers often lack the time, patience, and aptitude for formal planning. A possible solution to this problem is for managers to utilize some of the people who report to them. There is certainly no need for managers to do routine work. Have subordinates gather information for the situation analysis, develop sales and financial forecasts, and the like. In this way management can restrict its own participation to analysis, strategic discussions, and decisions.

Use of a Planning Coordinator

Many companies have found that designating someone to *coordinate* the planning process reduces the work of the chairman and the other members of the team. The title of this post varies; it might be Planning Coordinator, Director of Corporate Planning, or the like. The person's duties usually include recommending the planning format, scheduling meetings, keeping minutes, helping to gather data and assembling and distributing the plans. Usually the planning coordinator is a nonvoting, ex officio member of the planning team.

It is generally accepted that the planning coordinator's role is not to develop plans but to facilitate the process. To underscore this point, in one firm the planning coordinator is called Planning Consultant. In another firm, he is called Staff Assistant.

Do not underestimate the requirements for the job, however. As one of the leading authorities on planning, George Steiner, points out, a good planning coordinator should have a thorough understanding of the firm and its operations. He (or she) should also have a close working relationship with the president and the respect of its operating managers. He must be sensitive to the kind of information necessary (and acceptable) for managerial decision making, but never give the impression that he is making the decisions for managers. Overall, he should serve as a catalyst in the planning process.[1]

Steiner also emphasizes that operating managers should view the planning coordinator as someone available to help them, not as a watchdog who will turn them in as soon as something goes wrong. The coordinator, then, must not be responsible for seeing that the plans are carried out. The coordinator who must report to the president that the performance of one of the operating managers isn't up to snuff loses the trust not only of that manager but of the others as well. After all, anyone might be next. Who can remain open and free with a potential executioner?

Most smaller companies cannot afford a full-time coordinator. Many elect to settle for less than the ideal by using a part-time one. These persons usually lack many of the qualities listed above, or because of the nature of their job, perform fewer of the tasks that might be carried out by full-time planning coordinators.

Here are examples of the types of individuals six companies chose to use to fill the part-time coordinator's job. The first, the marketing manager of a medium-sized bank, was a relatively new assistant vice-president. Normally a person in this position would not be on the planning team, but top management felt that his contributions would be valuable. To openly make him a member, however, would create hostility among those in his echelon in management, and the bank wanted to avoid that. So they expanded his duties to include those of the planning coordinator. In this way they received the benefit of his input in the planning sessions, sidestepped the jealousy of other executives, and at the same time relieved top management of many routine chores.

In another company, of approximately 500 employees, the comptroller and the vice-president of advertising were appointed as joint planning coordinators and ex officio members of the planning team. Both of these executives were below the level of top management, but the president still wanted them to be on the planning team in order to help gather information as well as to increase their exposure to top level management's concerns.

The president of a third company ($8,000,000 in sales) solved the problem by appointing his secretary as planning coordinator.

Because the president knew she was so capable, this move would relieve him of many coordinating tasks. Besides, he wanted to upgrade her responsibility and create new challenges for her. At first her responsibilities were limited to scheduling meetings, keeping minutes, writing up and assembling the plans, and the like. As she came to know the job, her responsibilities increased.

In the fourth example, a small, job-shop, manufacturing company with $2,500,000 in sales, the planning had been carried out by two people—the owners. The formal planning was essentially for one year. In starting five-year comprehensive planning, they wanted to involve five others. Yet, except for the plant manager who had just joined the company about eight months earlier, these people did not have any experience in formal planning. The plant manager was considered to be at a higher echelon than the other four newly-appointed members of the planning team and, as a result, was in a management level all his own. The owners decided to make him the planning coordinator because of his knowledge of planning. This appointment would not create any jealousies. Although this role would expand the plant manager's duties, they felt that the additional exposure would broaden his understanding of the company, and they really wanted this person to "grow." Then, too, because of his experience in planning, quality of the plan would be improved and its completion within the prescribed planning cycle insured.

A scientific research oriented firm ($7,000,000 in sales) decided to use the assistant to the treasurer as planning coordinator. As a CPA, he was extremely capable and since he had been with the company for five years, he knew the firm. The planning team recognized that there was a danger that he might serve the treasurer (who was on the planning team) "too well," but it was commonly agreed that it was not a real threat to the planning process.

The last example, a division of a multibillion-dollar company, was just implementing a five-year plan. The division manager decided to use the vice-president finance as the planning coordinator. He chose to use this person since the position of vice-president finance was a job rotated within the corporate structure. As a result, it was viewed as being a position occupied by a person who was exempt from "power struggles" within the division. Furthermore, the vice-president finance had been serving as coordinator putting together the one-year plan.

In companies with no planning coordinator, the president usually assumes the responsibility for planning formats, scheduling the meetings, and putting together the plans. One president, of a company with $2,000,000 in sales, emphasized that he wanted to be the "scribe" in order to underscore the importance that he attached to the planning process. Actually, you'll find that if you stick to the procedure recommended in this book, you'll have less writing than you probably expect.

Whatever the case, it's usually not a good idea to assign the coordinator's duties to a member of the planning team. It gives that member additional power, which may threaten other members and foster rivalries.

The Use of Consultants

By now it should be clear: Consultants should not do the planning. Consultants should be used only to suggest planning procedures, to provide information (such as competitive data), or to evaluate the feasibility of particular plans. In certain instances you might wish them to *suggest* strategies. But remember, consultants should serve only in an advisory or facilitating capacity. Managers must do the planning.

The Role of the "Outside" Board of Directors

The role played by outside directors depends, of course, on the nature of the board. The boards of some companies are little more than rubber stamps. In others the boards play an active role. But at the very least the board should help formulate and approve objectives, be briefed on the results of the situation analysis, be briefed (and respond to) environmental forecasts, and be briefed (and respond to) strategy development and annual plans.

ORGANIZING FOR PLANNING IN A DECENTRALIZED COMPANY

The corporate planning team will include, quite obviously, top management of the corporation. In some instances, division managers are the top management, but the larger the company, the less likely it will be that division managers will sit on its corporate planning team. In larger firms, the corporate planning team is made up of corporate vice-presidents or executive vice-presidents.

The division planning teams closely resemble those of the centrally organized company (see Fig. 3-1). These planning teams set up planning timetables (within corporate limits), determine divisional strategies and action plans, discuss objectives, strategies, and forecasts with corporate management, and authorize the preparing of detailed plans for functional areas after corporate management approves their (divisional) plans.

Figure 3-2 depicts the organizational structure in a decentralized company. Note that the corporate planning coordinator assists the corporate planning team, and, in addition, helps the divisional planning teams and coordinators arrange formats, timing, and other planning procedures. These services are extremely important since the longer the chain of command the greater the opportunities for lack of coordination and confusion.

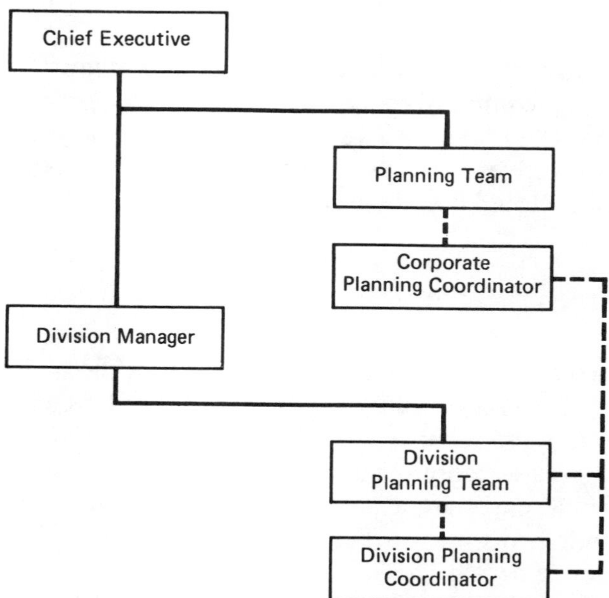

Figure 3-2 Organizational Planning Structure in a Diversified Company

4

Step 1: Establishing Objectives, Mission, and Policies

Before you can do any kind of planning, you must decide what you want your company to be like. This means establishing your objectives, your mission, and your policies. It's usually best to determine your objectives first. But, all three are interrelated, a fact the planning team should keep in mind.

ESTABLISHING OBJECTIVES

After you've decided who is going to be on the planning team, the next step is to set objectives. Remember that here goals and objectives are used interchangeably. Trying to differentiate between the two usually creates more misunderstanding than it's worth. As one company's planning manual admitted: "The previous edition [of this manual] made a distinction between *objective* and *goal* which has been abandoned because of the resulting confusion."[1]

Regardless of what you call them, make sure that your objectives don't emerge like some corporate goals—"to maximize profits," for example, or "to produce profits in order to return to shareholders adequate dividends and to have ample funds for long-term investments." These "objectives" are unlikely to cause any argument; they are vague enough to mean all things to all people. And that is precisely what is wrong with them. For example, what does "maximizing profits" really mean? Does it mean that the company can operate at a deficit for the next ten years in order to obtain large profits afterwards? If so, what is meant by "deficit" and "large profits"? Or does maximizing profits mean that a firm should have some earnings every year? Then, what is meant by "some" earnings? One thousand dollars? One million dollars?

Vague objectives can create confusion among those engaged in strategic planning even when only a few people are involved and they are in continual communication. Consider an actual example: A medium-sized bank with $300,000,000 in deposits had no specific long-range goals. Its top three executives, the real "shakers and movers," were asked to write down what they thought were the bank's five-year objectives for deposits. One executive wrote down $400,000,000. The second put down $800,000,000. The third would not participate. Clearly—at least between two of them—there was anything but agreement about what the bank was trying to be. How, then, could there be any real agreement about proper strategies for the bank to follow?

At the very outset of strategic planning make sure there is a common understanding among management about what the company wishes to accomplish both within and by the end of the planning horizon. Here's how to construct meaningful corporate objectives—objectives that provide direction for the planning process.

Interim Objectives and Objectives for the Planning Horizon

First determine your "planning horizon"—how far in the future you wish to plan. No single time span is proper to all because needs vary from company to company. The length of the planning horizon usually varies with "turnaround time"—firms with heavy, fixed commitments usually plan further into the future than companies without such investments. However, many firms have discovered that five years is about right. It's far enough ahead so that they can make strategic changes. On the other hand, a five-year span is not so far away that it seems "blue sky."

Occasionally some people object to a planning horizon as lengthy as five years. Usually they will cite the fashion goods industry: "How can you plan ahead for five years? Because of the rapid change within the industry, about six months is about as far as you can plan." As far as product planning goes, this is true. But such a narrow view of planning misses the essence of strategic planning. The benefit from strategic planning is taking the long-range view of the business and asking such basic questions as "Are there trends occurring in this industry that may make our business less (or more) viable in the future? Are there any actions that we should be taking today to protect against (or capitalize on) these trends?" Such actions might range from upgrading personnel, modernizing production facilities, investing more in research and development, or changing channels of distribution, to taking steps to change the major thrust of the business.

When you've decided upon your objectives for the end of your planning horizon, determine your objectives for the first year. If you're experienced in long-range planning, you may wish to set objectives for the second and third years as well. But if you're just starting, settle for the first and fifth year. Keep the process as simple as possible.

Corporate Level Objectives

The first objectives within the firm should be set at the corporate level. After these goals have been established, develop plans to achieve them. These plans become the goals for the next level of management, and so on.

Figure 4-1 illustrates this principle.

Too frequently top management fails to determine the company's objectives. The reason given usually goes something like this: "In our firm we can't do things this way. Actually, each division has to set its goals first. Then we take the sum of these goals—the composite—and this gives us the goals of the firm. This is the only way goals can be set realistically." What this really means is that lower-level managers decide the destiny of the company. There's a hand on the tiller all right, but it's three decks down, in the engine room. A judgment is unavoidable; when top management allows others to decide the system's objectives, the wrong people are in top management.

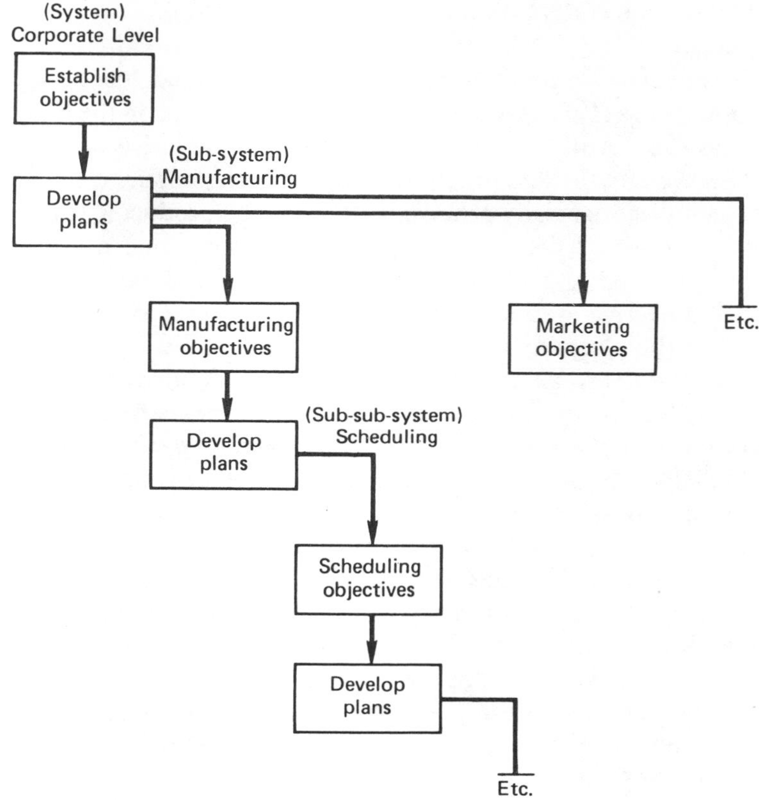

Figure 4-1. Hierarchy of Corporate Objectives

But let's backtrack for a moment. It might be argued, "If you've got competent functional area managers, they know what the corporation can reasonably expect to attain. For example, the marketing manager knows pretty well how much can be sold. The manager of manufacturing knows how much can be produced. So if you want realistic objectives, you are really just adding up the objectives of each functional area." You can't argue with this—for operational planning. As we know, usually operational planning is restricted to fine tuning. But such an argument overlooks the purpose—and the reason for—strategic planning. A more distant planning horizon enables top management to say, "Here's where we want to be in five years. Now, what changes (perhaps basic) need to be made so we can get there?"

Objectives with Minimum Process Restrictions

The president of a small electronics firm described his company's main objective as "to have the highest quality product on the market." Discussion revealed, however, that the firm's real desire was to reach a certain level of sales and profits. Follow-up analysis suggested several strategies more financially promising than that of producing the highest quality product. When the company acted upon one of these, its profits improved appreciably. In retrospect, the president realized that his objective was actually a strategy—several steps had been omitted in the planning process. Once the true objective was clearly specified, the firm was no longer bound to the pseudogoal of producing the highest quality product on the market. It was free to consider other alternatives and, as it turned out, more rewarding strategies.

In differentiating between goals and the means for accomplishing goals, it is also important that one recognize which echelon of management is under consideration: A goal at one level of management might be a "means" (plan) at another. For instance, the intent "to increase manufacturing capacity by 50 percent in five years" would be a goal for the manufacturing department, but it is not a goal at the corporate level. At the corporate level it would only be part of the master plan. The corporate goal should be expressed in terms of what it really wants to obtain: for example, $1,000,000 in net profit after taxes in five years.

Making Objectives Specific

It is always easier to agree on broad objectives than on specific ones. But a broad objective, by definition, leaves much open to interpretation. By contrast, a specific objective promotes unity of purpose: Everyone knows what must be accomplished. Knowing where you want to arrive also enables you to evaluate the various ways of getting there. Moreover, you're in a position to measure your progress en route and, if necessary, to make adjustments.

"Measure" is a key word, because a specific objective is concrete and measurable, whether in dollars, percentages, or proportions. For this reason, "maximizing profits" is not a specific objective, for how can you tell when the company has maximized profits? At best such a goal indicates a broad aim. Suppose, however, a company determines that over a five-year period it plans to increase its profits to $400,000 after taxes and its annual sales to $4,000,000. These are specific objectives because they describe exactly what the firm wants to achieve; progress toward objectives of this kind can be measured every step of the way. And when the firm gets there, it knows it.

Sometimes it's difficult to hammer objectives into specificity. The following process is typical. A planning team states its broad objective of "maximizing profits." The members must then forge an agreement about what maximization of profits actually involves. Reconciliation can be a monumental task. The members' concepts of an acceptable level of profits may vary widely. No doubt disputes of this nature explain why many companies have vague goals. Avoidance of establishing specific goals saves thought and argument, but in shirking the task, the firm, unfortunately, forfeits the benefits of management by objectives.

The process has a side benefit. An objective subjected to intense scrutiny, "pulled apart and put back together," its possible consequences weighed and balanced, can only emerge the better for it. Its ability to measure what the firm wishes to accomplish will be apparent to everybody.

Of course there are many cases in which quantitative terms cannot fully describe what one wishes to accomplish. In these instances a compromise is necessary, and you may have to express what you want to achieve in the most concrete qualitative terms that the situation permits.

Establishing Objectives for Every Key Area

Setting objectives would be far simpler if a company had only one major objective it wished to accomplish. But most firms have several. Consequently, the objectives for each key area must be concretely defined. Objectives for key areas help avoid ones that are overly broad. "Maximizing profits," besides not being specific, is too inclusive. The company might wish to optimize profits in order to be able to reinvest funds and pay dividends. If so, when properly broken down (and made specific), the objectives read something like this: earnings per share of $3.25; dividend of $0.75 per share.

A word of caution: Be sure that you establish objectives only for key areas. Lengthy lists that include trifling goals are impractical.

They can also obscure, through sheer numbers, the ones which really count. The common key areas are profitability, growth, dividends, stability, and—where information is available—relative ranking.

Profitability. To set objectives for profitability, most firms use one or more of the following measures: earnings per share (net profits), return on equity, and return on assets. (If you'd like a brief review of financial terms, see Appendix 4A at the end of this chapter.)

Earnings per share (net profits) is the most commonly used. However, the validity of profits—used by itself—has increasingly come under attack. Profits do not measure how effectively assets are being utilized. For example, a firm may have borrowed money at a time when interest rates were much lower than at present. Profits may be high, but return on assets could be lower than the going cost of capital. Eventually the firm will have to come into the capital market again. And a business that does not earn the going cost of capital will be in trouble sooner or later.

Although return on equity (net income divided by shareholders' equity) may be a good measure of shareholders' rate of return, it's still subject to the same criticism. It doesn't matter whether it's borrowed or invested capital. The firm's assets must meet the tests of the marketplace. There may also be another problem with the use of return on equity to evaluate profitability. Capital may have been invested a number of years ago and its value on the balance sheet is no longer a realistic figure.

Still, practically all firms do wish to set objectives for earnings per share (net profits) and/or return on equity. Some overcome the shortcomings of these objectives by also specifying a rate of return on assets or on invested capital.

Growth. The second key area is growth. Both shareholders and employees are usually interested in the firm registering growth. For the shareholders this quite often means increased profits and value of their stock; for employees, new job opportunities. Here, as always, the "golden mean" is desirable since sales growth, at the cost of profit margins, may cause earnings to fall.

Dividends. Dividend payment is also a prime consideration for many firms. This is especially true for smaller firms whose shareholders often consist of family who are dependent upon dividends for income.

Stability/Risk. Most companies are concerned with risk posture —or at least they should be. So you should set objectives for debt/equity ratio (long-term debt divided by shareholders' equity). Again, you should seek the "golden mean." If you are too conservative, you'll restrict your company's growth potential and may also conflict with the objective of paying higher dividends. On the other hand, if you take a stance that is too leveraged, you'll create undue risks for your company. Hanes Corporation, for example, believed that debt above 73 percent of equity was too risky. They lowered this through retained profits, debt retirements, and inventory cutbacks. They now keep the debt/equity ratio at 1 to 2 to maintain flexibility and ensure any necessary future financing.[2] Of course, the "correct" debt/equity ratio varies from industry to industry.

You may be able to increase your leverage through leasing. However a long-term lease—a twenty-year lease on a building, for instance —has the same effect as a long-term debt. Such a lease may help you get a loan today. But don't delude yourself. W. T. Grant was able to maintain a "respectable" balance sheet for years by leasing warehouses and the like. But when the company ran into cash flow problems, the leases had the same fixed commitments as long-term bank loans.

You may wish to use some other measure of stability besides debt/equity ratio. Appendix 4B gives a number of other key business ratios, according to industry classification.

Relative Ranking. When data is available and publicized, there is a fifth area—besides profitability, growth, dividends, and stability/risk, that is commonly used: relative ranking. Most top executives of a company are interested in maintaining, or achieving, a certain relative rank among firms with whom they are normally compared. This is for an obvious reason: If the firm is at the bottom or its rank is slipping, stockholders are not going to be satisfied with the present management. Therefore, many firms use relative ranking as a target. Mead, for example, set a long-term goal of being in the upper quartile of those companies against whom they are compared. A bank which ranked eighteenth out of eighteen set a five-year objective of being in the upper 50 percent and a one-year objective of moving up one place to seventeenth.

The sophisticated financial manager recognizes that no one financial measure is a suitable yardstick; exclusive reliance on return on assets may encourage a firm to make do with old equipment since that equipment's book value is low; a firm with a heavy debt burden must earn a high rate of return on shareholders' equity to offset the risk. And so on. So why not consider setting objectives for several financial areas? You may wish to use Mead's objectives (Fig. 4-2) as a pattern.

We have translated our long term goal of being in the upper quartile of those companies against which we are compared into specific numbers. We recognize that as markets, competitors and external factors such as the rate of inflation change—these numbers may have to be revised. Currently, these are the targets we are shooting for:

Financial goals	
Return on net assets	12%
Sustainable growth rate	10%
Debt to equity ratio	50%
Dividend payout	±30%
Return on equity	17%

These financial goals will produce a 17% return on equity. However, as you know, Return on Equity will vary as the actual debt/equity ratio moves around the 50% figure.

These goals are also designed to support a dividend which increases on a regular basis, a policy we have followed since 1972, and one which we think will be increasingly important to our shareowners.

Figure 4-2. Objectives of Mead

Source: Excerpt from "Executive Management Presentation to: Paper & Forest Products Analysts at the Princeton Club, New York, N.Y., February 8, 1977," with permission of Mead Corporation.

Exciting, Yet Believable Objectives

Mediocrity is no more interesting in a corporation than in an individual, and the company that sets up uninspiring objectives invites a potentially fatal case of passivity in its employees. Highly creative and aggressive people gradually wilt if the atmosphere around them is dulled. The mediocre quickly become even more so. On the other hand, absurdly high objectives are just as bad. It does little good to establish objectives at a high level if no one really believes that the company can achieve them. In such a case only half-hearted efforts will go into developing plans and putting them into action.

Where then, should a firm set its goals? Perhaps this has been best summarized by the former chairman of A.T.&T., Frederick R. Kappel: "Part of the talent or genius of the goal setter is the ability to distinguish between the possible and the impossible—but to be willing to get very close to the latter."[3] Note, however, that an attainable goal that nobody believes in is little better than one that really is impossible. Part of the "genius" of top management is to convince everybody that they *can* rise to the challenge.

It's helpful to have comparative data on what other firms have done to serve as a reference point. As one executive asked, "How can I be sure that objectives I set are realistic? I'd hate to stick my neck out for objectives that we possibly couldn't achieve." First, plot performance. Then make some trend lines. This will show you how ambitious your objectives are, given past performance. Then, possibly, your association has data on what firms in your industry are doing. This will help bracket reasonability. If you can't get industry data, why not use information in Table 4-1 to give you a rough guide?

Table 4-1 Annual Growth Rate of Earnings per Share of Fortune (501–1000) Industrials 1966–76

Rate of Growth of EPS	*Number of Companies*
Over 10%	151
5% to 10%	107
0% to 5%	71
Negative	63
Data not available	108
	500

Source: *Fortune,* June 1977.

Concerning growth rate, Appendix 4C is a table of compound growth rate. For example, it shows that if you wish to increase sales 10 percent annually, in five years your present sales would have to increase by 161 percent. This table is useful in two ways: It lets you know how much you would have to increase sales over a period of time in order to sustain a certain growth rate (the example above), and it also lets you work "backward." That is, if you want to double your sales in five years, what would be the approximate growth rate? The table points out it is approximately 15 percent.

Ranking Objectives in Order of Importance

There are two major problems in deciding what the firms objectives should be: The first is that there's never enough time or resources to work toward all of the things you'd like to accomplish. The second is deciding on the proper level of desired accomplishment. Of course the objective should be demanding and exciting, but where should one draw the line? For example, if the firm's sales are now at $5,000,000, why not $15,000,000 in five years? Then again, why not $20,000,000? Certainly the company would like to accomplish that. In fact, why not $50,000,000?

To handle the first problem, use a procedure recommended by Kepner and Tregoe. Place objectives in one of two groups: *must* objectives and *want* objectives.[4] Must objectives are absolutely essential. Want objectives are important, but not absolutely essential. Must objectives are to be attained at all costs. There is no hierarchy among these objectives. They all have to be reached. And here—on must objectives—is where you'll spend your resources.

Now for deciding the proper levels. For each must objective, determine the minimum acceptable amount necessary to create the necessary vitality and excitement in your company (stockholders, executives, workers, and even "external" members, such as suppliers and customers). These levels, then, become minimum acceptable levels of performance.

Anything besides the must objectives and minimum levels of performance, then, are really want objectives. If there is a surplus left over after allocating resources to achieve the must objectives, it can be used for achieving want objectives. Kepner and Tregoe's book provides further information how want objectives might be ranked and utilized. But for most companies, isolating the must objectives and minimum levels of acceptable performance provides adequate direction. So for all practical purposes you can forget about the objectives you placed on the want objective list.

Committing Objectives to Writing

The very act of transferring an idea to paper is a test of its worth. It is a little alarming how many flashes of inspiration fail this initial assay. Commitment to paper also serves to focus debate. Of course it is okay to hash out objectives verbally, but before final acceptance, write them down.

There is another reason why objectives should be in writing. Through time, we tend to forget. Having them in writing and in a prominent place in the corporate plan tends to remind you and to reinforce your original commitment.

Figure 4-3 gives an example of corporate objectives committed to paper. Textron's corporate objectives were set in 1972 for a ten-year time span, and progress was charted in their annual reports. Key areas were for sales, net income, and earnings per share.

Objectives Subject to Revision

Objectives that you set today may become obsolete within a short period of time. While working through the planning process, for instance, you might find that there is no way you can reach the predetermined objectives. Or, after the plan has been implemented, environmental conditions might change. When you replan you might find your previously set objectives impossible to attain. If this happens, change your objectives.

Then, too, you'll "roll over" your plan every year, at which time you'll reassess your planning horizon objectives. You may even find that they are too low and need to be revised upward.

Some companies are willing to change short-range objectives but are very sticky on the longer-range ones. For example, a manufacturing company that uses a seven-year planning horizon makes adjustments in its short-range goals (one year) in the event of an economic downturn. Its planning horizon goals, however, usually remain the same. The company's reasoning is as follows: In the short run management may be able, for example, to do little to counter a recession. But over a longer period of time, commitments to predetermined courses of action are not fixed the way they are in the short run, so managers have more leeway and should be able to adapt.

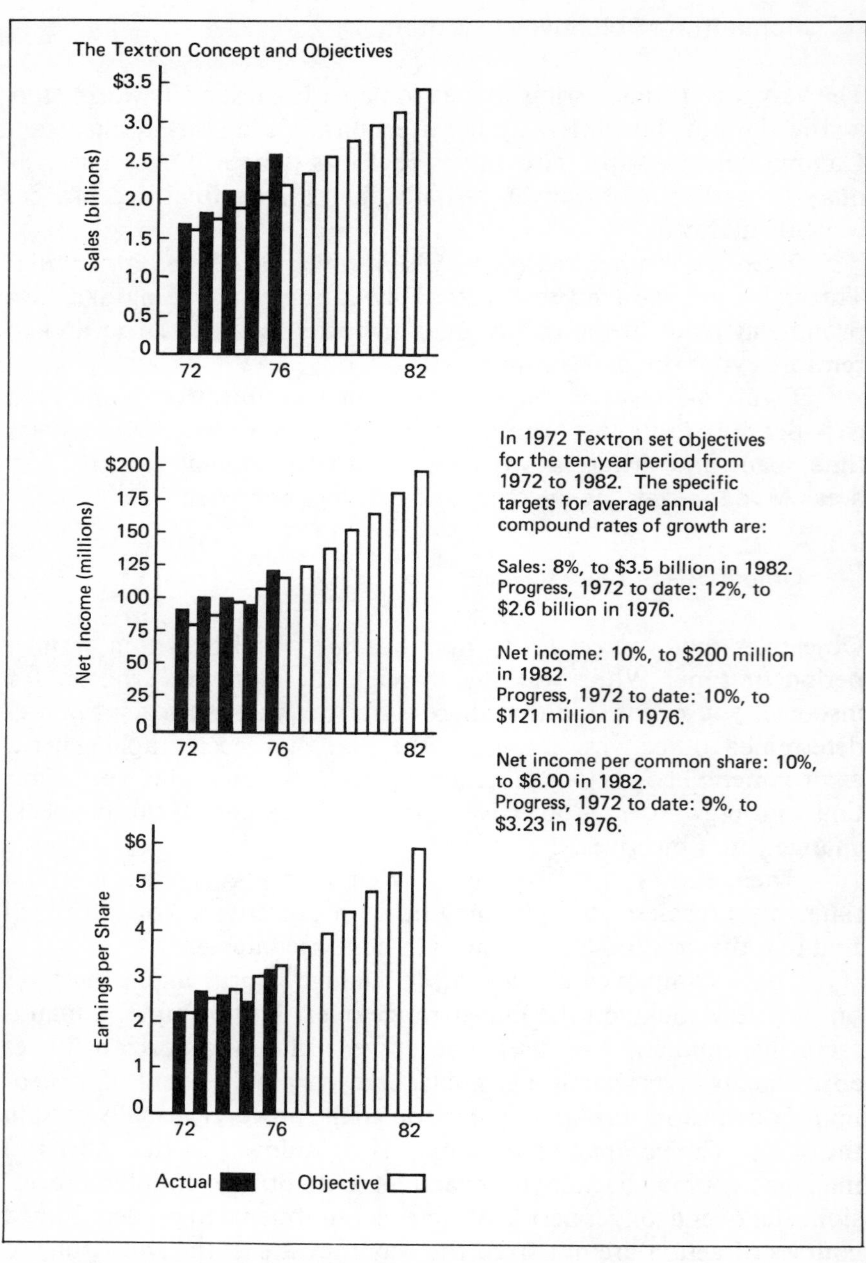
The Textron Concept and Objectives
Sales (billions)
$3.5
3.0
2.5
2.0
1.5
1.0
0.5
0
72
76
82
Net Income (millions)
$200
175
150
125
100
75
50
25
0
72
76
82
Earnings per Share
$6
5
4
3
2
1
0
72
76
82
Actual
Objective
In 1972 Textron set objectives for the ten-year period from 1972 to 1982. The specific targets for average annual compound rates of growth are:
Sales: 8%, to $3.5 billion in 1982.
Progress, 1972 to date: 12%, to $2.6 billion in 1976.
Net income: 10%, to $200 million in 1982.
Progress, 1972 to date: 10%, to $121 million in 1976.
Net income per common share: 10%, to $6.00 in 1982.
Progress, 1972 to date: 9%, to $3.23 in 1976.

Figure 4-3. Textron's Corporate Objectives, 1976
Source: Reprinted from Textron's 1976 Annual Report with permission of Textron Inc.

Before you set objectives, however, make sure that the planning team is also familiar with mission and policies. As pointed out previously, these three—objectives, mission, and policies—complement each other and may partly overlap.

STATING THE MISSION

After you have decided what it is that you want to achieve (objectives), the next step is to specify the mission. The mission stakes out broad areas of business in which the firm can, or perhaps cannot, operate. In other words, the mission decides the playing field.

It's still prior to the situation analysis or examination of the external environment. At first this might seem too soon to declare the mission. As a practical matter, however, the chief executive and everyone else involved in the planning process already have concepts of what the company should or should not be. Since these may not agree, it's best to get them out in the open. For example, when Frank Farwell left IBM to become the president of Underwood in 1955, he reportedly declared that he'd be "damned" if he would spend his life "peddling adding machines and typewriters." This statement does not specify what new directions Farwell had in mind, but the tone of his comment is clear: He felt that Underwood was an overly conservative firm that had depended too long on outdated technology.[5]

It's best to arrive at a common understanding of the general mission of the company early in the planning process. Although everyone may have a general idea of what this is, chances are that putting it in writing will help people to think it through more carefully. A carefully expressed mission helps narrow the search for suitable strategies by indicating what broad areas (industries, geographic areas) of business are acceptable. There's no point wasting time on ideas that the company is not prepared to accept.

After you've conducted the situation analysis and the examination of the environment, you may decide to revise the mission. Or you may wish to do so later because an unexpected opportunity has arisen. In any case, there's no harm done. The mission is not graven in stone. It expresses the philosophy of an evolving institution. Its function is perpetually contemporary: to let management know at any given time which areas of business are acceptable and which are not.

Following are examples of statements of mission:

- A manufacturer—"To remain primarily a manufacturing company emphasizing internal growth, international as well as domestic, and distinctive wood and related products which require innovation, special aesthetic features or fabrication, and significant marketing skills."[6]
- A manufacturer—(extracted from a series of statements) "To concentrate our efforts on opportunities in food-oriented and food-related business, building on existing bases in Agri-business, Food Processing and Restaurants/Food-Service by investing in those parts of these businesses which are healthy and growing."[7]

From the examples above you can see that the mission should point in the direction of acceptable strategies and to an industry or subindustry affected by identifiable external forces and where, hopefully, statistics will be available. Too broad a mission is not much help. You probably lose more than you gain by saying, "We're not in the bicycle business, but in the transportation business." What does transportation business mean? Air, surface, water, underwater, space? What mode of travel? Jet aircraft, glider, supercargo, sailboat, spaceship? To what class of customer? Industry, government, individual? J. Frank Leach, chief executive officer of Arcata Redwood Company, found his company in a similar trap. "The old acquisition policy [under the direction of the previous chief executive officer] was based on the rationale that the company was in the information-transfer business. I won't sit here and say that that was an unsound concept, but the company used it to go in too many directions."[8]

On the other hand, the mission should be stated broadly enough to allow for creative growth. It would be better to state the mission as being in "environmental cooling systems for industry" rather than in the "air conditioning business." When possible, the mission should describe both who the customers are and what services the firm performs for them.[9]

For a company that wishes to position itself more broadly as, for instance, a diversified manufacturing company, one might say as Textron does—that:

> [Our company] is founded on the principle of balanced diversification, designed on the one hand to afford protection against economic cycles

> and product obsolescence and on the other to provide a means for participating in new markets and new technologies. The key elements are balance and flexibility in a rapidly changing world.[10]

Although this statement of mission does not define acceptable industries, it does give guidance as to industries that would be more suitable than others. (Please note that more specific guidance is given in other Textron literature.)

STATING POLICIES

Now that you've decided what it is that the company should accomplish (objectives) and what types of general activities the company should or should not engage in (mission), the next step is to determine corporate policies. These are rules of behavior that govern top management action, both within the company and in the company's dealings with other businesses and the general public. Whereas the mission stakes out the playing field, policies specify the rules of the game.

Policies delineate courses of action that will be acceptable to the company and, like the acknowledgment of the mission, help to focus the search. For example, the owner-president of a company with 35 employees claimed that it was a policy of her company to provide jobs—and growth opportunities—for employees of the company. Another company (about 300 employees) had as a policy that the firm would not seek expansion through innovation. Rather the firm would grow by utilizing its marketing skills and by capitalizing on its well-known name. On the other hand, Textron (about 67,000 employees) has a policy "to be distinctive in its products and services—distinctive as to technology, design, service, and value. Superior performance will be achieved by way of excellence and quality."[11] Everyone involved in planning at Textron should know that the company has little interest in imitative and derivative products (or in products that hardly do the job). Some companies have policies concerning ownership: retention of family control or even sole ownership. Then too, some companies, in order to avoid overdependence on one or two customers, target the maximum percentage of total sales to any one customer. These examples point out how important it is that members of the planning team fully understand the firm's "rules of conduct"; it saves quite a bit of thrashing around.

Statements of policy need not be elegant. After all, all that you are trying to do is minimize confusion among members of the planning team. Of course, policies can be stated more elaborately and be used for public relations as well. Examine the policy on citizenship of Hewlett Packard which is set forth in the following two statements.[12]

> *To honor our obligations to society by being an economic, intellectual, and social asset to each nation and each community in which we operate.*
>
> All of us should strive to improve the environment in which we live. As a corporation operating in many different communities throughout the world, we must assure ourselves that each of these communities is better for our presence. This means building plants and offices that are attractive and in harmony with the community; it means solving instead of contributing to the problems of traffic and pollution; it means contributing both money and time to community projects.
>
> Each community has its particular set of social problems. Our company must help to solve these problems. As a major step in this direction, we must strive to provide worthwhile employment opportunities for people of widely different backgrounds. Among other things, this requires positive action to seek out and employ members of disadvantaged groups; and to encourage and guide their progress toward full participation at all position levels.
>
> As citizens of their community, there is much that HP people can and should do to improve it—either working as individuals or through such groups as churches, schools, civic or charitable organizations. At a national level, it is essential that the company be a good corporate citizen of each country in which it operates. Moreover our employees, as individuals, should be encouraged to contribute their support to the solution of national problems.
>
> The betterment of our society is not a job to be left to a few; it is a responsibility to be shared by all.

Among other things, this policy points out the necessity for having plants "that are attractive and in harmony with the community." In planning or acquiring facilities, then, this policy points out what character of buildings would be acceptable. But most important of all, it notifies everyone that "The betterment of our society is not a job to be left to a few; it is a responsibility to be shared by all."

Another policy of HP's, on "growth," specifies that—regardless of the playing field—growth is important to the company. Of course, growth is built into the corporate objectives, but declaring it also as a policy helps to clarify its importance. Management will know full well that the strategies it develops must lead to growth, as this statement makes it clear:

> *To let our growth be limited only by our profits and our ability to develop and produce technical products that satisfy real customer needs.*
>
> How large should a company become? Some people feel that when it has reached a certain size there is no point in letting it grow further. Others feel that bigness is an objective in itself. We do not believe that large size is important for its own sake; however, for at least two basic reasons, continuous growth is essential for us to achieve our other objectives.
>
> In the first place, we serve a rapidly growing and expanding segment of our technological society. To remain static would be to lose ground. We cannot maintain a position of strength and leadership in our field without growth.
>
> In the second place, growth is important in order to attract and hold high caliber people. These individuals will align their future only with a company that offers them considerable opportunity for personal progress. Opportunities are greater and more challenging in a growing company.

On the whole, the larger the company the greater the need for written policies, but each company must determine for itself how codified a system it requires. Generally speaking, a policy deserves to be put on paper when it saves time, improves communications, or clarifies murky areas of action. To be effective, it must also be narrow enough to govern managerial activity without obstructing individual initiative and creativity. Nor should it require continual adjustment; its purpose is to ensure stability, not undercut it. Of course, times do change, and policies must be accommodated to fit them.

GETTING THE JOB DONE

You should be able to set objectives, mission, and policies in several meetings. A guiding rule is not to strive for perfection. One president remarked that his planning team had been trying to decide upon proper corporate objectives for three months. They had been meeting one afternoon every other week, but in spite of all this time spent, they still hadn't arrived at any conclusions. No one had ever told him it could be done in a few hours. In retrospect, he realized that they could have set tentative objectives—and mission and policies, too—in two meetings. Revisions could have been made, if necessary, as they progressed through the planning cycle.

In the same manner, consider the output of your first "pass" as being tentative. Don't try to get your objectives, mission, and policies perfect—or 100 percent reconciled. If you strive for perfection you, too, will get "hung up" and won't get through the planning efforts. And even imperfect goals, mission, and policies can provide a start. You can make reconciliations later on.

Naturally, objectives, mission, and policies—like many other aspects of planning—reflect the stature of the president. He or she will have the final say, and in some instances may overwhelm the sentiments of the majority of the planning team. Why, then, have a planning team? Simply because it allows the other top managers of the firm a systematic means of voicing their opinions.

At the first meeting, have the planning team determine key objective areas. You'll probably want to use some measure for the key areas of growth, earnings, and stability, but take no more than an hour to decide what these should be.

The next step will be to analyze your company's track record in these key areas (this will help to assure that the amounts you set will be perceived as being reasonable). If, for example, sales, return on assets and earnings are your key objective areas, plot on a graph your sales, return on assets, and earnings for the past five years. Extend the trend lines out for the next five years to improve your perspective. You probably won't have all the information you'll need at this meeting, however, so assign someone to put it together for the next meeting.

But don't stop now. Have the planning team also arrive at a consensus as to whether it sees the company as a single-industry, diversified, or conglomerate type of firm. If they see it as a single-industry or diversified company, have the team specify general restrictions, such as unacceptable types of products, services, or geographic locations. Then have the team specify, in very general terms, customers and products and/or services. (See the examples in the previous section on mission for ideas.) If the team sees the company as being highly diversified, write out the general corporate purpose (use Textron's as a guide). Allow about an hour or two, but no more, for this job. As you go through the process you'll gain insights that will help you to better define your company's mission.

At the close of the first meeting, briefly discuss policies. Think about past discussions or actions of management in the company. Are there any major areas that have caused confusion in the past? If so, these areas need policies. Also reflect on new restrictions, as well as any old ones, that the government is really interested in enforcing. You can prevent trouble by making sure that management in your company is aware of them. And a good way to ensure this is to specify them as a policy. At this meeting, though, the policy discussion should be short. Set up a task force to prepare tentative policies for discussion at the next meeting.

At the second meeting, with the help of the data you've collected, analyze your track record for your key objective areas. This will help "bracket in" acceptability and reasonability. Remember, the first year's objectives will probably have to be close to the trend line unless your company has been sloppily managed. Of course, your five-year objectives can have considerable stretch, which is one of the reasons for using a planning horizon of that length. In addition, give some thought to these questions while you're setting quantitative amounts: What kind of sales, return on assets, and earnings are necessary as far as your stockholders are concerned? What kind of growth rate is necessary to provide challenges and advancement for your key employees? What is your labor situation? If you make high profits, will this encourage labor unions to make more demands? If so, you might wish to set profits somewhat lower and aim instead for growth. Finally, how much growth can you effectively handle, given your present resources (management, labor, finances, and physical facilities)? In some cases, there may be great potential for growth. In others, consolidation may be a better alternative.

Finalize the policies you discussed last time (or, if necessary, have the task force amend and/or add to the tentative policies; at the next meeting, as part of the agenda, you can finalize them).

The purpose of objectives, mission, and policies is to provide guidelines for action. Your objectives tell you what you want to accomplish; your mission, what general areas of business are acceptable; and your policies, what rules of conduct are permissible. The next step is to take a close look at your company's strengths and weaknesses.

CASE EXAMPLE

For clarity, a case example is given of a hypothetical company working through the planning process, from setting objectives through formulating strategy. The case example will be continued in each chapter illustrating the recommended procedures.

Acme Metalworking Company is a small limited-line manufacturer of office equipment for the home. The company markets office desks to mass merchandisers under their private labels. The firm is located in a Georgia metropolitan area.

Prior to World War II, Acme was a small job shop employing 8 people. During the war, government contracts were secured for various items. One was for metal desks. By the end of the war the firm had expanded to just under 50 employees and had been incorporated. After the government contracts terminated, a contract for budget low-price metal desks with a large mail-order firm enabled the president to keep his plant largely intact. Through efficiency in manufacturing and by expanding its sales to other national mass merchandisers, the company has grown until now it has 286 employees: 240 are in manufacturing, 46 are clerical and executive. Several years ago the president, who was the founder of the company, retired and turned the company over to his son.

Acme's income statement and balance sheet for the year just ending are shown in Table 4-2. Until last year Acme had a severe cash problem. They had built a new plant and moved in during a severe recession. The recession had caused a slump in sales, and coupled with the new plant expenditures, Acme's cash position was extremely weak.

Since desks are capital expenditure items, their purchase is postponable. Consequently, sales are vulnerable to recessions. Because of the rise in the price of steel, the current market situation favors products priced at the lower end of the price line. Top-quality desks are almost priced out of the market.

The dominant distribution channel is through mass merchandisers. Running a distant second are the channels through wholesalers. Typically consumers purchase through mass merchandisers; businesses tend to purchase through dealer-office supply houses. Dealer-office supply houses carry a full line of office equipment including desks, chairs, and file cabinets. Dealers usually buy from wholesalers. This

Table 4-2 Income Statement and Balance Sheet of Acme Metalworking Company

Consolidated Income Statement ($000)	
Sales	12,100
Cost of goods sold (including selling costs)	8,460
Depreciation	900
Interest	740
Pretax income	2,000
Income tax	800
Net income	1,200

Balance Sheet ($000)

Assets		Liabilities	
Current assets		Current liabilities	
Cash	200	Accounts payable	500
Marketable securities	100	Bank note	1,900
Accounts receivable	1,300	Long-term debt	5,500
Inventories	1,500	Total liabilities	7,900
Long-term assets		Shareholders' equity	
Land	800	Common stock	100
Plant & equipment	9,000	Retained earnings	4,900
Total assets	12,900	Total liabilities & equity	12,900

simplifies ordering, and, of more importance, most dealers cannot buy from manufacturers in lots that make shipments from manufacturers feasible unless dealers carry large inventories. As a result, manufacturers usually sell through wholesalers rather than directly to dealers. Wholesalers prefer to deal with full-line manufacturers because of ease in ordering, ability to operate with smaller inventories, and ease in merchandising. Large dealers who do buy from manufacturers prefer to deal with full-line manufacturers for the same reason. In recent years there has been a winnowing out of both small wholesalers and dealers.

Today, Acme faces only one major competitor. Because of economies of scale in manufacturing low-price desks—coupled with price competition—smaller firms are not competitive. As a result, firms producing such products are getting bigger or dropping out. West Coast firms are unable to compete east of the Mississippi because of freight costs. For the same reason, Acme cannot compete west of the

Rockies. This problem decreases in direct proportion to the size of the order, however: The larger the volume of shipment, the greater the feasibility of more distant shipments.

Acme's formal planning horizon has been one year. Although the company has been very successful, the president believes the company has reached a size where it no longer has the flexibility that it once had. He feels that it is now the time for his company to extend its planning horizon to five years. Another impetus for a five-year plan came just recently when one of their key customers was interested in knowing Acme's five-year plan so better future relationships could be planned.

The planning team chosen by the president consists of the five top executives of the firm—himself and the vice-presidents of manufacturing, finance, marketing, and personnel.

Objectives

The planning team set the following objectives for Acme:

	First Year	*Fifth Year*
Return on assets	9%	12%
Sales	14,000,000	25,000,000
Debt/equity	1.1 to 1	1 to 1
Profits	1,400,000	2,500,000
Dividends	350,000	600,000

Although there have been "peaks and valleys," sales and profits have averaged about 15 percent a year for the past five years, so the objectives for the next five years almost follow a trend line. Yet the planning team feels that they have been extremely fortunate in securing this growth rate during the past and, that if they could continue this rate of growth for the next five years, they would be making excellent progress. They believe that interest rates will be higher during the next five years and therefore have decided they will have to utilize assets more efficiently. They also feel they should drop their debt/equity ratio to 50 percent given the relative volatility of their industry. Acme has a good cash position and the planning team is willing to "take it on the chin" for a year, but in general they want to realize increments of growth during the five-year period.

Mission

The team sees no reason why manufacturing should be limited to budget low-price office desks for the home. Yet they believe that their "playing field," at least initially, should be limited to manufacturing nontechnical metal products. They recognize that if they can't find a suitable strategy within this boundary, they might have to change their mission in order to bring other alternatives into the scope of their search. But at least for now, this will be their mission: the manufacture and marketing of nontechnical metal products.

Policies

Concerning policies, the planning team set forth three "rules of conduct":

- Increase the transfer of stock to key executives, but retain family control.
- Acme Metalworking Company will not tolerate any unethical (and obviously illegal) conduct on the part of any employee.
- Acme Metalworking Company will seek to maintain stability of employment—at all levels—within the company.

The policies on conduct and stability will be made public throughout the company while the policy on ownership will remain privy to members of the planning team.

APPENDIX 4—A Explanation of P. & L. and Balance Sheets and Common Ratios

Consolidated Income Statement ($000)

Sales	12,100
Cost of goods sold (including selling costs)	8,460
Depreciation	900
Interest	740
Pretax income	2,000
Income tax	800
Net income	1,200

Consolidated Balance Sheet ($000)

Assets		Liabilities	
Current assets		Current liabilities	
Cash	200	Accounts payable	500
Marketable securities	100	Bank note	1,900
Accounts receivable	1,300	Long-term debt	5,500
Inventories	1,500		
Total current assets	3,100	Total liabilities	7,900
Long-term assets		Shareholders' equity	
Land	800	Common stock	100
Plant and equipment	9,000	Retained earnings	4,900
	9,800		5,000
Total assets		Total liabilities & equity	12,900
Current & long-term	12,900		

Common Ratios

Liquidity ratios

Current ratio:

Current assets ($3,100) compared with current liabilities ($2,400) = 1.29 to 1

Quick ratio or acid test:

Deducting inventories from current assets and comparing the remainder ($1,600) to current liabilities ($2,400) = .66 to 1

Profitability ratios

Return on assets:

Net income ($1,200) compared with total assets ($12,900) = 9%

Return on invested capital:

Net income ($1,200) compared with shareholders' equity ($5,000) and long-term debt ($5,500) = 11.4%

Return on shareholders' equity:

Net income ($1,200) compared with shareholders' equity ($5,000) = 24%

Leverage ratios

Debt/equity:

Long-term debt ($5,500) compared to owners equity ($5,000) = 1.1 to 1

Current liabilities to equity:

Current liabilities ($2,400) to owners equity ($5,000) = .48 to 1

Times interest earned:

Earnings before interest and taxes ($2,740) compared with interest ($740) = 3.7 to 1

APPENDIX 4—B Key Business Ratios*

HOW THE RATIOS ARE FIGURED

Although terms like "median" and "quartile" are everyday working language to statisticians, their precise meaning may be vague to some businessmen.

In the various ratio tables, three figures appear under each ratio heading. The center figure in bold type is the **median;** the figures immediately above and below the median are, respectively, the **upper** and **lower quartiles.** To understand their use, the reader should also know how they are calculated.

First, year-end financial statements from concerns in the survey (almost exclusively corporations with a tangible net worth over $100,000) are analyzed by Dun & Bradstreet statisticians. Then each of 14 ratios is calculated individually for every concern in the sample.

These individual ratio figures, entered on data-processing cards, are segregated by line of business, and then arranged in order of size

*Source: 1976 statistics from 125 lines of retailing, wholesaling and manufacturing & construction developed by the business economics division of Dun & Bradstreet, Inc. Copyright: DUN & BRADSTREET, INC., 1978. Reprinted with permission.

—the best ratio at the top, the weakest at the bottom. The figure that falls in the middle of this series becomes the **median** for that ratio in that line of business. The figure halfway between the median and the top of the series is the **upper quartile;** the number halfway between the median and the bottom of the series is the **lower quartile.**

In a statistical sense, each median then is the **typical ratio figure** for all concerns studied in a given line. The upper and lower quartile figures typify the experience of firms in the top and bottom halves of the sample, respectively.

Current Assets to Current Debt. Current Assets are divided by total Current Debt. Current Assets are the sum of cash, notes and accounts receivable (less reserves for bad debt), advances on merchandise, merchandise inventories, and listed Federal, State and Municipal securities not in excess of market value. Current Debt is the total of all liabilities falling due within one year. This is one test of solvency.

Net Profits on Net Sales. Obtained by dividing net earnings of the business, after taxes, by net sales (the dollar volume less returns, allowances, and cash discounts). This important yardstick in measuring profitability should be related to the ratio which follows.

Net Profits on Tangible Net Worth. Tangible Net Worth is the equity of stockholders in the business, as obtained by subtracting total liabilities from total assets, and then deducting intangibles. The ratio is obtained by dividing Net Profits after taxes by Tangible Net Worth. Tendency is to look increasingly to this ratio as a final criterion of profitability. Generally, a relationship of at least 10 percent is regarded as a desirable objective for providing dividends plus funds for future growth.

Net Profits on Net Working Capital. Net Working Capital represents the excess of Current Assets over Current Debt. This margin represents the cushion available to the business for carrying inventories and receivables, and for financing day-to-day operations. The ratio is obtained by dividing Net Profits, after taxes, by Net Working Capital.

Net Sales to Tangible Net Worth. Net Sales are divided by Tangible Net Worth. This gives a measure of relative turnover of invested capital.

Net Sales to Net Working Capital. Net Sales are divided by Net Working Capital. This provides a guide as to the extent the company is turning its working capital and the margin of operating funds.

Collection Period. Annual net sales are divided by 365 days to obtain average daily credit sales and then the average daily credit sales are divided into notes and accounts receivable, including any discounted. This ratio is helpful in analyzing the collectibility of receivables. Many feel the collection period should not exceed the net maturity indicated by selling terms by more than 10 to 15 days. When comparing the collection period of one concern with that of another, allowances should be made for possible variations in selling terms.

Net Sales to Inventory. Obtained by dividing annual Net Sales by Merchandise Inventory as carried on the balance sheet. This quotient does not yield an actual physical turnover. It provides a yardstick for comparing stock-to-sales ratios of one concern with another or with those for the industry.

Fixed Assets to Tangible Net Worth. Fixed Assets are divided by Tangible Net Worth. Fixed Assets represent depreciated book values of building, leasehold improvements, machinery, furniture, fixtures, tools, and other physical equipment, plus land, if any, and valued at cost or appraised market value. Ordinarily, this relationship should not exceed 100 percent for a manufacturer, and 75 percent for a wholesaler or retailer.

Current Debt to Tangible Net Worth. Derived by dividing Current Debt by Tangible Net Worth. Ordinarily, a business begins to pile up trouble when this relationship exceeds 80 percent.

Total Debt to Tangible Net Worth. Obtained by dividing total current plus long-term debts by Tangible Net Worth. When this relationship exceeds 100 percent, the equity of creditors in the assets of the business exceeds that of owners.

Inventory to Net Working Capital. Merchandise Inventory is divided by Net Working Capital. This is an additional measure of inventory balance. Ordinarily, the relationship should not exceed 80 percent.

Current Debt to Inventory. Dividing the Current Debt by Inventory yields yet another indication of the extent to which the business relies on funds from disposal of unsold inventories to meet its debts.

Funded Debts to Net Working Capital. Funded Debts are all long-term obligations, as represented by mortgages, bonds, debentures, term loans, serial notes, and other types of liabilities maturing more than one year from statement date. This ratio is obtained by dividing

Funded Debt by Net Working Capital. Analysts tend to compare Funded Debts with Net Working Capital in determining whether or

Table 4B-1 Retailing

Retailing

Line of Business (and number of concerns reporting)	Current assets to current debt	Net profits on net sales	Net profits on tangible net worth	Net profits on net working capital	Net sales to tangible net worth	Net sales to net working capital	Collection period	Net sales to inventory	Fixed assets to tangible net worth	Current debt to tangible net worth	Total debt to tangible net worth	Inventory to net working capital	Current debt to inventory	Funded debts to net working capital
	Times	Per cent	Per cent	Per cent	Times	Times	Days	Times	Per cent	Per cent	Per cent	Per cent	Per cent	Per cent
5531	2.72	4.04	15.94	25.84	7.51	8.88	**	6.8	15.2	45.9	101.6	102.0	61.0	21.5
Auto & Home	**1.79**	**1.41**	**8.21**	**11.27**	**4.54**	**6.39**	**	**5.8**	**27.6**	**105.0**	**166.2**	**123.0**	**95.3**	**53.0**
Supply Stores (53)	1.38	0.47	2.33	3.68	3.18	4.86	**	3.8	53.3	185.8	290.0	179.4	146.3	111.2
5641	4.44	4.46	17.03	19.83	7.12	9.47	**	5.6	5.9	32.4	68.5	88.5	32.0	26.2
Children's & Infants'	**2.66**	**2.45**	**9.06**	**11.35**	**4.95**	**5.14**	**	**4.3**	**21.7**	**61.0**	**103.6**	**113.0**	**51.0**	**41.7**
Wear Stores (41)	1.79	0.44	0.92	1.59	3.04	3.17	**	2.9	45.4	116.0	186.5	162.5	84.2	78.7
5611	4.52	4.64	15.49	20.51	5.68	6.24	**	6.3	7.5	22.4	45.0	69.3	36.3	10.8
Clothing & Furnishings	**2.75**	**2.21**	**7.14**	**8.26**	**3.49**	**4.19**	**	**4.4**	**16.5**	**47.5**	**88.1**	**92.4**	**61.8**	**28.1**
Men's & Boys' (223)	1.84	0.48	1.54	2.07	2.38	2.69	**	3.1	37.2	90.3	153.1	131.1	93.0	52.0
5311	4.39	3.38	12.91	17.84	6.01	7.29	**	7.1	6.4	13.7	26.7	50.1	28.2	3.5
Department Stores (338)	**2.71**	**1.59**	**6.25**	**7.71**	**4.10**	**4.97**	**	**5.5**	**22.9**	**40.4**	**73.1**	**77.4**	**52.1**	**25.2**
	2.00	0.02	0.11	0.15	2.67	3.22	**	4.2	49.5	77.3	125.7	121.6	85.8	53.5
Discount Stores (125)	2.96	2.86	17.10	20.20	7.99	9.32	**	6.9	2.8	36.6	53.2	68.7	40.8	4.0
	2.26	**1.40**	**10.89**	**12.84**	**6.31**	**6.77**	**	**5.2**	**14.7**	**61.5**	**98.3**	**127.9**	**55.8**	**27.2**
	1.76	0.47	4.91	4.82	4.21	4.34	**	4.1	35.5	93.4	152.0	174.4	78.7	53.4
Discount Stores,	3.17	5.45	15.83	17.78	6.18	6.62	**	5.4	9.0	38.9	49.1	97.6	40.6	10.3
Leased Departments (24)	**2.66**	**2.62**	**9.35**	**9.72**	**4.47**	**5.08**	**	**4.6**	**19.7**	**55.1**	**90.1**	**126.2**	**53.1**	**24.8**
	2.02	1.36	5.59	5.79	3.76	4.31	**	4.0	34.8	110.5	152.1	160.2	66.1	35.9
5651	6.23	5.33	16.48	19.35	4.18	5.62	**	5.4	4.1	16.1	44.2	53.9	37.0	12.9
Family Clothing	**2.84**	**2.39**	**6.67**	**8.51**	**3.16**	**3.92**	**	**3.8**	**16.5**	**44.1**	**76.3**	**102.0**	**57.1**	**28.8**
Stores (103)	2.08	0.55	1.61	1.80	1.78	2.21	**	2.8	37.3	72.5	139.4	146.5	80.0	68.9
5712	5.00	5.35	14.06	15.24	5.30	5.36	27	6.0	5.2	22.2	47.3	37.2	49.5	13.7
Furniture Stores (159)	**3.27**	**2.30**	**7.21**	**7.34**	**2.62**	**2.85**	**78**	**4.4**	**12.0**	**47.8**	**87.6**	**66.3**	**69.2**	**23.4**
	1.98	0.75	1.54	1.99	1.66	1.72	162	3.4	25.6	91.3	188.1	111.2	99.0	49.3
5541	3.48	6.96	22.68	75.18	6.44	17.35	**	25.8	27.1	18.8	49.1	45.4	78.7	17.0
Gasoline Service	**1.81**	**3.19**	**15.07**	**40.97**	**3.76**	**10.65**	**	**12.2**	**36.4**	**44.9**	**72.6**	**69.3**	**119.2**	**45.8**
Stations (80)	1.47	1.57	8.71	17.63	2.63	6.06	**	7.8	59.1	72.4	114.7	117.1	216.6	99.8
5411	2.22	1.60	16.72	45.16	16.07	42.24	**	26.5	38.9	39.2	65.1	98.0	71.4	20.5
Grocery Stores (136)	**1.68**	**0.93**	**11.77**	**26.71**	**11.64**	**24.34**	**	**17.0**	**73.1**	**67.7**	**101.7**	**150.6**	**100.3**	**64.1**
	1.34	0.53	5.60	15.19	8.49	17.03	**	13.7	51.7	103.4	160.0	227.6	140.1	114.0
5251	6.15	6.25	16.96	25.90	4.57	6.30	**	6.6	9.0	12.9	29.3	60.1	30.6	11.0
Hardware Stores (89)	**3.09**	**3.23**	**10.83**	**14.99**	**2.61**	**3.66**	**	**4.3**	**18.3**	**34.3**	**69.6**	**80.2**	**58.5**	**28.2**
	1.98	1.67	4.15	7.02	1.70	2.42	**	3.4	40.5	68.6	131.9	121.1	91.5	80.2

** Not computed. Necessary information as to the division between cash sales was available in too few cases to obtain an average collection period usable as a broad guide.

not long-term debts are in proper proportion. Ordinarily, this relationship should not exceed 100 percent.

Table 4B-1 Retailing (cont.)

Line of Business (and number of concerns reporting)	Current assets to current debt	Net profits on net sales	Net profits on tangible net worth	Net profits on net working capital	Net sales to tangible net worth	Net sales to net working capital	Collection period	Net sales to inventory	Fixed assets to tangible net worth	Current debt to tangible net worth	Total debt to tangible net worth	Inventory to net working capital	Current debt to inventory	Funded debts to net working capital
	Times	Per cent	Per cent	Per cent	Times	Times	Days	Times	Per cent	Per cent	Per cent	Per cent	Per cent	Per cent
5722	3.48	4.38	15.41	17.94	6.43	7.50	16	7.3	6.8	32.4	59.8	61.5	53.6	12.0
Household Appliance	**2.40**	**1.75**	**8.40**	**9.96**	**4.25**	**4.84**	**27**	**5.0**	**14.4**	**61.0**	**133.8**	**95.0**	**75.7**	**32.7**
Stores (87)	1.47	0.70	1.93	2.48	2.40	3.15	52	3.7	38.6	153.7	285.0	136.2	126.6	64.0
5944	5.51	8.44	14.02	17.72	3.06	3.26	**	3.6	3.4	18.0	44.4	67.7	28.2	8.4
Jewelry Stores (93)	**3.50**	**4.19**	**7.28**	**8.43**	**2.09**	**2.28**	**	**2.7**	**9.6**	**34.4**	**79.8**	**89.4**	**55.8**	**27.5**
	2.09	1.79	3.55	4.84	1.20	1.76	**	1.8	24.5	69.8	156.4	128.7	79.4	43.8
5211	4.88	4.90	15.82	21.27	5.95	7.46	34	10.1	10.9	18.5	47.2	50.3	43.7	11.7
Lumber & Other Bldg.	**2.78**	**2.53**	**8.60**	**11.36**	**3.61**	**4.44**	**49**	**6.2**	**24.4**	**48.9**	**92.3**	**75.7**	**78.5**	**32.9**
Mtls. Dealers (159)	1.92	1.20	3.68	4.66	2.38	3.16	64	4.4	42.5	82.9	152.5	99.0	131.2	58.2
5399	4.89	3.60	16.35	25.38	7.67	9.12	**	8.0	10.0	16.6	50.7	77.6	30.4	9.1
Miscellaneous General	**2.43**	**2.06**	**9.80**	**13.79**	**4.75**	**5.60**	**	**4.7**	**25.0**	**45.3**	**99.2**	**103.6**	**55.7**	**38.2**
Mdse. Stores (103)	1.81	0.93	3.70	4.88	2.42	3.14	**	3.3	44.4	85.6	170.5	166.8	86.2	67.4
5511	1.99	1.88	17.07	26.34	14.84	18.30	**	8.8	9.4	72.0	109.4	116.9	71.3	6.1
Motor Vehicle	**1.57**	**1.04**	**11.44**	**15.50**	**9.89**	**14.11**	**	**7.3**	**21.7**	**124.3**	**180.6**	**196.3**	**87.7**	**23.6**
Dealers (74)	1.30	0.54	5.71	7.03	7.02	9.72	**	5.7	49.7	193.8	263.5	264.2	108.0	91.5
5231	4.50	5.32	18.27	29.63	5.15	6.27	**	9.9	7.7	16.1	28.3	65.1	30.6	10.7
Paint, Glass &	**3.51**	**3.53**	**10.73**	**14.33**	**3.18**	**4.35**	**	**5.1**	**25.9**	**34.5**	**76.5**	**89.7**	**57.2**	**28.9**
Wallpaper Stores (33)	2.06	1.27	6.01	6.73	1.61	2.52	**	3.5	44.6	73.1	117.5	108.1	97.7	63.2
5732	3.18	7.03	38.32	51.78	10.18	10.77	**	6.7	7.3	28.3	83.5	61.8	46.1	13.0
Radio & Television	**1.96**	**3.25**	**21.74**	**26.16**	**5.43**	**6.21**	**	**5.3**	**23.0**	**74.3**	**165.5**	**116.8**	**78.7**	**33.0**
Stores (63)	1.35	2.19	8.11	14.29	2.62	4.16	**	3.9	50.0	180.6	272.7	215.1	124.2	76.9
5261-5191	3.47	4.91	24.96	48.77	5.88	10.67	**	13.4	15.8	18.7	33.7	58.3	53.8	10.8
Retail & Wholesale	**2.05**	**3.58**	**15.77**	**26.27**	**4.16**	**7.49**	**	**7.7**	**30.7**	**52.1**	**77.0**	**87.6**	**111.5**	**28.8**
Nurseries, Lawn, Garden	1.42	1.95	6.48	11.11	2.66	4.58	**	5.3	49.2	91.0	122.3	140.4	171.0	62.0
and Farm Supplies (60)														
5661	3.84	4.13	12.86	16.46	5.56	6.50	**	4.7	6.5	27.0	60.3	85.0	35.6	14.4
Shoe Stores (97)	**2.61**	**1.61**	**6.09**	**7.04**	**3.71**	**4.52**	**	**3.9**	**17.1**	**53.4**	**106.8**	**123.1**	**55.0**	**31.1**
	1.81	0.00	0.00	0.00	2.66	3.52	**	2.7	34.7	92.3	151.9	157.1	75.2	50.4
5331	6.21	5.00	15.25	22.61	5.66	7.10	**	5.2	7.4	10.6	32.8	86.4	22.7	9.0
Variety Stores (65)	**3.50**	**2.41**	**9.69**	**11.28**	**3.63**	**4.21**	**	**4.0**	**19.1**	**30.0**	**71.6**	**107.1**	**37.2**	**36.3**
	2.09	1.15	5.00	5.45	2.71	3.28	**	3.0	46.6	69.5	170:2	149.1	60.4	76.6
5621	4.76	5.99	16.85	21.96	5.44	6.69	**	8.8	8.6	19.8	33.7	50.3	47.2	15.5
Women's Ready-to-	**2.76**	**2.37**	**7.83**	**9.77**	**3.40**	**4.12**	**	**5.8**	**18.7**	**45.9**	**82.8**	**75.1**	**76.8**	**33.3**
Wear Stores (190)	1.92	0.52	1.67	1.74	1.65	2.72	**	4.1	40.6	82.3	149.1	115.1	110.7	78.8

** Not computed. Necessary information as to the division between cash sales was available in too few cases to obtain an average collection period usable as a broad guide.

Table 4B-2 Wholesaling

Wholesaling

Line of Business (and number of concerns reporting)	Current assets to current debt	Net profits on net sales	Net profits on tangible net worth	Net profits on net working capital	Net sales to tangible net worth	Net sales to net working capital	Collection period	Net sales to inventory	Fixed assets to tangible net worth	Current debt to tangible net worth	Total debt to tangible net worth	Inventory to net working capital	Current debt to inventory	Funded debts to net working capital
	Times	Per cent	Per cent	Per cent	Times	Times	Days	Times	Per cent	Per cent	Per cent	Per cent	Per cent	Per cent
5075 & 78 Air Condtg.	3.24	3.20	14.55	14.73	6.25	7.72	42	8.0	6.3	30.0	71.8	67.2	52.2	9.5
& Refrigtn. Equipt.	**2.27**	**2.08**	**10.54**	**11.49**	**4.59**	**5.18**	**46**	**5.0**	**10.2**	**82.5**	**130.3**	**96.3**	**88.6**	**20.4**
& Supplies (49)	1.57	1.28	6.54	7.38	3.15	3.33	58	4.0	21.0	155.8	224.1	126.4	134.1	41.1
5013 Automotive	3.63	4.37	15.33	19.30	6.13	7.35	29	7.5	6.3	34.3	57.8	64.8	47.0	13.8
Parts & Supplies	**2.28**	**2.50**	**10.76**	**12.27**	**4.09**	**4.96**	**36**	**5.8**	**16.0**	**55.4**	**107.7**	**87.4**	**83.1**	**24.7**
(158)	1.68	1.09	4.74	6.30	3.03	3.71	48	4.2	32.9	129.6	173.1	128.9	119.7	45.1
5181 & 82 Beer, Wine	3.58	3.23	19.04	33.62	11.87	18.55	3	16.4	14.8	34.8	62.0	80.0	56.3	16.1
& Alcoholic Beverages	**2.12**	**1.79**	**12.53**	**16.25**	**7.95**	**11.39**	**15**	**9.8**	**27.5**	**58.7**	**132.5**	**118.4**	**82.3**	**35.3**
(109)	1.52	0.82	6.89	7.13	5.15	7.50	26	7.0	51.9	135.2	210.9	178.4	110.3	67.5
5161 Chemicals &	2.47	4.95	19.55	28.71	8.90	10.76	35	16.0	12.0	42.9	63.7	53.9	102.0	5.5
Allied Products	**2.16**	**3.08**	**14.57**	**20.19**	**5.79**	**7:53**	**42**	**12.5**	**21.6**	**67.8**	**92.4**	**69.6**	**154.0**	**15.0**
(50)	1.68	1.93	9.52	13.84	3.51	5.46	47	9.3	39.2	111.1	175.5	95.4	208.1	43.6
5137 Clothing & Acces-	3.13	3.08	16.46	20.24	10.15	12.48	27	20.3	3.0	36.1	59.2	44.7	68.4	6.5
sories, Women's, Children's	**1.86**	**1.46**	**9.57**	**9.60**	**5.61**	**6.29**	**41**	**10.1**	**5.9**	**75.3**	**95.2**	**73.8**	**148.9**	**13.6**
& Infants' (68)	1.44	0.42	2.05	2.32	3.18	4.03	59	6.3	12.9	173.6	263.9	134.9	245.5	37.3
5136 Clothing & Fur-	3.88	6.48	18.46	20.60	10.55	11.88	25	9.4	2.5	31.8	60.7	59.2	46.8	5.7
nishings, Men's & Boys'	**2.62**	**1.92**	**10.17**	**11.96**	**4.94**	**5.66**	**36**	**6.1**	**6.1**	**56.9**	**98.3**	**85.2**	**76.1**	**14.3**
(66)	1.46	0.57	4.21	4.62	2.25	3.05	58	3.5	14.5	189.1	227.5	127.1	147.8	36.8
5081 Commercial	3.68	4.46	14.53	20.49	6.56	8.53	33	8.5	5.4	29.2	42.2	51.1	59.5	7.5
Machines & Equipment	**2.22**	**2.06**	**9.89**	**11.00**	**4.21**	**5.32**	**52**	**6.0**	**11.3**	**56.0**	**93.7**	**81.5**	**117.2**	**17.4**
(58)	1.64	1.12	3.37	4.07	2.50	3.31	79	4.5	39.0	114.5	163.7	128.4	175.9	51.3
5145 Confectionery	4.39	2.35	16.79	21.59	15.66	16.09	10	20.2	5.5	25.8	64.7	58.7	50.0	19.6
(37)	**2.66**	**0.90**	**10.43**	**11.38**	**9.04**	**10.90**	**16**	**12.7**	**17.9**	**50.8**	**134.1**	**82.1**	**79.1**	**30.7**
	1.88	0.47	4.00	5.15	4.95	6.88	22	9.4	43.4	100.2	225.6	113.8	106.3	92.4
5143 Dairy Products	2.36	2.63	15.98	39.25	16.36	35.09	14	54.0	13.4	33.3	42.2	40.6	105.6	7.6
(53)	**1.72**	**1.27**	**9.18**	**18.01**	**8.81**	**14.84**	**25**	**26.6**	**36.8**	**61.0**	**96.3**	**57.0**	**212.2**	**40.5**
	1.31	0.30	1.73	3.28	5.25	11.66	30	16.5	60.8	104.2	185.9	100.0	344.5	78.6
5122 Drugs, Drug	2.44	1.75	12.70	14.14	11.61	12.41	27	8.2	7.8	63.6	98.7	83.4	70.4	10.3
Proprietaries &	**1.80**	**1.09**	**7.41**	**8.24**	**8.40**	**9.21**	**32**	**7.2**	**15.8**	**113.4**	**163.3**	**110.5**	**102.0**	**23.1**
Sundries (92)	1.49	0.31	3.75	3.89	5.97	6.23	44	5.9	34.4	175.1	266.8	153.4	129.5	49.0
5063 Electrical Appa-	3.02	3.00	14.34	17.65	8.84	9.97	35	9.8	7.3	44.5	59.6	65.8	68.3	6.2
ratus & Equipment	**2.25**	**1.52**	**8.58**	**9.68**	**6.65**	**6.76**	**43**	**6.6**	**15.7**	**77.5**	**111.9**	**89.0**	**96.4**	**18.2**
(131)	1.69	0.74	3.52	4.20	4.45	4.71	51	5.6	30.0	127.3	228.1	118.1	141.6	37.2
5064 Electrical Appli-	2.55	2.71	14.29	16.78	9.71	10.44	27	8.2	4.6	56.2	76.9	71.1	72.4	5.4
ances, TV & Radio Sets	**1.90**	**1.45**	**8.75**	**9.97**	**6.46**	**7.23**	**38**	**5.9**	**8.9**	**92.9**	**151.3**	**102.7**	**93.4**	**20.2**
(96)	1.59	0.75	4.51	4.81	4.03	4.64	49	4.6	20.9	165.5	267.0	167.9	115.5	43.1
5065 Electronic Parts	3.28	4.23	19.03	20.46	6.03	6.31	28	7.4	6.6	38.8	69.0	60.2	56.2	9.5
& Equipment	**2.52**	**2.63**	**11.45**	**11.81**	**4.27**	**4.56**	**39**	**5.7**	**12.6**	**68.7**	**115.9**	**90.8**	**87.2**	**26.0**
(53)	1.74	1.15	6.06	6.09	3.31	3.58	53	3.4	22.1	112.7	236.4	140.6	101.6	39.4
5083 Farm & Garden	2.66	4.34	21.92	24.91	6.84	8.30	18	6.8	10.8	50.7	65.6	80.7	63.6	9.3
Machinery & Equipment	**1.97**	**2.72**	**12.73**	**15.47**	**4.79**	**5.41**	**36**	**4.2**	**19.1**	**90.3**	**129.1**	**117.7**	**87.6**	**15.3**
(143)	1.52	1.56	6.03	6.62	3.53	4.05	55	3.1	31.0	166.0	214.5	179.2	113.0	42.2
5139 Footwear	3.18	3.63	16.32	19.38	7.61	7.65	40	8.4	1.4	37.4	87.7	47.2	77.0	6.9
(62)	**2.20**	**1.05**	**6.17**	**7.22**	**4.99**	**5.04**	**55**	**5.9**	**3.7**	**84.9**	**128.4**	**69.5**	**115.5**	**21.1**
	1.60	0.26	2.78	3.09	3.38	3.55	80	3.8	9.8	158.8	241.3	137.9	185.3	27.7
5148 Fresh Fruits	3.41	3.17	17.31	37.07	18.68	25.83	9	129.5	12.8	21.9	56.4	11.4	105.8	13.9
& Vegetables	**1.89**	**1.17**	**12.07**	**15.62**	**7.76**	**14.06**	**14**	**62.0**	**40.7**	**54.8**	**118.0**	**28.7**	**236.8**	**39.9**
(77)	1.37	0.40	2.86	4.13	5.08	8.93	28	24.4	64.0	135.0	252.0	61.6	529.6	112.2

Table 4B-2 Wholesaling (cont.)

Line of Business (and number of concerns reporting)	Current assets to current debt	Net profits on net sales	Net profits on tangible net worth	Net profits on net working capital	Net sales to tangible net worth	Net sales to net working capital	Collection period	Net sales to inventory	Fixed assets to tangible net worth	Current debt to tangible net worth	Total debt to tangible net worth	Inventory to net working capital	Current debt to inventory	Funded debts to net working capital
	Times	Per cent	Per cent	Per cent	Times	Times	Days	Times	Per cent	Per cent	Per cent	Per cent	Per cent	Per cent
5021 & 23 Furniture	3.34	2.65	17.06	19.27	9.98	11.34	28	10.8	7.1	43.8	68.3	57.6	62.6	9.3
& Home Furnishings	**2.26**	**1.41**	**9.94**	**11.20**	**6.09**	**6.44**	**41**	**6.7**	**12.3**	**74.8**	**145.6**	**88.2**	**102.6**	**19.6**
(77)	1.50	0.52	2.51	3.14	4.74	4.97	53	5.1	29.5	178.8	240.6	182.4	143.0	51.8
5141 Groceries	3.09	1.40	14.27	20.36	22.14	25.61	7	18.0	12.4	47.8	80.0	87.0	52.3	18.6
General Line	**1.90**	**0.59**	**7.50**	**9.46**	**14.09**	**17.16**	**11**	**13.0**	**30.6**	**93.5**	**142.7**	**131.6**	**83.5**	**42.6**
(168)	1.52	0.24	3.00	3.40	8.29	8.41	19	9.1	65.9	163.8	229.5	177.6	108.8	79.4
5072 Hardware	4.17	4.39	14.70	17.22	6.09	6.64	27	8.3	6.5	26.4	58.9	71.1	39.4	9.3
(162)	**2.73**	**2.41**	**9.57**	**11.21**	**3.89**	**4.76**	**38**	**5.5**	**12.9**	**52.1**	**95.0**	**94.6**	**64.5**	**23.1**
	1.89	1.13	4.45	5.41	2.83	3.09	47	3.8	27.4	99.0	152.0	121.6	98.2	39.2
5084 Industrial	3.00	4.17	17.12	25.11	9.32	12.86	34	15.3	9.3	36.5	67.0	55.1	71.0	9.7
Machinery & Equipment	**1.94**	**2.27**	**11.39**	**14.66**	**5.24**	**6.25**	**42**	**7.9**	**20.7**	**76.9**	**114.4**	**75.0**	**123.3**	**49.3**
(95)	1.49	0.96	6.92	8.23	3.23	4.11	54	4.6	44.3	129.5	189.8	114.8	218.8	72.9
5031 & 39 Lumber &	3.76	2.85	13.32	17.86	7.90	9.90	28	11.0	8.5	32.3	62.3	58.6	54.2	6.2
Construction Materials	**2.26**	**1.26**	**8.38**	**9.68**	**5.51**	**6.63**	**40**	**7.4**	**19.7**	**61.3**	**109.6**	**87.2**	**87.8**	**24.2**
(134)	1.65	0.35	2.13	2.51	3.69	4.52	53	5.7	41.7	116.5	188.5	121.1	152.8	56.4
5147 Meats &	2.94	2.27	15.25	20.50	22.83	28.14	12	62.7	6.3	41.5	78.5	34.0	89.8	21.0
Meat Products	**2.18**	**0.64**	**10.36**	**13.14**	**12.85**	**16.44**	**20**	**28.6**	**24.2**	**59.8**	**151.9**	**59.8**	**129.5**	**48.0**
(53)	1.57	0.18	4.55	6.50	7.22	10.87	26	19.1	50.3	140.0	228.1	83.8	285.3	79.6
5051 Metals Service	4.08	3.70	13.97	17.93	6.18	9.31	29	8.0	6.9	21.9	50.4	62.0	44.7	1.6
Centers & Offices	**2.27**	**2.28**	**8.60**	**12.22**	**3.93**	**5.44**	**37**	**5.7**	**17.5**	**60.1**	**102.5**	**88.7**	**78.0**	**14.3**
(85)	1.69	0.92	4.44	5.93	2.77	3.49	48	4.0	39.3	112.2	151.3	129.5	115.3	32.2
5198 Paints, Varnishes,	5.18	3.52	18.84	26.90	6.14	8.32	26	8.8	8.6	19.2	55.2	52.6	46.1	14.2
& Supplies	**3.71**	**2.03**	**10.00**	**11.62**	**3.88**	**5.30**	**35**	**6.8**	**19.5**	**32.3**	**94.0**	**77.1**	**74.5**	**32.4**
(35)	1.70	1.20	4.64	6.49	3.18	3.49	46	6.1	34.7	75.0	148.4	122.1	118.9	66.6
5111-12-13 Paper &	3.60	3.01	14.36	19.54	8.61	10.45	31	15.6	8.5	27.6	62.3	53.2	63.7	7.7
Paper Products	**2.36**	**1.55**	**9.63**	**12.80**	**5.51**	**6.97**	**41**	**9.7**	**18.4**	**62.0**	**110.0**	**72.9**	**99.9**	**26.2**
(121)	1.71	0.58	3.70	5.71	4.12	4.87	48	5.8	39.1	118.7	168.2	108.2	159.7	47.8
5171 & 72 Petroleum &	2.48	2.28	15.19	36.01	12.02	20.37	18	38.1	26.3	37.2	56.1	34.1	110.6	13.5
Petroleum Products	**1.80**	**1.27**	**8.87**	**16.29**	**7.67**	**11.68**	**25**	**20.8**	**51.0**	**67.8**	**106.7**	**70.1**	**169.2**	**44.7**
(98)	1.30	0.28	4.23	7.66	4.75	9.02	36	13.8	81.3	116.3	183.0	104.8	269.3	103.9
5133 Piece Goods	3.53	2.90	14.59	17.36	8.72	10.21	22	10.7	1.8	37.6	67.1	53.1	63.8	3.2
(116)	**2.15**	**1.48**	**9.49**	**10.76**	**5.79**	**6.03**	**44**	**6.5**	**5.1**	**88.9**	**109.3**	**86.5**	**101.2**	**11.3**
	1.57	0.75	3.23	3.33	3.55	3.70	63	5.1	12.6	159.5	227.5	133.5	152.0	21.5
5074 Plumbing	4.15	2.94	13.39	16.04	6.31	6.98	33	8.9	7.7	26.7	46.9	61.3	49.2	8.0
& Heating Equipment	**2.77**	**1.81**	**7.38**	**8.65**	**4.41**	**4.83**	**42**	**6.2**	**15.6**	**54.9**	**90.0**	**79.3**	**75.1**	**18.4**
& Supplies (184)	2.02	0.47	3.18	3.95	3.01	3.53	51	4.6	30.8	93.7	127.3	106.1	119.3	42.3
5144 Poultry &	2.56	2.42	18.57	27.24	16.15	26.11	17	76.3	6.8	36.1	42.9	13.4	106.5	10.8
Poultry Products	**1.86**	**0.95**	**12.87**	**14.66**	**10.70**	**15.81**	**24**	**42.6**	**17.4**	**71.5**	**110.4**	**54.4**	**169.7**	**29.7**
(49)	1.43	0.27	3.99	4.91	4.27	8.77	33	12.6	59.9	112.7	142.6	118.0	308.8	86.9
5093 Scrap & Waste	4.23	4.22	12.61	24.10	6.27	11.37	12	16.1	10.0	17.8	44.9	39.9	56.2	18.4
Materials	**2.08**	**1.90**	**7.24**	**12.83**	**3.44**	**7.26**	**30**	**10.2**	**40.1**	**43.6**	**122.6**	**67.8**	**120.5**	**42.4**
(68)	1.46	0.44	0.69	1.71	1.83	4.00	43	6.3	74.0	95.3	242.7	113.8	181.2	170.5
5014 Tires & Tubes	2.03	4.54	23.22	35.89	9.55	10.88	34	9.2	14.9	67.1	89.5	71.4	94.5	10.8
(35)	**1.63**	**1.70**	**10.57**	**14.00**	**6.20**	**8.28**	**42**	**6.9**	**31.2**	**116.8**	**171.1**	**117.9**	**131.5**	**30.3**
	1.38	0.98	4.40	7.28	4.56	5.75	52	4.1	51.1	203.2	250.7	190.7	160.2	56.9
5194 Tobacco &	3.14	1.50	17.54	18.08	21.60	22.16	12	27.6	6.7	44.0	60.2	57.6	62.1	6.9
Tobacco Products	**2.24**	**0.94**	**10.06**	**11.89**	**13.14**	**14.41**	**16**	**17.9**	**12.2**	**67.7**	**96.1**	**84.4**	**90.3**	**15.1**
(92)	1.69	0.53	4.81	5.26	7.62	9.88	21	14.9	23.4	135.2	184.5	122.8	158.4	43.4

Table 4B-3 Manufacturing & Construction

Manufacturing & Construction

Line of Business (and number of concerns reporting)	Current assets to current debt	Net profits on net sales	Net profits on tangible net worth	Net profits on net working capital	Net sales to tangible net worth	Net sales to net working capital	Collection period	Net sales to inventory	Fixed assets to tangible net worth	Current debt to tangible net worth	Total debt to tangible net worth	Inventory to net working capital	Current debt to inventory	Funded debts to net working capital
	Times	Per cent	Per cent	Per cent	Times	Times	Days	Times	Per cent	Per cent	Per cent	Per cent	Per cent	Per cent
2873-74-75-79	3.73	5.97	18.79	31.32	5.44	8.66	23	16.6	22.9	25.6	44.1	33.5	96.9	8.9
Agricultural Chemicals	**2.50**	**3.53**	**13.07**	**20.29**	**3.52**	**5.43**	**45**	**9.7**	**35.3**	**40.3**	**56.5**	**70.6**	**119.2**	**17.4**
(51)	1.75	1.78	5.92	10.59	2.08	3.12	65	5.6	60.7	79.9	128.5	100.1	183.8	60.5
3724-28 Airplane Parts	3.94	6.51	19.17	23.76	4.50	5.11	30	10.3	28.7	25.7	41.3	50.2	62.9	13.9
& Accessories	**2.68**	**5.13**	**13.77**	**16.27**	**2.63**	**3.58**	**47**	**5.4**	**48.7**	**43.3**	**62.8**	**72.0**	**98.5**	**38.3**
(63)	1.85	2.38	6.00	7.25	1.84	3.02	60	3.9	61.6	71.3	120.6	100.7	147.2	70.4
2051-52	3.48	4.13	17.01	38.87	9.56	19.29	21	40.2	50.4	18.4	52.6	27.1	105.3	21.4
Bakery Products	**2.01**	**1.86**	**9.63**	**24.79**	**5.55**	**12.41**	**24**	**25.8**	**76.3**	**46.5**	**84.9**	**59.5**	**171.6**	**69.4**
(68)	1.26	0.92	4.06	7.83	4.15	7.55	30	17.6	117.5	81.7	151.9	118.8	328.4	154.6
3312-13-15-16-17 Blast	3.01	5.70	15.08	31.08	3.50	6.96	34	6.8	52.2	28.0	59.8	72.0	56.6	46.7
Furnaces, Steel Wks. &	**2.25**	**4.05**	**9.13**	**17.53**	**2.51**	**5.33**	**40**	**5.2**	**82.9**	**36.1**	**83.0**	**91.4**	**80.7**	**76.0**
Rolling Mills (52)	1.80	2.15	6.22	11.27	2.10	3.53	47	4.1	104.6	64.3	125.1	111.3	107.4	110.3
2331 Blouses & Waists,	2.68	4.00	21.52	25.52	13.20	15.06	27	16.2	3.6	46.6	62.3	54.8	95.8	7.1
Women's & Misses'	**1.71**	**2.11**	**11.86**	**16.01**	**7.43**	**9.10**	**33**	**11.6**	**9.8**	**100.0**	**105.1**	**92.1**	**140.2**	**19.6**
(49)	1.47	0.77	7.77	9.57	4.60	5.20	51	6.8	25.4	205.3	241.0	124.8	232.0	37.1
2731-32 Books; Publish-	4.02	8.53	16.13	19.65	3.56	4.23	41	8.1	9.8	21.5	45.0	53.2	53.7	12.4
ing, Publishing &	**2.65**	**5.03**	**9.60**	**13.54**	**2.17**	**2.94**	**57**	**5.0**	**27.8**	**41.0**	**60.7**	**67.8**	**92.7**	**23.6**
Printing (48)	1.86	1.56	4.48	5.97	1.52	2.16	72	3.1	49.9	73.7	124.1	97.2	234.6	80.3
2211 Broad Woven	3.65	4.48	12.66	21.01	3.28	6.06	42	10.0	38.4	21.5	42.2	54.1	55.1	21.0
Fabrics, Cotton	**2.97**	**2.85**	**8.09**	**13.67**	**3.05**	**4.55**	**57**	**7.6**	**54.2**	**31.2**	**72.6**	**70.0**	**80.4**	**41.4**
(42)	2.24	1.90	4.60	6.99	2.21	3.56	66	5.9	66.7	48.1	114.7	88.7	106.2	78.0
2032-33-34-35-37-38	2.61	3.93	14.85	19.50	5.33	13.54	15	8.7	38.9	40.5	70.2	87.5	65.0	18.3
Canned & Preserved	**1.82**	**2.00**	**7.51**	**11.15**	**3.83**	**6.65**	**23**	**4.4**	**62.6**	**66.9**	**120.4**	**129.3**	**91.0**	**46.1**
Fruits & Vegbls. (76)	1.24	0.50	0.70	0.80	2.79	4.25	31	3.5	94.0	123.9	188.2	257.9	130.4	108.5
2751 Commercial	3.92	5.36	12.20	23.21	4.69	8.16	35	**	32.2	18.5	39.4	**	**	13.2
Printing except Litho-	**2.44**	**2.86**	**9.32**	**13.36**	**3.06**	**6.45**	**45**	**	**47.6**	**35.0**	**61.4**	**	**	**43.9**
graphic (53)	1.79	1.21	5.28	8.57	1.86	3.17	55	**	77.9	57.6	104.8	**	**	87.0
3661-62 Communica-	3.40	7.70	20.37	22.74	3.73	5.67	46	7.4	18.2	30.9	55.7	60.5	54.7	12.8
tion Equipment	**2.47**	**4.79**	**11.90**	**14.44**	**2.64**	**3.77**	**59**	**4.5**	**37.1**	**50.5**	**103.8**	**76.3**	**84.1**	**31.0**
(61)	1.79	1.92	5.86	7.40	2.04	2.60	82	3.9	57.4	94.8	172.8	92.8	117.7	59.1
3271-72-73-74-75 Con-	3.99	5.94	15.03	24.84	3.97	8.80	34	22.2	39.1	18.8	52.6	28.6	65.3	19.9
crete, Gypsum & Plaster	**2.35**	**2.40**	**8.49**	**12.94**	**2.88**	**4.85**	**45**	**10.0**	**62.0**	**35.5**	**81.2**	**51.5**	**130.1**	**57.2**
Products (68)	1.67	0.86	3.35	4.72	1.94	3.62	66	6.1	90.9	77.9	149.9	83.3	232.8	115.5
2065-66-67 Confec-	4.14	6.29	19.06	31.93	5.59	17.12	10	10.4	34.1	20.3	49.7	64.0	56.5	12.7
tionery & Related	**2.36**	**3.43**	**10.07**	**16.42**	**3.87**	**6.99**	**21**	**8.1**	**53.7**	**32.3**	**57.6**	**86.3**	**90.9**	**59.2**
Products (33)	1.51	(0.11)	1.20	1.65	2.88	4.85	31	5.0	90.4	58.3	124.9	151.2	135.7	216.8
3531-32-33-34-35-36-37	4.07	8.03	23.38	28.63	4.10	5.01	37	6.3	21.0	27.3	53.9	58.7	50.7	12.6
Const., Min. & Handling	**2.68**	**4.69**	**14.30**	**16.52**	**2.77**	**3.42**	**57**	**4.1**	**39.1**	**45.4**	**82.6**	**83.2**	**69.5**	**37.8**
Machy. & Equipt. (93)	1.92	2.01	5.58	6.49	2.16	2.63	76	3.0	54.8	75.3	117.6	102.5	119.7	58.8
2641-42-43-45-46-47-48-	4.46	4.59	14.55	22.27	4.12	7.24	29	10.0	25.9	19.8	37.1	48.8	63.2	5.6
49 Convtd. Paper & Pa-	**2.92**	**2.64**	**10.27**	**12.93**	**3.19**	**4.86**	**38**	**7.9**	**46.5**	**36.4**	**65.5**	**69.5**	**82.5**	**29.6**
perboard Prods. (55)	2.18	0.89	2.83	6.93	2.33	3.64	50	5.8	77.5	49.3	103.5	100.1	117.4	76.2
3421-23-25-29 Cutlery,	4.93	6.94	16.33	24.29	3.82	5.08	37	5.7	23.9	18.8	37.0	58.8	41.9	10.6
Hand Tools & General	**3.27**	**4.79**	**11.62**	**15.75**	**2.39**	**3.56**	**46**	**4.5**	**35.8**	**30.9**	**72.9**	**82.4**	**65.1**	**30.1**
Hardware (89)	2.36	2.45	5.97	7.83	1.94	2.67	59	3.2	58.4	57.7	111.3	98.4	89.2	66.9
2021-22-23-24-26	2.00	1.98	14.58	33.84	12 97	33.57	19	49.4	44.8	37.6	73.6	51.7	137.2	29.9
Dairy Products	**1.47**	**1.10**	**10.47**	**18.21**	**9.01**	**19.44**	**27**	**27.9**	**65.2**	**87.2**	**125.2**	**86.0**	**240.5**	**59.1**
(103)	1.23	0.23	2.08	2.37	5.87	12.06	32	17.3	90.3	144.0	225.5	139.5	371.2	158.4
2335 Dresses: Women's	3.22	2.70	16.22	21.33	12.54	14.03	34	17.0	4:2	37.2	71.4	42.6	90.1	4.7
Misses' & Juniors'	**1.97**	**0.92**	**7.88**	**8.75**	**7.86**	**8.25**	**51**	**9.9**	**9.6**	**85.2**	**127.7**	**69.9**	**133.1**	**21.1**
(85)	1.50	0.20	1.14	1.40	4.23	4.72	61	6.6	18.6	183.5	305.2	101.2	223.8	58.0

( ) Indicates Loss

** Not computed. Printers carry only current supplies such as paper, ink, and binding materials rather than merchandise inventories for re-sale.

Table 4B-3 Manufacturing & Construction (cont.)

Line of Business (and number of concerns reporting)	Current assets to current debt	Net profits on net sales	Net profits on tangible net worth	Net profits on net working capital	Net sales to tangible net worth	Net sales to net working capital	Collection period	Net sales to inventory	Fixed assets to tangible net worth	Current debt to tangible net worth	Total debt to tangible net worth	Inventory to net working capital	Current debt to inventory	Funded debts to net working capital
	Times	Per cent	Per cent	Per cent	Times	Times	Days	Times	Per cent	Per cent	Per cent	Per cent	Per cent	Per cent
2831-33-34	3.58	10.54	18.76	30.51	3.75	5.82	43	6.6	34.0	28.0	48.3	48.5	69.9	19.7
Drugs	**2.43**	**6.62**	**13.71**	**19.62**	**2.58**	**3.61**	**53**	**5.5**	**57.4**	**43.4**	**85.0**	**71.4**	**95.9**	**55.5**
(67)	1.84	2.84	3.43	8.68	1.69	2.53	72	4.2	85.6	78.6	137.5	102.5	135.7	113.7
3641-43-44-45-46-47-48	3.89	6.17	18.29	22.48	6.22	8.09	34	6.3	15.7	24.5	46.4	54.8	47.0	11.6
Electric Lighting & Wiring Equipment	**2.59**	**3.33**	**11.79**	**14.60**	**3.18**	**4.59**	**45**	**4.5**	**34.0**	**47.3**	**76.3**	**74.1**	**73.0**	**31.1**
(53)	1.91	0.72	2.41	4.06	2.05	3.05	62	4.0	64.1	92.3	187.4	116.8	105.4	61.6
3612-13 Elec. Trans. &	3.67	7.05	20.15	25.54	4.66	5.46	44	7.0	19.8	28.8	42.6	52.5	55.5	13.0
Distribution Equipment	**2.48**	**4.29**	**15.02**	**17.74**	**3.58**	**4.28**	**59**	**5.4**	**31.5**	**48.7**	**113.1**	**74.7**	**82.9**	**27.2**
(53)	1.68	2.45	6.32	10.71	2.50	3.00	72	3.9	53.4	91.0	156.7	110.5	116.3	62.0
3621-22-23-24-29	4.04	6.12	17.11	23.84	4.25	5.12	48	5.9	27.7	30.9	50.3	60.5	62.1	15.8
Electrical Industrial Apparatus	**2.67**	**4.03**	**11.89**	**14.22**	**2.96**	**3.78**	**59**	**4.6**	**41.2**	**49.5**	**76.5**	**78.2**	**82.7**	**31.3**
(69)	1.94	1.77	7.13	9.15	2.31	2.90	71	3.4	56.3	101.8	149.9	101.9	119.6	71.7
1731	3.38	4.10	19.02	23.07	6.89	8.54	**	**	9.7	35.1	58.6	**	**	8.4
Electrical Work	**2.32**	**2.24**	**10.23**	**13.00**	**4.75**	**5.99**	**	**	**17.6**	**69.9**	**113.4**	**	**	**26.8**
(113)	1.68	0.79	1.63	2.20	3.15	4.17	**	**	38.4	121.2	186.1	**	**	63.8
3671-72-73-74-75-76-	3.65	8.07	21.61	27.83	3.84	4.81	47	6.8	23.6	31.1	59.1	53.8	59.2	18.9
77-78-79 Electronic Compnts. & Acces.	**2.63**	**4.76**	**12.36**	**16.43**	**2.98**	**3.53**	**60**	**5.1**	**39.0**	**49.5**	**88.4**	**74.7**	**89.4**	**37.9**
(90)	1.94	2.82	5.40	8.26	2.02	2.45	71	3.9	64.6	84.3	143.3	92.1	125.0	65.6
3811 Engineering, Laboratory &	4.22	7.31	19.51	24.12	3.28	4.04	58	5.6	21.5	25.4	57.7	48.7	44.6	23.9
Scientific Instruments	**2.65**	**4.59**	**14.06**	**15.45**	**2.67**	**3.33**	**69**	**4.4**	**36.6**	**44.6**	**81.6**	**70.8**	**73.3**	**33.8**
(50)	2.11	2.18	5.89	6.02	1.83	2.35	84	3.5	49.8	73.7	140.6	96.9	113.6	60.1
3441-42-43-44-46-48-49	4.34	5.56	20.41	25.81	4.73	6.87	34	10.6	19.7	22.7	50.4	43.2	53.6	11.2
Fabricated Structural Met. Prodts.	**2.57**	**2.95**	**10.46**	**12.86**	**3.20**	**5.07**	**50**	**6.6**	**36.1**	**50.7**	**92.7**	**71.6**	**94.3**	**32.8**
(168)	1.77	0.77	1.67	2.97	2.36	3.38	66	4.7	60.0	93.0	162.7	104.2	173.0	74.3
3523 Farm Machinery	3.93	6.16	21.24	26.06	4.98	8.80	25	6.3	26.4	32.8	79.0	71.9	51.7	20.0
& Equipment	**2.32**	**3.34**	**12.83**	**15.79**	**3.54**	**4.92**	**42**	**4.3**	**39.1**	**61.9**	**119.3**	**112.3**	**76.3**	**43.0**
(73)	1.59	1.73	4.58	5.89	2.49	2.99	63	3.1	62.0	139.1	211.0	178.8	116.0	69.3
3143-44-49	3.66	4.36	17.28	19.75	5.69	6.71	40	7.4	10.5	32.8	65.3	59.6	54.3	9.1
Footwear	**2.39**	**2.70**	**9.72**	**11.98**	**4.13**	**4.56**	**56**	**5.4**	**18.6**	**60.5**	**90.9**	**88.9**	**82.4**	**26.7**
(65)	1.94	1.44	4.63	6.43	2.85	3.33	68	3.7	35.1	97.6	180.9	111.7	108.4	52.6
1541-42 General	2.24	2.80	18.08	29.16	12.93	19.46	**	**	9.1	53.6	105.4	**	**	15.8
Building Contractors	**1.54**	**1.50**	**9.42**	**14.86**	**7.10**	**10.60**	**	**	**22.4**	**116.2**	**196.1**	**	**	**36.0**
(129)	1.27	0.56	3.68	5.64	3.62	4.74	**	**	49.2	202.6	302.8	**	**	96.5
3561-62-63-64-65-66-67-68-	3.75	6.73	17.13	23.97	4.20	5.43	44	7.2	22.9	26.3	40.7	55.8	53.3	9.4
69 Gen. Industrl. Machy. & Equipment	**2.66**	**4.08**	**11.49**	**17.07**	**2.92**	**3.81**	**56**	**5.0**	**36.4**	**45.2**	**73.1**	**71.2**	**76.7**	**22.3**
(119)	1.90	2.14	7.33	9.23	2.02	2.73	70	3.6	60.8	79.0	130.3	98.6	119.5	55.9
2041-43-44-45-46-47-48	3.45	3.85	17.02	30.36	7.66	14.98	18	21.0	28.8	23.2	53.5	46.6	64.0	28.6
Grain Mill Products	**2.25**	**2.00**	**13.78**	**21.52**	**5.49**	**8.85**	**25**	**13.3**	**53.6**	**56.2**	**99.6**	**80.5**	**100.1**	**49.3**
(83)	1.62	1.20	6.54	9.50	3.97	6.80	38	9.2	77.5	86.6	159.9	106.5	163.9	88.1
3431-32-33 Heating	5.30	6.57	19.30	24.20	3.74	4.21	33	6.2	17.5	18.7	45.7	56.9	43.3	8.3
Equipt. & Plmbg. Fixtures	**3.41**	**5.20**	**13.15**	**16.88**	**2.55**	**3.21**	**43**	**4.5**	**28.3**	**34.6**	**70.9**	**75.7**	**54.1**	**27.3**
(48)	2.32	2.06	6.00	6.37	2.02	2.45	63	3.5	49.1	53.2	106.9	95.5	89.9	64.7
1622-23-29 Hvy. Construction,	2.86	5.32	19.03	28.38	6.50	17.80	**	**	32.0	24.5	74.3	**	**	18.9
except Hwy. & Street	**1.85**	**1.83**	**11.69**	**15.18**	**3.86**	**7.66**	**	**	**51.3**	**65.3**	**93.5**	**	**	**53.6**
(93)	1.39	0.41	1.76	1.89	1.98	4.00	**	**	83.4	93.8	137.1	**	**	90.3
2251-52	5.04	5.00	11.83	20.10	5.03	7.70	31	10.5	21.6	12.2	53.3	50.1	47.8	11.7
Hosiery	**2.67**	**2.06**	**4.30**	**7.15**	**3.28**	**4.49**	**48**	**7.5**	**39.3**	**38.7**	**74.8**	**81.3**	**79.3**	**38.8**
(46)	1.93	0.57	(2.20)	(2.21)	2.34	3.73	59	5.0	59.8	65.6	95.9	111.9	137.8	54.8
3631-32-33-34-35-36-39	4.39	6.37	23.07	28.25	6.35	6.39	37	7.0	19.2	26.9	60.6	52.1	54.3	11.1
Household Appliances	**2.44**	**3.54**	**11.72**	**14.12**	**3.34**	**4.28**	**49**	**5.3**	**29.2**	**53.0**	**102.1**	**79.4**	**82.4**	**39.8**
(52)	1.82	1.13	5.43	6.21	2.73	3.34	68	4.3	55.8	100.0	160.7	114.2	123.9	68.7

( ) Indicates Loss

** Not computed. Building Trades contractors have no inventories in the credit sense of the term. As a general rule, such contractors have no customary selling terms, each contract being a special job for which individual terms are arranged.

Table 4B-3 Manufacturing & Construction (cont.)

Line of Business (and number of concerns reporting)		Current assets to current debt	Net profits on net sales	Net profits on tangible net worth	Net profits on net working capital	Net sales to tangible net worth	Net sales to net working capital	Collection period	Net sales to inventory	Fixed assets to tangible net worth	Current debt to tangible net worth	Total debt to tangible net worth	Inventory to net working capital	Current debt to inventory	Funded debts to net working capital
		Times	Per cent	Per cent	Per cent	Times	Times	Days	Times	Per cent	Per cent	Per cent	Per cent	Per cent	Per cent
3711-13 Passenger Car,		3.69	3.16	15.07	25.65	7.56	12.39	20	8.2	25.0	30.8	46.3	72.0	54.4	9.4
Truck & Bus Bodies		**2.25**	**2.25**	**9.83**	**12.43**	**4.75**	**4.99**	**41**	**4.5**	**42.6**	**62.8**	**86.4**	**102.5**	**83.6**	**38.3**
	(59)	1.46	0.35	4.77	5.11	2.59	3.08	53	3.8	57.6	135.5	143.9	150.2	136.4	64.6
2911 & 1311		1.65	5.76	28.47	62.92	8.23	21.74	22	35.0	39.3	57.7	84.4	50.0	137.5	20.5
Petroleum Refining		**1.44**	**3.13**	**16.94**	**41.82**	**5.46**	**13.87**	**34**	**13.6**	**78.5**	**94.7**	**144.6**	**102.4**	**205.0**	**55.7**
	(57)	1.21	1.65	12.16	23.32	3.18	6.56	54	7.7	139.1	151.9	250.6	165.5	324.4	194.0
2821-22-23-24 Plastics		2.93	4.28	11.30	25.64	5.41	8.39	42	11.0	36.9	23.0	54.2	50.3	78.2	26.9
Materials & Synthetics		**2.23**	**3.25**	**8.81**	**13.64**	**3.54**	**6.40**	**50**	**8.3**	**61.8**	**47.8**	**101.5**	**67.3**	**116.1**	**74.8**
	(42)	1.68	1.69	5.46	10.86	2.06	3.28	64	5.9	101.1	86.5	144.0	101.8	154.4	119.5
1711 Plumbing, Heating		2.66	3.42	18.26	25.44	8.44	11.41	**	**	10.2	39.0	77.2	**	**	8.9
& Air Conditioning		**1.81**	**1.61**	**9.35**	**11.10**	**5.37**	**8.16**	**	**	**22.5**	**94.6**	**156.2**	**	**	**26.1**
	(102)	1.48	0.69	3.57	3.64	3.35	4.61	**	**	46.3	158.3	232.6	**	**	69.1
2421 Sawmills &		3.71	7.25	19.74	38.38	4.31	8.27	17	14.6	28.4	15.0	49.3	47.5	52.4	36.1
Planing Mills		**2.28**	**3.28**	**10.35**	**20.52**	**2.59**	**6.57**	**28**	**7.1**	**46.7**	**38.7**	**95.3**	**93.0**	**100.0**	**69.2**
	(65)	1.46	1.49	5.06	6.65	1.64	3.08	43	5.0	89.2	76.2	193.7	137.9	163.0	199.3
3451-52 Screw Machine		8.06	8.17	17.10	29.43	3.15	6.26	37	11.6	26.8	16.6	39.3	43.0	49.6	13.0
Products		**2.78**	**4.63**	**9.65**	**16.38**	**2.58**	**4.36**	**42**	**6.7**	**47.0**	**34.5**	**69.8**	**59.5**	**81.4**	**46.7**
	(70)	2.06	2.16	5.16	8.51	1.90	3.07	52	5.0	64.2	49.0	94.2	94.3	140.7	75.1
2321-22 Shirts, Under-		2.94	4.47	18.28	18.93	6.65	6.80	21	7.2	4.5	42.2	55.1	58.0	64.0	7.7
wear & Nightwear,		**2.30**	**2.78**	**11.28**	**12.33**	**4.42**	**4.85**	**40**	**5.4**	**14.7**	**71.0**	**96.6**	**95.2**	**87.4**	**22.4**
Men's & Boys'	(58)	1.80	0.92	6.59	8.58	3.57	3.81	68	4.1	26.2	102.4	129.7	133.0	128.4	44.1
2841-42-43-44 Soap,		3.52	7.13	19.07	24.71	4.89	8.36	35	13.1	25.8	25.9	39.9	44.2	71.1	8.7
Detergents, Perfumes &		**2.39**	**4.12**	**13.22**	**19.06**	**3.53**	**4.68**	**45**	**7.8**	**38.4**	**47.8**	**73.2**	**60.3**	**110.1**	**27.6**
Cosmetics	(76)	1.74	2.10	8.03	11.14	2.58	3.86	60	6.0	62.3	88.4	136.9	84.6	181.9	56.6
2086 Soft Drinks,		3.45	8.46	29.43	62.45	6.22	15.14	15	20.7	51.2	14.4	32.1	37.1	79.3	10.3
Bottled & Canned		**2.23**	**5.38**	**19.75**	**50.00**	**3.55**	**9.48**	**19**	**16.8**	**69.4**	**30.7**	**87.5**	**56.2**	**125.2**	**68.6**
	(59)	1.48	3.03	13.73	34.70	2.59	6.26	27	12.4	122.6	63.3	170.9	107.3	189.9	181.0
3551-52-53-54-55-59		3.77	6.64	18.94	25.82	3.63	5.17	47	6.9	22.1	23.7	38.6	53.2	48.5	9.1
Special Industry		**2.44**	**4.58**	**11.37**	**16.67**	**2.45**	**3.31**	**59**	**5.0**	**28.5**	**44.9**	**61.0**	**79.0**	**82.5**	**21.6**
Machinery	(75)	2.00	2.27	5.62	7.17	1.78	2.43	76	3.7	41.3	64.1	98.9	99.6	110.9	42.3
2337 Suits & Coats,		3.45	2.19	16.75	17.36	11.16	13.54	24	14.4	3.2	33.0	52.2	45.1	91.3	1.9
Women's & Misses'		**1.93**	**1.13**	**7.64**	**8.77**	**7.72**	**8.51**	**35**	**9.2**	**8.1**	**89.4**	**140.2**	**78.2**	**142.2**	**9.3**
	(63)	1.55	0.06	1.94	2.02	4.34	5.32	57	6.2	12.6	166.6	270.5	132.4	224.1	15.4
2311 Suits, Coats &		3.25	3.19	14.41	15.30	9.92	10.00	19	9.8	2.0	43.0	76.5	51.5	63.3	12.7
Overcoats, Men's &		**2.24**	**1.95**	**7.20**	**7.95**	**5.28**	**5.43**	**56**	**6.2**	**9.3**	**89.2**	**147.8**	**92.0**	**91.5**	**31.6**
Boys'	(85)	1.55	0.75	0.90	0.93	3.00	3.67	86	4.2	29.0	164.3	285.5	153.4	162.5	77.3
3841-42-43 Surgical,		5.54	7.50	19.50	26.87	3.37	4.42	46	7.0	13.7	17.3	35.1	48.6	35.2	8.6
Medical & Dental Instru-		**3.08**	**5.30**	**13.91**	**18.70**	**2.59**	**3.14**	**59**	**4.6**	**25.0**	**29.8**	**50.9**	**66.0**	**73.4**	**21.9**
ments	(57)	2.36	3.58	9.50	11.84	1.82	2.40	69	3.6	47.8	50.3	85.9	86.8	115.0	37.8
3942-44-49 Toys,		4.21	4.66	19.10	19.15	4.96	5.89	42	8.3	18.8	20.2	35.1	54.1	49.5	2.6
Amusement & Sporting		**2.72**	**3.20**	**11.52**	**12.25**	**3.18**	**4.18**	**60**	**5.9**	**37.2**	**47.6**	**79.5**	**72.3**	**83.6**	**25.1**
Goods	(65)	1.93	0.87	2.81	3.75	2.46	2.64	93	3.3	61.8	81.4	146.2	93.6	128.5	71.4
2327 Trousers, Men's		3.27	3.39	21.31	21.40	7.31	7.36	11	11.4	3.8	48.4	50.6	62.4	73.8	4.1
& Boys'		**2.15**	**1.94**	**11.00**	**11.94**	**5.59**	**5.84**	**57**	**6.2**	**15.8**	**74.9**	**85.0**	**86.0**	**86.0**	**20.6**
	(49)	1.87	0.80	4.19	5.91	4.20	4.25	75	4.7	33.1	120.5	154.9	115.5	126.9	39.0
2341 Underwear &		3.32	1.82	11.74	12.50	9.54	10.16	38	8.8	4.4	48.1	67.7	63.5	75.4	12.9
Nightwear, Women's &		**1.86**	**1.32**	**7.32**	**7.87**	**5.69**	**6.33**	**53**	**5.8**	**7.3**	**95.9**	**114.1**	**104.8**	**115.2**	**20.8**
Children's	(51)	1.52	0.45	2.36	2.38	3.40	4.22	65	4.1	25.3	173.1	182.1	141.7	168.6	57.4
2511-12 Wood House-		4.67	4.61	12.00	18.54	4.33	6.55	33	8.6	18.7	19.7	42.0	57.8	44.3	12.7
hold Furniture &		**2.89**	**2.16**	**6.45**	**9.49**	**2.96**	**4.23**	**45**	**6.2**	**38.3**	**34.9**	**76.7**	**80.9**	**64.7**	**44.0**
Upholstered	(114)	2.05	0.71	2.71	3.49	2.26	3.11	55	3.9	59.8	73.8	132.0	110.2	88.6	71.9
2328 Work Clothing,		5.38	5.73	15.68	17.35	7.69	7.73	17	8.6	7.5	20.7	47.3	52.6	37.4	6.3
Men's & Boys'		**3.61**	**4.27**	**11.19**	**13.89**	**3.32**	**3.92**	**42**	**4.5**	**14.3**	**33.2**	**83.5**	**68.8**	**54.3**	**23.1**
	(40)	1.94	1.82	5.40	6.32	2.38	2.51	57	3.8	27.0	91.3	207.8	126.8	109.0	44.2

** Not computed. Building Trades contractors have no inventories in the credit sense of the term. As a general rule, such contractors have no customary selling terms, each contract being a special job for which individual terms are arranged.

Table 4B-3 Manufacturing & Construction (cont.)

Line of Business (and number of concerns reporting)		Current assets to current debt	Net profits on net sales	Net profits on tangible net worth	Net profits on net working capital	Net sales to tangible net worth	Net sales to net working capital	Collection period	Net sales to inventory	Fixed assets to tangible net worth	Current debt to tangible net worth	Total debt to tangible net worth	Inventory to net working capital	Current debt to inventory	Funded debts to net working capital
		Times	Per cent	Per cent	Per cent	Times	Times	Days	Times	Per cent	Per cent	Per cent	Per cent	Per cent	Per cent
2812-13-16-19		3.10	8.28	21.68	44.53	4.32	10.53	41	14.2	46.4	27.9	53.2	39.7	104.4	30.0
Industrial Chemicals		**2.00**	**5.62**	**16.35**	**25.92**	**2.84**	**6.53**	**50**	**9.0**	**74.7**	**40.0**	**97.0**	**68.3**	**124.4**	**72.1**
	(67)	1.56	3.21	8.80	14.67	1.90	3.53	61	6.4	107.4	75.0	132.5	97.1	230.1	123.3
3822-23-24-25-29 In-		3.80	6.46	17.53	19.67	3.67	4.24	51	5.8	22.6	28.1	48.0	55.3	59.8	11.6
struments, Measuring &		**2.73**	**4.28**	**11.92**	**14.62**	**2.89**	**3.40**	**67**	**4.3**	**39.1**	**49.5**	**75.3**	**76.4**	**75.5**	**28.1**
Controlling	(71)	2.06	1.58	5.36	6.56	1.97	2.51	79	3.5	50.0	73.5	125.1	90.5	120.2	45.7
3321-22-24-25		4.28	6.74	16.55	38.14	3.40	8.41	37	23.5	38.0	18.9	35.4	26.5	60.0	12.7
Iron & Steel		**2.85**	**3.53**	**11.11**	**22.39**	**2.65**	**5.74**	**44**	**11.3**	**60.6**	**31.4**	**49.6**	**61.3**	**155.4**	**31.8**
Foundries	(57)	1.75	1.89	5.26	8.26	2.00	3.31	54	7.0	97.5	46.8	82.3	85.6	274.1	86.4
2253 Knit Outerwear		3.32	2.73	13.69	18.40	9.08	9.10	30	11.5	10.8	39.4	60.2	53.6	81.0	26.5
Mills		**1.99**	**0.97**	**4.45**	**4.99**	**4.67**	**6.13**	**42**	**6.7**	**33.4**	**77.0**	**108.7**	**87.0**	**117.0**	**46.1**
	(68)	1.43	(0.08)	(0.71)	(2.45)	3.05	4.16	61	4.1	71.0	168.5	215.9	139.3	160.8	82.5
2082		2.70	5.50	18.40	69.52	3.95	20.16	2	17.1	73.4	23.7	43.2	53.2	109.2	42.7
Malt Liquors		**2.04**	**4.36**	**13.58**	**41.42**	**3.25**	**11.06**	**14**	**13.8**	**82.8**	**30.1**	**64.2**	**96.7**	**147.9**	**73.8**
	(16)	1.45	2.81	9.38	30.56	2.45	6.01	24	11.7	109.1	40.8	88.4	172.4	165.9	216.7
2515 Mattresses &		4.15	4.39	14.80	16.88	6.34	8.46	29	11.5	12.2	20.6	54.1	41.7	60.7	14.3
Bedsprings		**2.71**	**1.94**	**6.34**	**9.80**	**4.12**	**5.12**	**44**	**8.7**	**24.9**	**38.2**	**76.1**	**70.9**	**83.7**	**35.6**
	(47)	1.89	0.32	1.33	2.46	2.21	3.33	50	5.7	43.6	82.7	105.4	95.9	137.3	54.6
2011 Meat Packing		3.71	1.40	13.34	23.11	16.72	32.74	11	61.6	34.4	18.1	44.0	41.6	66.2	14.3
Plants		**2.37**	**0.75**	**6.38**	**13.12**	**10.30**	**17.84**	**14**	**33.6**	**57.8**	**44.5**	**81.5**	**57.8**	**97.2**	**49.2**
	(64)	1.89	0.06	0.08	0.40	7.31	12.14	17	18.5	73.2	83.4	145.8	83.5	146.7	102.2
3465-66-69		3.74	7.26	24.74	40.45	4.95	8.63	32	12.1	33.3	25.5	46.5	44.4	67.9	8.6
Metal Stampings		**2.36**	**4.61**	**14.02**	**24.83**	**3.44**	**5.52**	**44**	**8.5**	**52.2**	**42.8**	**90.4**	**69.8**	**115.7**	**46.9**
	(91)	1.58	2.50	5.67	11.57	1.83	3.61	51	6.5	78.5	83.9	158.1	104.5	178.0	106.5
3541-42-44-45-46-47-49		4.79	4.90	12.22	17.87	3.86	6.06	40	12.4	27.7	17.9	49.4	33.6	51.4	14.5
Metalworking Machy. &		**2.73**	**3.07**	**7.51**	**10.14**	**2.50**	**3.68**	**55**	**5.9**	**42.2**	**40.4**	**88.5**	**74.4**	**83.9**	**41.5**
Equipment	(135)	1.90	1.14	2.31	3.48	1.66	2.56	70	3.4	65.3	71.4	192.4	105.9	169.3	102.7
2431		3.26	3.77	18.39	21.94	7.12	8.56	30	8.3	22.2	31.0	67.2	57.3	60.2	17.4
Millwork		**2.43**	**2.12**	**9.15**	**11.88**	**4.15**	**5.72**	**41**	**6.2**	**41.5**	**47.6**	**113.6**	**78.4**	**84.6**	**51.8**
	(58)	1.74	1.38	4.23	6.35	2.73	4.33	50	4.6	69.7	109.5	187.3	132.4	111.6	82.8
3592-99 Misc. Machy.,		4.72	6.30	17.63	36.30	3.67	6.71	32	11.8	23.5	14.6	44.9	31.9	55.2	11.5
except Electrical		**2.48**	**4.02**	**10.61**	**20.64**	**2.61**	**4.40**	**45**	**6.8**	**48.0**	**37.5**	**73.8**	**64.3**	**97.9**	**37.0**
	(81)	1.70	2.22	4.54	6.86	1.82	3.39	56	4.7	73.9	69.7	107.8	89.0	175.0	75.7
3714 Motor Vehicle		3.36	5.66	17.35	26.00	4.31	6.06	37	8.3	29.3	30.3	47.4	61.1	59.7	10.4
Parts & Accessories		**2.58**	**4.14**	**12.30**	**17.43**	**3.22**	**4.18**	**46**	**5.7**	**48.4**	**48.4**	**82.0**	**82.0**	**85.1**	**36.3**
	(95)	2.11	2.77	7.78	8.81	2.52	3.34	54	4.1	65.8	65.6	123.9	102.4	125.3	67.4
3361-62-69 Nonferrous		3.61	5.42	15.36	29.56	4.49	8.08	39	13.1	31.1	24.3	35.8	35.8	66.9	9.5
Foundries		**2.66**	**3.77**	**10.73**	**15.88**	**3.08**	**4.69**	**45**	**8.2**	**51.9**	**39.3**	**64.7**	**69.1**	**103.5**	**26.3**
	(56)	1.80	1.83	5.01	9.35	2.39	3.80	55	5.9	73.2	63.0	104.8	85.7	174.3	66.2
2541-42 Office &		3.69	4.70	14.00	23.53	5.99	9.63	38	19.8	14.4	26.8	52.5	35.5	71.7	26.5
Store Fixtures		**2.17**	**2.32**	**7.29**	**10.42**	**3.60**	**5.83**	**51**	**8.5**	**34.1**	**53.8**	**95.7**	**69.3**	**114.2**	**67.7**
	(54)	1.62	0.13	0.73	1.57	2.31	3.55	61	5.9	69.3	97.7	176.5	103.9	197.7	95.2
3572-73-74-76-79 Office,		3.49	8.21	17.11	22.05	4.31	4.40	59	4.7	21.0	32.7	65.7	63.5	63.1	11.4
Computing & Account-		**2.57**	**4.45**	**11.64**	**14.30**	**2.71**	**3.15**	**80**	**3.8**	**33.7**	**55.1**	**121.0**	**73.8**	**74.9**	**50.5**
ing Machines	(61)	2.09	0.83	3.00	3.75	1.80	2.21	108	3.2	62.7	88.1	203.2	99.3	103.9	86.9
2361-63-69 Outerwear,		2.86	2.99	17.54	21.05	8.48	10.24	28	10.0	7.2	60.8	119.1	68.8	49.9	16.3
Children's & Infants'		**1.97**	**1.58**	**10.08**	**11.55**	**6.70**	**7.03**	**47**	**6.6**	**14.2**	**93.1**	**167.3**	**95.1**	**96.3**	**27.6**
	(33)	1.52	0.62	4.21	5.28	4.51	5.15	55	5.2	30.4	166.1	242.0	135.3	149.3	50.9
2851 Paints, Varnishes,		3.72	4.36	16.61	21.82	4.94	7.00	31	11.5	23.1	27.2	48.1	57.1	59.0	16.3
Lacquers & Enamels		**2.54**	**2.80**	**8.96**	**13.59**	**3.52**	**5.51**	**45**	**6.2**	**37.8**	**41.3**	**77.7**	**76.8**	**79.7**	**29.3**
	(101)	1.88	1.26	4.12	6.64	2.42	3.70	62	5.0	57.7	79.6	142.8	103.6	113.7	71.2
2621 Paper Mills, except		3.15	6.90	15.42	41.81	4.32	10.41	30	13.2	56.3	21.6	56.1	52.1	79.9	57.0
Building Paper		**2.25**	**3.59**	**7.08**	**13.26**	**2.98**	**6.53**	**38**	**8.6**	**95.0**	**36.5**	**76.5**	**77.4**	**103.6**	**96.0**
	(42)	1.80	1.54	3.62	4.51	1.95	4.84	49	6.8	122.1	60.4	131.9	106.0	183.7	162.8
2651-52-53-54-55		4.25	5.98	17.06	30.38	6.18	12.71	23	13.9	31.2	17.5	45.0	42.5	49.6	14.3
Paperboard Containers		**2.37**	**3.94**	**12.48**	**20.14**	**3.37**	**5.50**	**32**	**8.6**	**47.0**	**40.4**	**81.5**	**65.6**	**83.2**	**60.7**
& Boxes	(62)	1.79	1.89	7.11	8.86	2.13	3.66	41	6.5	92.3	65.1	139.8	107.0	147.5	123.9

APPENDIX 4—C Table of Compound Growth Rates

Year	*1%*	*2%*	*3%*	*4%*	*5%*
1	101%	102%	103%	104%	105%
2	102	104	106	108	110
3	103	106	109	113	116
4	104	108	113	117	122
5	105	110	116	122	128
6	106	113	119	127	134
7	107	115	123	132	141
8	108	117	127	137	148
9	109	120	131	142	155
10	111	122	134	148	163

Year	*6%*	*7%*	*8%*	*9%*	*10%*
1	106%	107%	108%	109%	110%
2	112	115	117	119	121
3	119	123	126	130	133
4	126	131	136	141	146
5	134	140	147	154	161
6	142	150	159	168	177
7	150	161	171	183	195
8	159	172	185	199	214
9	169	184	200	217	236
10	179	197	216	237	259

Year	*15%*	*20%*	*30%*	*40%*	*50%*
1	115%	120%	130%	140%	150%
2	132	144	169	196	225
3	152	173	219	274	338
4	175	207	286	384	506
5	201	249	371	538	759
6	231	299	483	753	1139
7	266	358	628	1054	1709
8	306	430	816	1476	2563
9	352	516	1060	2066	3844
10	405	619	1379	2893	5767

5

Step 2: Conducting the Situation Analysis

Corporate plans are based on assumptions about company strengths and weaknesses. It follows, then, that the accuracy of your assumptions, in part, determines the effectiveness of your strategies. A thorough appraisal of your company will point out strengths which can be capitalized on for internal expansion, diversification, or both. Conversely, it should indicate internal weaknesses, which unless corrected, signify that certain strategies should be avoided.

Surprisingly, many firms do not have a solid grasp of what makes them successful. An executive vice-president of one of the largest marketing research companies in the United States once commented on this puzzling fact. Many of his company's clients, he said, lacked well-organized data bases. In fact, many did not even have a list of their key customers. It's easy to understand how such companies might overlook both market opportunities and ways to improve their operating efficiency.

Take an actual case. A bank was considering closing a branch located on the ground floor of a high-rise office building. The branch had $60,000,000 in deposits. Management believed the loss would be minimal as the branch was located only one block from the bank's main office and most depositors would probably switch to the main office. Still, because of the size of the potential loss, they brought in a consultant to do a feasibility study. The consultant's findings projected that the bank would lose over one-half of these deposits if it closed the branch. His findings were based on the fact that most of the large depositors of the branch were lawyers located in the building. Because of its convenience, they used the branch to deposit funds for trust accounts and the like. If the bank closed the branch, it would be at a location disadvantage to two other banks (in fact, three, if another bank placed a branch in the vacated office space). Consequently, the bank did not close down the branch. The bank was wise in bringing in a consultant for this study, but one wonders at the opportunities the bank might have been (and still is) missing because of lack of similar understanding of other parts of its business.

The situation analysis offers another benefit. All companies have an abundance of beliefs about the firm's strengths and weaknesses. Unfortunately, too many of these beliefs are myths. They may have been fact at one time, but times and conditions change and to further complicate communications, often—even among top management—there's no common agreement on myths. The situation analysis provides the planning team with a common factual understanding as to what the firm's strengths and weaknesses are.

You may feel that a formal situation analysis would be a waste of time in your case because your planning team already has an accurate understanding of your company. Perhaps it does. But it is hard for anyone who is deeply involved in what he or she is doing to be completely objective about it. If management has committed itself to a course of action, even subconsciously, it becomes easy to downplay or even ignore evidence of potential weaknesses in that course. At the same time, it is easy to perceive strengths that do not exist. A formal study helps to minimize these possibilities.

So conduct a formal evaluation of your company's resources and capabilities before you form strategic plans. Include every major functional area within the organization. For instance, in a centralized firm (or a division within a diversified corporation), there should be an audit of major areas such as manufacturing, R & D, finance, marketing, and manpower. These individual analyses would then be consolidated into a summary statement of the firm's present strengths and weaknesses.

The members of the planning team should take an active role in the analysis. This will help them to better understand the firm's points of leverage and vulnerability. It's fine to use staff to assemble data, providing that the managers involve themselves in every step of the process. This includes determining what information will be gathered, analyzing their respective divisions, and coordinating the final report. Don't make the mistake of assigning middle management to prepare the reports for the functional areas. Let the functional area managers know that this is their job, and that you expect them to do it.

Intense involvement will help managers to better internalize and accept the results and, in addition, to think of the corporation as a system rather than as a number of disjointed functional areas. You may get reactions like that of the plant manager of a chemical company who had been with the company for twenty years: "You know, this is the first time I've ever felt as if I really understood our company." He went on to say, "And it's the first time I've really felt like a part of top management."

CONDUCTING THE ANALYSIS

The following recommends the "ideal" way of conducting the situation analysis. For a number of reasons, some of the suggested guidelines may be too complicated for you at this time. Later on methods of simplifying the process are given. But read through the "ideal" process first. You'll develop a better understanding of the "ideal" and consequently know better where to make shortcuts—and the potential dangers of doing so.

Getting bogged down in the situation analysis is an all too common problem. There are some rules of thumb that can make the difference between success and chaos.

Keeping the Task Manageable

On the first go-around, don't try to gather all the facts you'd like to have. It's impractical—if not impossible—to make a complete diagnosis of your firm. Accept the fact that you'll have to make "best estimates" about many things. If you try to gather everything, you'll never finish the planning cycle. And you'll have the same experience as the firm that started formal planning with a zest but never got any further than the situation analysis—because the president had insisted on gathering all the facts.

Planning is a continuous process. It is something you'll be doing year after year, and through time your methods will grow increasingly sophisticated. The first time through you'll no doubt find areas where you lack information you'd really like to have but can't take the time to gather. But make plans to begin collecting data; you'll be better prepared for the next cycle. In any case, keep in mind that a shirt-sleeve analysis carried out by management will likely prove more useful than a comprehensive analysis that management has little or no part in; the thought process is usually more important than the written report.

Setting up Timetables

Decide at the outset when the situation analysis must be completed. The length for this job pretty much depends, of course, on a host of variables—the nature of the business, difficulties in retrieving information, the scope of the analysis, and so on. But people are going to spend only a small part of their working time on it. There will have to be committee meetings—and you know how hard it is to arrange mutually acceptable times. A ballpark estimate for conducting the situation analysis would be about two months.

Besides a completion date deadline, set up timetables for each task. If you allow people a nebulous period of time to complete a job, you invite procrastination. Moreover, only timetables enable coordination of the various stages of the overall effort. Decide on what needs to be done and set dates for every step as well as for the completion of the functional area analyses and their consolidation. In addition, functional area managers should set up timetables for completing tasks within their individual areas of analysis. For example, if marketing wishes to make an analysis of its key customers, it should decide at the beginning when this task must be finished.

Finally, adhere to these timetables.

Keeping the Situation Analysis Relevant

There are all sorts of information that are "interesting" or "nice to know," and there may be a place for it—but not in the situation analysis. Limit your study to information that suggests action. For instance, manufacturing will be looking for ways to improve productivity.

Marketing will be looking for insights into possible opportunities for product line expansion and/or pruning, new products, geographic extension, and the like. If the situation analysis fails to provide insights of this sort, it's a waste of time.

Deciding What Should Be Analyzed

No single format will fit the needs of all corporations, and for a basic reason. The evaluation must include the firm's significant areas, and those that are "significant" will vary from company to company. Even so, there is much common ground.

Regardless of the company, or the industry it's operating in, there must be an analysis of absolute strengths and competitive posture. Looking first at absolute strengths, this analysis highlights what "tools" the company has to work with. For example, what kind of production facilities does the company have? How much working capital? What is its customer base? What kind of skills do its employees possess? The purpose of this analysis is to assure that each member of the planning team will better understand the strengths and weaknesses of the other functional areas. And, of course, such an examination forces functional area heads to make a systematic analysis of the points of leverage (and vulnerabilities) of their own departments—no small benefit!

The following lists indicate areas of absolute strengths that could be covered in a single-industry manufacturing firm. Naturally, you'll need to adapt this list to meet the particular needs of your company.

Manufacturing

- Production facilities (plant, processes)
- Factory capacity and loadings
- Manufacturing expense analysis and ratios
- Productivity ratios
- Quality control costs and ratios
- Manufacturing engineering
- Raw materials availability
- Raw materials cost ratios
- Warehouse capacity (raw materials, work-in-process, and finished goods)

- Inventory control and cost ratios
- Patents
- In-process research
- Engineering expense analysis and ratios

Marketing

- Total sales
- Product categories
  - Sales
  - Profitability
- Territory
  - Sales
  - Profitability
- Customers
  - Sales
  - Profitability
- Customer dependence
- Market growth rate
- Key buying influences (price, reciprocity, quality, service, etc).

Personnel

- Operating employees
  - Age/skill analysis
  - Turnover
  - Recruitment/available labor pool
  - Industrial relations (including unionization status)
  - Training
  - Comparative wage rates
- Managerial staff
  - Age/skill analysis
  - Turnover
  - Recruitment
  - Training
- Professional and technical employees
  - Age/skill analysis
  - Turnover
  - Recruitment
  - Training
- Sales personnel
  - Age/skill analysis
  - Turnover
  - Recruitment
  - Training

Finance

- Net profit
- Return on assets
- Return on equity
- Cash flow
- Debt/equity ratio
- Working capital
- Acid test
- Current ratio
- Interest coverage
- Credit reputation
- Open lines of credit
- Age of accounts receivable
- Bad debt loss
- Accounting practices (including budgetary and auditing procedures)

For some of these factors you may wish to (and should) gather data to establish historical trends. Many companies go back five years. Use charts and graphs if they will make the relevance of the data more obvious.

The analysis of competitive posture is usually more difficult. It's more subjective. But it needs to be done. For example, many ratios—such as debt/equity—are only meaningful when compared with other firms in the same industry. Another situation: Total sales may be less meaningful than market share (sales may be climbing but the company's market share may be dropping precipitously, foreboding all kinds of trouble). The planning team is the logical group to perform this analysis, because the conclusions they reach will have a major impact on strategy selection.

The following suggestions may be helpful. You will have to complete a separate analysis for each product line and, of course, adopt to suit your own situation.

- Description of Competitors
  - List and description of competitive products
  - Principal competitors
  - Your company's present and historical market share
- Competitive Profile—see Figure 5-1.

	Competitive Advantage				Neutral			Competitive Disadvantage			
	Among the Best				Average			Below Average			
FUNCTIONAL AREA	10	9	8	7	6	5	4	3	2	1	Comments
Manufacturing											
Raw materials costs					✓						
Raw materials availability											
Production facilities	✓										
Manufacturing efficiency	✓										
Warehousing	✓										
Patents											Not applicable
Research & Development										✓	No new products in development
Marketing											
Product quality			✓								
Competitive price		✓									
Market share				✓							
Customer relations		✓									
Distribution network					✓						
Personnel											
Operating personnel	✓										
Professional & Technical											Not applicable
Sales Personnel											Not applicable
Management		✓									
Finance			✓								
Credit reputation											
Working capital						✓					

Figure 5-1. Competitive Profile for _____

You won't be able to examine everything the way you'd like to, so concentrate on gathering the information that will be of real help to you in laying out strategy. There are no hard and fast rules as to how detailed or time-consuming your examination should be, but two common-sense rules offer a measure of assistance.

First, take a hard look at those items that could really make a difference. For example, major products should receive much closer examination than those which are "incidental." As for minor items —these are important, yes. But the greatest potential for increased sales and profits probably lies in the major items. You may have to lump many minor items together and make a cursory examination of them—especially the first time through the planning process.

The second general rule: Consider how thoroughly you know the various elements, and spend more time evaluating those you don't know so well.

Nothing makes these choices easy, but it may help if you keep the following questions in mind: How much will it cost in terms of time and/or money to get this information? And how much might it cost in profits if I don't?

Devising Forms

Have all functional area managers prepare forms appropriate for their individual areas. Do so before you start collecting data. First of all, forms will force you to think about what you're going to do before you start to do it. Specifically, forms will make you decide both what it is you're going to analyze and how deeply you will be going into it. Forms will also make it easier to delegate some of the routine chores of gathering information, since they will enable subordinates to better understand what data you want them to get.

Forms serve another important function. Since functional area managers conduct their own analyses, they may find it difficult to be objective. They may be afraid to "tell it like it is" because a straightforward report will reveal past errors (either theirs or their superior's). Even if they try to be frank, they may subconsciously distort the presentation to make their past efforts look better than they were. You can help avoid self-serving situation analysis reports by presenting, discussing, and revising forms at a planning team meeting before any information is gathered. Not only will this create a unity of thought about what information is needed, but it will also produce data that are more objective.

Figures 5-2a through 5-5f are sample forms for various functional areas. Of course, the best they can do is to provide ideas. For some companies these forms may be far too complex; for others, too simplistic. And, in all cases the sample forms do not tell you precisely the kind of information you should gather. Then, you may decide that graphs or some other form of presentation may be more appropriate than forms. Additional examples of forms, charts, and graphs may be found in Robert S. Kuehne, *Business Systems Factomatic:* A Portfolio of Successful Forms, Reports, and Records and Procedures (Englewood Cliffs, N.J.) Prentice-Hall, Inc.

But regardless of what kind of information is gathered or how it is presented, it should not be viewed as busywork. The process should serve two basic purposes: first, to help functional area managers take a closer, more objective look at their operations. This examination should point to areas where they could take action to improve productivity. Second, the situation analysis should provide a better, more uniform understanding of the firm. Hopefully, afterwards you'll wind up with the manager of production more of a marketing man, the marketing man more of a finance man. And so on. That's what you want. Your top managers to have a more "global" perspective. And one that's based on fact instead of myths.

Analyzing Available Secondary Information First

You may have to go out in the field in order to determine comparative production costs, gross margins, market shares, and the like. But be sure that you don't go through the painstaking and costly trouble of gathering information that is already available. For example, cost-of-doing-business ratios may be available for your industry through your association, or those published by Dun and Bradstreet may be of help. (Appendix 5A gives cost of doing business ratios for corporations for 190 lines of business. Also, Appendix 4B gives key financial ratios. These may give you some rough guidelines.)

So analyze available secondary information first. Not only can you save time, but you learn right away about areas in which your information is poor. Also, the more you know at the outset, the more efficiently you'll go about collecting information—and the right information. But the above is pretty "academic" for your first time

MANUFACTURING EXPENSE ANALYSIS (current dollars)

	19_	19_	19_	19_	End of Last Year
Sales Volume (in dollars)					
Direct labor costs					
Dollar cost					
Cost/sales ratio					
Engineering costs					
Dollar cost					
Cost/sales ratio					
Indirect labor costs					
Dollar cost					
Cost/sales ratio					
Operating expenses					
Dollar cost					
Cost/sales ratio					
Depreciation					
Dollar cost					
Cost/sales ratio					

Concluding Comment:

Figure 5-2a Manufacturing

QUALITY CONTROL ANALYSIS (current dollars)

	19_	19_	19_	19_	End of Last Year
Sales Volume (in dollars)					
Prevention (quality control design program)					
Dollar cost					
Cost/sales ratio					
Appraisal (plant and field inspection)					
Dollar cost					
Cost/sales ratio					
Internal failure					
Dollar cost					
Cost/sales ratio					
External failure					
Dollar cost					
Cost/sales ratio					

Concluding Comment:

Figure 5-2b Manufacturing (continued)

DISTRIBUTION AND INVENTORY CONTROL ANALYSIS (current dollars)

	19_	19_	19_	19_	End of Last Year
Sales Volume (in dollars)					
Inventory					
Raw Materials					
Inventory/Sales Ratio					
Work in Process					
Dollar Volume					
Inventory/Sales Ratio					
Finished Goods					
Dollar Volume					
Inventory/Sales Ratio					
Distribution					
Inbound					
Dollar Costs					
Distribution Costs/ Sales Ratio					
Outbound					
Dollar Costs					
Distribution Costs/ Sales Ratio					

Concluding Comment:

Figure 5-2c Manufacturing (continued)

ANALYSIS OF TOTAL SALES

	End of 19_	End of 19_	End of 19_	End of 19_	End of Last Year
Total Sales Volume					
Current Dollars					
Constant Dollars					
Contribution to Margin					
Current Dollars					
Constant Dollars					

Concluding Comment:

Figure 5-3a Marketing

ANALYSIS OF MAJOR PRODUCT LINES

	End of 19__	End of 19__	End of 19__	End of 19__	End of Last Year
Product line 1					
Sales (current $)					
Contribution to margin					
Estimated market growth rate					
Estimated market share					
Estimated share of largest competitors					
Key buying influences					
User franchise (excellent-good-poor)					
•					
•					
•					
Product line n					
Sales (current $)					
Contribution to margin					
Estimated market growth rate					
Estimated market share					
Estimated share of largest competitors					
Key buying influences					
User franchise (excellent-good-poor)					

Concluding Comment:

Figure 5-3b Marketing (continued)

KEY CUSTOMER ANALYSIS (Customers who account for more than 10% of the total sales volume)

Customer	End of 19_	End of 19_	End of 19_	End of 19_	End of Last Year
Customer 1					
Sales (current $)					
Profitability					
Relationship (Excellent-good-poor)					
Estimated share of customer's purchases					
•					
•					
•					
Customer n					
Sales (current $)					
Profitability					
Relationship (Excellent-good-poor)					
Estimated share of customer's purchases					

Concluding Comment:

Figure 5-3c Marketing (continued)

TERRITORIAL ANALYSIS

	End of 19_	End of 19_	End of 19_	End of 19_	End of Last Year
Territory 1					
Sales (current $)					
Selling Costs					
Territory Coverage (Excellent-good-poor)					
•					
•					
•					
Territory n					
Sales (current $)					
Selling Costs					
Territory Coverage (Excellent-good-poor)					

Concluding Comment:

Figure 5-3d Marketing (continued)

PROFITABILITY AND DIVIDENDS

Measure of Profitability	End of 19_	End of 19_	End of 19_	End of 19_	End of Last Year
Net profit					
Current dollars					
Constant dollars					
Dividends					
Current dollars					
Constant dollars					
Return on assets					
Current dollars					
Constant dollars (when applicable)					
Return on equity					
Current dollars					
Constant dollars (when applicable)					

Concluding Comment:

Figure 5-4a Finance

LIQUIDITY AND STABILITY

Measures of Liquidity and stability	End of 19_	End of 19_	End of 19_	End of 19_	End of Last Year
Cash flow					
Current dollars					
Constant dollars					
Working capital					
Current dollars					
Constant dollars					
Debt-Equity Ratio					
Acid Test					
Current Ratio					
Interest Coverage					

Concluding Comment:

Figure 5-4b Finance (continued)

CREDIT AND RECEIVABLES

Measures	End of 19_	End of 19_	End of 19_	End of 19_	End of Last Year
Open lines of credit					
Current dollars					
Constant dollars					
Bad-debt loss (% of sales)					
Age of accounts receivables					

Credit reputation (Qualitative statement):

Concluding Comment:

Figure 5-4c Finance (continued)

LABOR INCREASE (DECREASE)

Type of Employee	End of 19_	End of 19_	End of 19_	End of 19_	End of Last Year
Semi-skilled					
Skilled					
Lath operators					
•					
•					
•					
Tool grinders					
Clerical					
Sales					
Technical					
Management					

Concluding Comment:

Figure 5-5a Personnel

LABOR TURNOVER

Type of Employee	End of 19_	End of 19_	End of 19_	End of 19_	End of Last Year
Semi-skilled					
Skilled					
Lath operators					
•					
•					
•					
Tool grinders					
Clerical					
Sales					
Technical					
Management					

Concluding Comment:

Figure 5-5b Personnel (continued)

WAGE RATES (Including Fringe - constant dollars)

Type of Employee	Average End of 19_	Average End of 19_	Average End of 19_	Average End of 19_	Average End of 19_
Semi-skilled					
Skilled					
Lath operators					
•					
•					
•					
Tool grinders					
Clerical					
Sales					
Technical					

Qualitative statements (including industry averages, working conditions, etc.)

Semi-skilled:

Skilled:

Clerical:

Sales:

Technical:

Concluding Comment

Figure 5-5c Personnel (continued)

INDUSTRIAL RELATIONS

Unionization status (qualitative statements, including dates for new labor legislation):

Production days lost through strikes:

19_	19_	19_	19_	Last Year
___	___	___	___	___

Production days lost through absenteeism:

19_	19_	19_	19_	Last Year
___	___	___	___	___

Concluding Comment:

Figure 5-5d Personnel (continued)

CRITICAL SKILL AGE ANALYSIS

Type of Employee	Reaching 65 Next Year		Reaching 65 Within Next 5 Years	
	Number	%	Number	%
Semi-skilled				
Skilled				
Lath operators				
•				
•				
•				
Tool grinders				
Sales				
Technical				

Qualitative statements concerning top management:

Concluding Comment:

Figure 5-5e Personnel (continued)

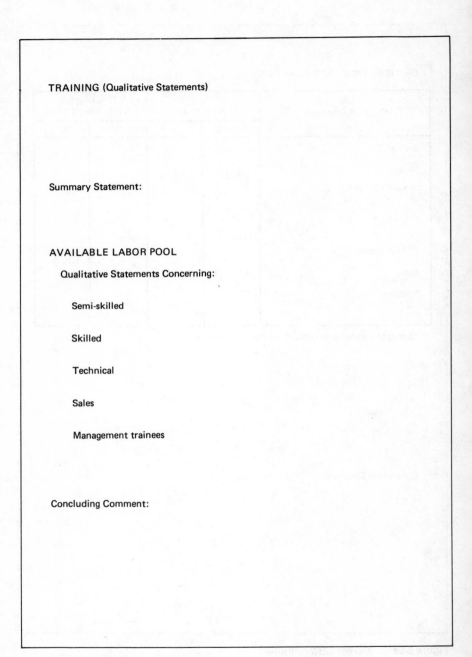

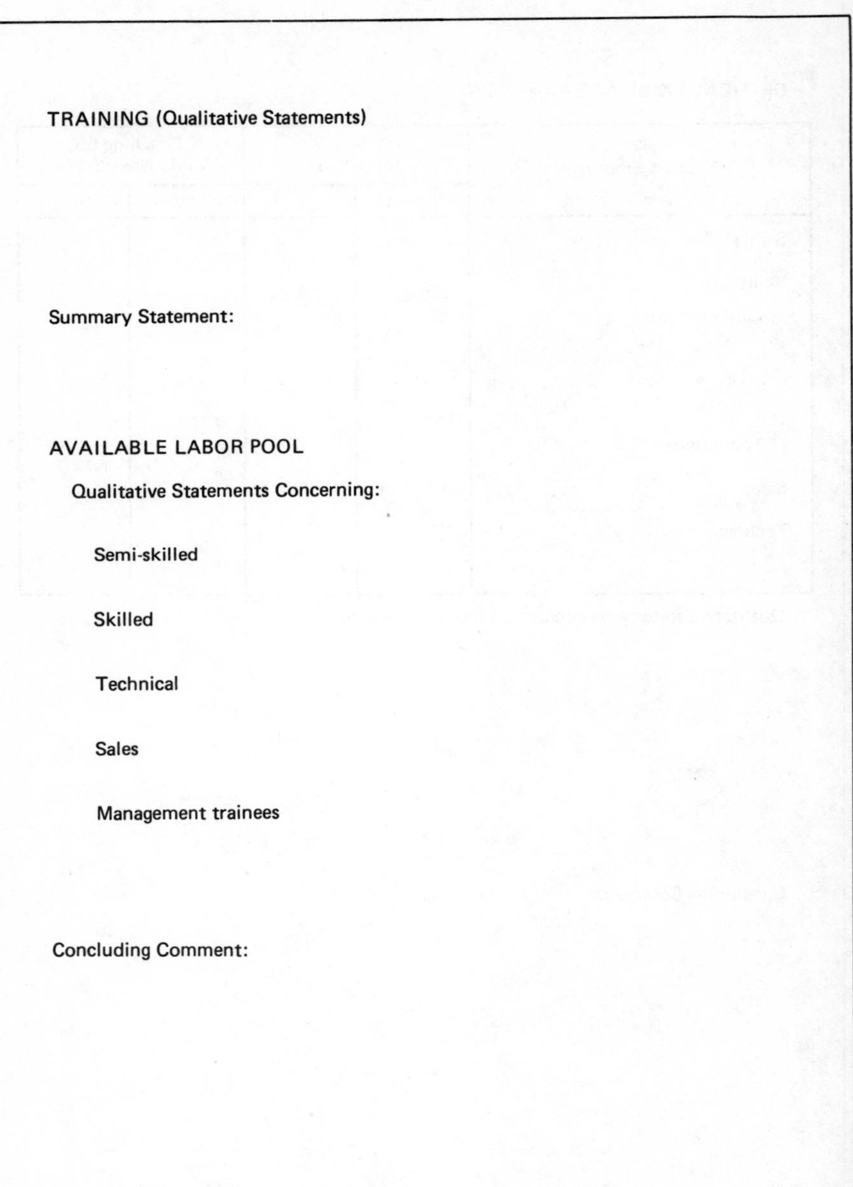
TRAINING (Qualitative Statements)

Summary Statement:

AVAILABLE LABOR POOL

Qualitative Statements Concerning:

Semi-skilled

Skilled

Technical

Sales

Management trainees

Concluding Comment:

Figure 5-5f Personnel (continued)

through the situation analysis. If you only have two months to complete it, you're not going to be able to do much primary research. About all that you'll be able to gather is information from company records, trade associations, syndicated industry studies, and the like. And you'll have to depend on "best estimates." But once you've identified the areas where you really need information, you can begin gathering data right away for the next planning cycle. Next time you'll have much better information. (Always keep in mind you can't do everything the way you'd like to the first time through. However, you can take steps now so that the next time you'll have more of the kinds of data you'd like to have.)

Thoroughness in Collecting Data

The temptation to collect data in slipshod fashion can be great, especially under the pressure of timetables. But this temptation must be resisted, and for a number of reasons: Accurate information is more likely to lead you to correct conclusions. Others will be more inclined to accept your findings if they trust your methods. If you do it right the first time, there will be no need to backtrack again (and again) for information you should already have.

Keeping Orderly Records

It is as important to keep your findings in an orderly manner as it is to be thorough. Doing so minimizes errors. It simplifies tabulating and collating the results, as well as the job of preparing periodic reviews. It enables the speedy return of documents to their original departments. Moreover, orderly record-keeping means that your progress is apparent at a glance, and it builds confidence in your audit.

Summarizing Findings

Each functional area should summarize its key problems and opportunities *on one page* to show the following:

A. Absolute strengths and weaknesses.
   1. List the absolute *major* strengths of the functional area.
   2. List the absolute *major* weaknesses of the functional area.

B. Present competitive posture.
   1. List the *major* points of leverage of the functional area.
   2. List the *major* points of vulnerability of the functional area.

Absolute strengths and weaknesses (Category A) are those that are independent of competition. For example, the firm may have a sizeable cash surplus. List the amount. On the other hand, the firm's managers may be close to retirement. List this as well.

Category B contains the points of strength and weakness that reflect the company's current competitive position. The company might enjoy a superior distribution system, for instance, while its manufacturing division may be hard pressed by innovations in production methods developed by competitors.

Normally only a few issues developed in the situation analysis are "key." These should be summarized on one page. The rest of the analysis serves as backup material.

Have each planning team member present his or her situation analysis to the group. (Copies should be delivered to the planning team several days before the meeting to make sure that everyone has a chance to analyze them ahead of time.) Thrash out any differences, and then consolidate all the important corporate issues *on one page.* This, then, is the consolidated situation analysis of the firm.

Examples of summary pages at the corporate level appear in Figures 5-6 and 5-7.

GETTING THE JOB DONE

Here are the basic steps to follow while conducting, in an "ideal" way, the situation analysis (simplified procedures are given later on).

First, the planning team sets up a timetable for completion of the major steps and completion date of the situation analysis. At this time you may also wish to put together a description of competitors. At any rate, it should be completed before the functional areas undertake their own analyses.

Second, the functional areas prepare forms which they circulate to the planning team members.

Third, the functional areas present the forms at a meeting of the planning team. The planning team discusses each of the forms separately, and, the forms are accepted or, when necessary, revised.

CORPORATE STRENGTHS

☐

Technical capability in the design, manufacture, and use of <u>metal</u> containers for "hard-to-hold" applications

☐

Good working relationships with major suppliers of metals.

☐

A major position as a supplier of filling equipment for soft drink and beer cans

CORPORATE LIMITATIONS

☐

Much smaller market share than the two major companies in the industry

☐

Limited financial resources for supporting research and development

☐

Outmoded manufacturing plants not located near concentrations of potential customers

Source: E. Raymond Corey, "Key Options in Market Selection and Product Planning," *Harvard Business Review,* 53 (September-October, 1975), 119–128. Reprinted with permission of the publisher.

Figure 5-6

Part 1: Weaknesses/Limiting Factors

	Weaknesses/Limiting Factors	Immediate Strategic Implications
1.	Management	
	a. Chief executive aged 65, no obvious successor.	a. Recruitment, merger, or sale of business.
	b. Weak middle management.	b. Recruitment training (Position can be improved but some weakness will remain for five years).
2.	Marketing	
	a. 80 percent for profits emanate from product A.	a. If market declining and market share constant,
		i. Reduce dependence.
		ii. Changed market strategy to improve performance.
		iii. Cost reduction to improve position--introduce value analysis.
	b. 25 products contribute no profit.	b. If profit potential low, cease production, re-deploy resources.

Part 2: Strengths

1. People

   a. A high level of technical expertise in production departments.

2. Marketing

   a. Strong image among consumers, particularly for quality, performance and after-sales service.

   b. Five established brand names.

3. Finance

   a. $1,000,000 available for expansion, from own resources. Up to $4. m loan capital can be raised without difficulty.

Source: Modified from D. H. Hussey, *Introducing Corporate Planning* (New York: Pergamon Press, 1971), p. 60. With permission of the publisher.

Figure 5-7

Fourth, each functional area undertakes its own situation analysis, ending with a one-page summary backed by the supporting documents, which it circulates to planning team members for review.

Fifth, functional areas present their situation analyses at a meeting of the planning team. The planning team discusses each situation analysis separately and accepts the analysis or, when necessary, has it revised.

Finally, the planning team reaches (or hammers out) a general agreement on the company's major strengths and weaknesses. It consolidates its findings into a one-page summary.

You can always make variations on this procedure. For instance, if the president's presence will inhibit discussion of the forms devised by the functional areas—as it well might—it would be wiser to have the functional areas debate their proposed forms among themselves and then forward amended forms to the president for his or her approval.

It may be that, at this time, you feel the above procedure is just too complicated for your planning situation; particularly the steps involved with the form design and form approval. Then simplify. For example, in one company each functional area manager prepared a list of strengths of his or her own area, the overall strengths and weaknesses of functional area interface, and, in addition, statistical data to support these conclusions. The president just filled out a list of points of leverage and vulnerability of the firm. These lists were circulated to members of the planning team ten days prior to a meeting where there was an evaluation of lists and data, consolidation, and, where necessary, assignments for future study.

In another company, the president had each of his planning team members fill out one-page summaries (on flip chart paper) of the strengths and weaknesses of their own functional areas. These were then discussed at a planning team meeting. At the same time, overall company strengths and weaknesses were agreed upon.

In another case, the planning team merely decided on company strengths and weaknesses at a planning team meeting.

There are many other variations. While deciding the process best for your company, keep in mind, the more the procedure is simplified, the more you run the risk of losing objectivity as well as perpetuating "myths". However, on the other hand you have to consider practicalities. A simplified procedure may be the only way to get strategic planning started and to get through the planning cycle.

Accept the fact that the situation analysis will take time. But don't charge it all off to long-range planning. By now it should be quite evident that the situation analysis will have many spill-offs that will help you make your present operations more efficient. In fact, you'll probably find that it will more than pay for itself with increased immediate profits.

It's important to recognize that how the situation analysis is handled will set the tone for the remaining steps of the planning process. This is the first time it's going to take independent work on the part of the planning team members. It's up to the president to make sure that the job is done thoroughly by everyone. If one, several, or all of the members do haphazard jobs, the president must send them back and have them redo their work until it's right. This will let the planning team know that there's real importance attached to the planning function.

CASE EXAMPLE

After the planning team at Acme set objectives, mission, and policies (Chapter 4), they assessed their major strengths and weaknesses. Each functional area manager analyzed his or her own area. The summary reports for each area follow.

Manufacturing

Production Facilities

- New and efficient production facilities. Highly automated, including automatic feed and electrodeposition painting. Since the plant is highly automated, there is a high volume break-even point. In fact, fixed costs exceed variable labor costs (at 80 percent capacity, direct labor is only 16 percent; administrative, selling expense, and factory overhead is 19 percent). Once the plant reaches a certain volume, additional production is extremely profitable.
- Electrodeposition painting is not adaptable to color changes for short production runs.
- Excess capacity: currently running only one shift.

Production Efficiency

- Limited line with volume production gives economies of scale. Output has a good, consistent quality for its price bracket.

Warehousing

- The company usually carries a large finished goods inventory enabling it to offer prompt shipments. In fact, in many instances the ability to ship within two weeks has given the company a competitive edge.
- Excess warehouse capacity.

Research and Development

- No new products in development.

Marketing

- Accounts with all national mass merchandisers. (In this sense the market is more or less saturated. Growth can only come through increases in market size.)
- Good relations with key customers. Acme is considered a very reliable supplier.
- The company is extremely vulnerable to three key customers: one for 30 percent, another for 20 percent, and the third for 10 percent.
- Only one product, and no new products in development.
- Since sales have been to companies under their private labels, Acme lacks consumer identity.
- No experience marketing to wholesalers, manufacturers representatives, or consumer markets.
- Sales have increased 15 percent compounded annually for the past five years.

Financial

- Age of accounts receivable: 43 days.
- Bad debt loss: 0.1 percent.
- Open line of credit to $3,000,000; interest rate: 0.5 percent over prime.
- Return on assets: 9 percent.
- Debt/equity: 1.1 to 1.
- Working capital: $700,000.
- Acid test: .66 to 1.
- Current ratio: 1.29 to 1.
- Return on equity: 24 percent.
- Return on invested capital: 11.4 percent.
- Interest coverage: 2.7 times.

Personnel

- Stable labor force with no unionization. Relatively good available pool of hard-working, dependable workers in the area.
- Young, aggressive top management. The president and vice president of manufacturing, late 50s; vice presidents of marketing and personnel in their mid-30s.

Competitive Posture

- The company faces one major competitor—a full-line producer. (For relative rating, see chart [Fig. 5-8].)
- Although there are no figures available, it is believed that the company is gaining in market share.

After analyzing the functional area situation analysis, the planning team consolidated the reports into a summary statement (see Table 5-1) for the corporation.

Table 5-1 Situation Analysis Summary Statement for Acme Metalworking Company

	Points of Leverage	*Points of Vulnerability*
Manpower	Young, aggressive good management team	
	Favorable labor situation	
Production	New, efficient highly automated production facilities	High volume break-even point
		Electrodeposition painting is not adaptable to color changes for short production runs
	Excess capacity in manufacturing and warehousing	No new products in development
Financial	Strong financial position	
	Open line of credit to $3,000,000	
Marketing	Good relations with key customers	Overdependence on key customers
	Low marketing costs	No consumer franchise
		One product whose sales volume is highly susceptible to recessions
		Large inventory of finished goods

	Competitive Advantage				Neutral			Competitive Disadvantage			
	Among the Best				Average			Below Average			
FUNCTIONAL AREA	10	9	8	7	6	5	4	3	2	1	Comments
Manufacturing											
Raw materials costs					√						
Raw materials availability											
Production facilities	√										
Manufacturing efficiency	√										
Warehousing	√										
Patents											Not applicable
Research & Development										√	No new products in development
Marketing											
Product quality			√								
Competitive price		√									
Market share				√							
Customer relations		√									
Distribution network					√						
Personnel											
Operating personnel	√										
Professional & Technical											Not applicable
Sales Personnel											Not applicable
Management		√									
Finance			√								
Credit reputation											
Working capital						√					

Figure 5-8 Competitive Profile for ACME Product Line

APPENDIX 5—A Cost of Doing Business*

DEFINITIONS

Explanation. Following are summaries of the Internal Revenue Service definitions applicable to the IRS data used by Dun & Bradstreet, Inc. as a basis for computing the ratios in this study.

Description of the Sample. Statistical information was estimated from a sample, selected before audit, of income tax returns filed in the district offices of the Internal Revenue Service and the Office of International Operations.

Business Receipts (Sales). Represent gross receipts, less allowances, rebates, and returns, from the principal business activity. The term reflects income arising out of the sale of goods and services and in some cases other income, such as dividends, interest, rents, and royalties, when such income constitutes the principal business activity. An example of the latter would be rental income in the case of real estate operators or manufacturers who lease instead of sell their product. In computing the ratios presented business receipts were expressed as the base (100%).

*Key business ratios in 190 lines compiled by Dun & Bradstreet, Inc. Reprinted with permission.

Cost of Goods Sold. Reflects operations involving merchandise as an income-producing factor. It represents the sum of opening inventory, merchandise purchased, labor, and material and supply costs, less closing inventory. In transcribing these data from returns identifiable amounts of such items as taxes paid, depreciation, depletion, amortization, advertising, and contributions under pension plans were excluded from costs of goods sold and transferred to their respective deduction categories.

Gross Margin. Equals business receipts less cost of goods sold.

Compensation of Officers. Includes amounts reported in the income statement as salaries, wages, stock bonuses, bonds or other benefits, if identified as having been paid for personal services rendered.

Rent. Rent paid on business property is deductible as an ordinary and necessary expense. Identifiable amounts of taxes and other expenses paid by lessees in connection with rent paid are included in their respective deduction headings.

Repairs. This includes cost of labor and supplies, and other costs necessary for incidental repairs to the property. It does not include capital expenditures which add to the property value, improvements which appreciably prolong its life, or expenditures for restoring or replacing property.

Bad Debts. Bad debts may be deducted when there is reasonable certainty that they are uncollectible. A debt which is deducted as uncollectible, if subsequently collected, must be reported as income for the year in which collected.

Interest. This deduction is permitted for interest paid or accrued in connection with business indebtedness.

Taxes. State and local taxes paid or accrued on business property or incurred in conducting business are allowable deductions. Also included are Federal import and excise duties and taxes.

Amortization, Depreciation and Depletion. Amortization is the sum of deductions taken in lieu of depreciation for Government-certified emergency facilities for the national defense and the amounts of deferred expenses written off for research and experimental expenditures, exploration and development expenditures. Depreciation is a deduction of a reasonable allowance for the exhaustion, wear and tear, or obsolescence of property used in a trade or business, or of property held for the production of income. Depletion is deduction from income for a wasting asset such as a mineral deposit, or a stand of timber to recover its cost.

Advertising. Includes advertising identified as a cost of sales or operations, as well as separately identified as a business deduction.

Pension and Other Employee Benefits. Includes pension and other deferred compensation plans and also such other benefits as health, accident, sickness, death and other welfare plans.

Cost of Doing Business Ratios—Corporations

The following operating ratios for 190 lines of business have been derived to provide a guide as to the average amount spent by corporations for these items. They represent a percentage of business receipts as reported by a representative sample of the total of all Federal Income Tax returns* filed for 1974-75.

Industry	Total Number of Returns Filed	Cost of Goods Sold	Gross Margin	SELECTED OPERATING EXPENSES								
				Compensation of Officers	Rent Paid on Business Property	Repairs	Bad Debts	Interest Paid	Taxes Paid†	Amortization Depreciation Depletion	Advertising	Pension & Other Employee Benefit Plans
		%	%	%	%	%	%	%	%	%	%	%
ALL INDUSTRIES	1,965,894	72.44	27.56	1.86	1.32	0.78	0.45	4.66	2.62	3.45	0.86	1.28
CONTRACT CONSTRUCTION	185,563	81.89	18.11	3.49	0.64	0.55	0.32	1.41	2.11	1.97	0.22	0.93
General Building Contractors & Operative Builders	74,694	87.46	12.54	2.67	0.44	0.30	0.22	1.83	1.46	1.23	0.24	0.54
Heavy Construction Contractors	14,895	80.12	19.88	2.25	0.79	1.14	0.31	1.54	2.14	3.96	0.10	1.10
Special Trade Contractors	95,974	76.27	23.73	5.13	0.79	0.51	0.43	0.84	2.87	1.77	0.26	1.30
RETAILERS & WHOLESALERS	602,423	78.02	21.98	1.68	1.33	0.32	0.26	1.05	1.41	0.91	0.89	0.45
RETAIL TRADE	386,772	71.37	28.63	1.81	2.26	0.43	0.30	1.23	1.81	1.21	1.54	0.52
Building Materials, Garden Supplies, & Mobile Home Dealers	31,319	73.31	26.69	2.98	1.33	0.45	0.65	1.30	1.87	1.23	1.05	0.54
General Merchandise Stores	10,996	63.46	36.54	0.38	2.66	0.46	0.55	2.47	2.31	1.39	2.62	0.64
Food Stores	26,335	78.96	21.04	0.61	1.48	0.41	0.05	0.38	1.20	0.97	0.88	0.69
Automotive Dealers & Service Stations	63,863	82.77	17.23	1.72	1.06	0.26	0.17	1.24	1.18	0.79	0.81	0.27
Motor Vehicle Dealers	32,965	84.53	15.47	1.44	0.91	0.21	0.15	1.33	0.96	0.71	0.87	0.26
Gasoline Service Stations	12,662	80.44	19.56	1.95	1.35	0.39	0.14	0.57	2.08	1.05	0.21	0.21
Other Automotive Dealers	18,236	70.71	29.29	3.86	2.00	0.43	0.37	1.34	1.83	1.16	1.17	0.44
Apparel & Accessory Stores	38,529	60.52	39.48	3.50	5.47	0.34	0.30	0.84	2.19	1.14	2.18	0.60
Furniture & Home Furnishings Stores	36,044	64.54	35.46	4.18	3.02	0.35	0.62	1.33	2.04	0.99	3.40	0.50
Eating & Drinking Places	76,601	46.12	53.88	3.54	4.94	1.23	0.13	1.35	3.81	2.81	1.73	0.44
Drug Stores & Proprietary Stores	20,316	70.31	29.69	3.01	3.05	0.28	0.11	0.66	1.67	0.88	1.12	0.51
Liquor Stores	12,074	80.10	19.90	3.04	1.68	0.32	0.06	0.52	2.03	0.77	0.50	0.18
Other Retail Stores	70,695	65.13	34.87	3.75	2.69	0.45	0.54	1.02	2.07	1.63	2.05	0.53
WHOLESALE TRADE	214,975	83.64	16.36	1.56	0.55	0.22	0.23	0.90	1.07	0.65	0.33	0.38
Groceries & Related Products	20,870	88.15	11.85	1.05	0.46	0.23	0.14	0.46	0.67	0.51	0.22	0.33
Machinery, Equipment & Supplies	45,391	74.88	25.12	2.75	0.71	0.26	0.34	1.09	1.15	1.02	0.42	0.60
Motor Vehicles & Automotive Equipment	18,292	78.86	21.14	2.02	0.91	0.19	0.23	1.21	1.12	0.64	1.03	0.40
Drugs, Chemicals & Allied Products	7,801	79.83	20.17	0.94	0.46	0.24	0.22	0.98	1.06	1.41	0.29	0.33
Apparel, Piece Goods & Notions	10,137	78.48	21.52	2.97	1.19	0.09	0.39	1.19	1.43	0.42	0.49	0.45
Farm-Product Raw Materials	7,161	93.76	6.24	0.40	0.18	0.23	0.07	0.62	0.30	0.42	0.07	0.11
Electrical Goods	13,728	76.42	23.58	2.26	0.79	0.17	0.47	1.11	1.14	0.48	0.88	0.57
Hardware, Plumbing & Heating Equipment	10,375	76.49	23.51	2.63	0.83	0.19	0.54	0.82	1.25	0.58	0.33	0.72
Alcoholic Beverages	4,619	79.02	20.98	1.37	0.50	0.20	0.10	0.45	5.15	0.52	0.55	0.50
Lumber & Construction Materials	9,956	81.57	18.43	2.09	0.55	0.29	0.50	1.17	1.15	0.90	0.29	0.43
Metals & Minerals, except Petroleum & Scrap	4,340	85.66	14.34	1.17	0.28	0.16	0.16	0.70	0.73	0.42	0.06	0.37
Petroleum & Petroleum Products	8,981	89.35	10.65	1.00	0.51	0.29	0.14	0.51	1.39	0.83	0.10	0.25
Paper & Paper Products	4,683	78.92	21.08	2.29	0.77	0.17	0.28	0.65	0.95	0.42	0.18	0.55
Other Wholesale Trade, Durable & Nondurable Goods Combined	48,641	83.96	16.04	1.68	0.57	0.22	0.25	1.43	1.05	0.55	0.37	0.37

Appendix 5—A (continued)

Industry	Total Number of Returns Filed	Cost of Goods Sold	Gross Margin	SELECTED OPERATING EXPENSES								
				Compensation of Officers	Rent Paid on Business Property	Repairs	Bad Debts	Interest Paid	Taxes Paid†	Amortization Depreciation Depletion	Advertising	Pension & Other Employee Benefit Plans
		%	%	%	%	%	%	%	%	%	%	%
MANUFACTURING	211,563	74.83	25.17	0.86	0.83	1.20	0.23	1.74	2.59	3.38	0.93	1.63
Food & Kindred Products	15,060	79.42	20.58	0.54	0.63	0.76	0.14	1.25	2.47	1.72	1.87	0.82
Meat Products	2,310	87.44	12.56	0.40	0.66	0.52	0.11	0.82	1.00	1.16	0.60	0.68
Dairy Products	2,076	82.64	17.36	0.44	0.60	0.82	0.17	0.88	1.26	1.62	1.27	0.83
Canned & Preserved Fruits & Vegetables	987	74.41	25.59	0.62	0.77	1.07	0.16	2.09	1.85	2.01	2.20	1.06
Grain Mill Products	1,930	82.38	17.62	0.51	0.50	0.91	0.17	1.30	0.97	1.32	2.27	0.76
Bakery Products	1,897	69.80	30.20	0.94	0.99	0.88	0.11	1.06	2.19	1.99	1.86	1.58
Sugar & Confectionery Products	937	78.44	21.56	0.47	0.63	1.12	0.09	1.07	2.43	1.75	0.91	0.74
Beverage Industries	2,239	69.70	30.30	0.55	0.64	0.78	0.15	1.67	7.62	2.72	3.38	0.94
Malt Liquors & Malt	51	65.16	34.84	0.29	0.48	1.18	0.20	0.82	17.16	3.10	2.62	1.47
Alcoholic Beverages, except Malt Liquors & Malt	208	74.17	25.83	0.29	0.63	0.35	0.06	2.60	6.02	1.41	3.54	0.63
Bottled Soft Drinks & Flavorings	1,980	68.77	31.23	0.98	0.76	0.89	0.21	1.41	2.33	3.66	3.76	0.85
Other Food & Kindred Products	2,684	78.68	21.32	0.74	0.48	0.60	0.12	1.41	1.80	1.65	2.69	0.58
Tobacco Manufacturers	63	63.29	36.71	0.20	1.71	0.76	0.10	3.33	9.16	2.64	3.79	1.52
Textile Mill Products	6,274	78.41	21.59	1.18	0.89	0.83	0.32	1.98	2.21	2.84	0.69	0.85
Weaving Mills & Textile Finishing	672	77.28	22.72	0.67	0.76	1.15	0.27	1.79	2.50	3.38	0.66	1.04
Knitting Mills	2,146	78.23	21.77	1.57	1.22	0.42	0.33	2.41	2.23	2.54	1.31	0.60
Other Textile Mill Products	3,456	79.90	20.10	1.60	0.88	0.65	0.39	2.00	1.85	2.33	0.42	0.73
Apparel & Other Textile Products	16.106	76.66	23.34	2.39	1.17	0.20	0.32	1.51	2.29	0.94	0.70	0.81
Men's & Boys' Clothing	2,270	77.06	22.94	1.63	1.10	0.18	0.42	2.02	2.18	1.00	0.93	0.83
Women's & Children's Clothing	8,853	76.93	23.07	2.49	1.21	0.17	0.25	1.26	2.33	0.85	0.58	0.79
Other Apparel & Accessories	2.181	75.66	24.34	3.30	1.08	0.19	0.28	1.32	2.28	0.60	0.51	0.93
Misc. Fabricated Textile Products not elsewhere classified	2,802	75.12	24.88	3.32	1.24	0.36	0.38	1.34	2.45	1.46	0.75	0.78
Lumber & Wood Products	13.508	76.00	24.00	1.44	0.99	1.01	0.28	2.60	2.64	8.47	0.39	0.79
Logging, Sawmills, & Planing Mills	4.353	73.71	26.29	1.29	1.18	1.05	0.13	2.88	3.13	13.45	0.20	0.68
Millwork, Plywood & Related Products	4.428	76.65	23.35	1.20	0.84	1.12	0.34	2.50	2.34	7.98	0.47	0.95
Other Wood Products, including Wood Bldgs. & Mobile Homes	4.727	78.03	21.97	1.98	0.97	0.80	0.38	2.41	2.44	2.70	0.53	0.72
Furniture & Fixtures	6,931	72.99	27.01	2.48	1.34	0.45	0.38	1.45	2.62	1.89	0.92	1.21
Paper & Allied Products	3.765	68.68	31.32	0.84	0.79	2.26	0.17	1.44	2.53	4.23	0.58	1.63
Pulp, Paper & Board Mills	349	71.15	28.85	0.25	0.67	2.77	0.12	1.60	2.39	4.59	0.38	1.84
Other Paper Products	3,416	66.24	33.76	1.42	0.91	1.75	0.22	1.28	2.67	3.87	0.78	1.42
Printing & Publishing	29,271	64.62	35.38	3.02	1.49	0.54	0.83	1.43	3.00	2.90	0.84	1.77
Newspapers	5,724	65.12	34.88	1.92	0.96	0.59	0.68	1.21	3.52	3.62	0.15	2.29
Periodicals	2.326	65.44	34.56	2.42	1.35	0.34	0.97	1.10	2.02	1.99	0.82	1.41
Books, Greeting Cards & Misc. Publishing	4.877	60.01	39.99	2.34	2.43	0.42	1.74	2.21	2.76	2.29	2.82	1.57
Commercial and Other Printing & Printing Trade Services	16.344	66.33	33.67	4.64	1.53	0.65	0.42	1.34	3.00	2.90	0.42	1.52
Chemicals & Allied Products	9.860	64.95	35.05	0.70	0.95	1.72	0.20	1.51	2.15	3.86	3.01	1.79
Industrial Chemicals, Plastics Materials & Synthetics	2.987	66.74	33.26	0.51	0.92	2.48	0.18	1.58	2.25	5.29	0.81	2.22
Drugs	643	56.27	43.73	0.63	1.04	0.65	0.19	1.39	2.40	2.39	7.28	1.78
Soap, Cleaners, & Toilet Goods	1.913	66.27	33.73	0.59	0.82	0.86	0.25	0.80	1.64	1.66	6.69	1.23
Paints & Allied Products	1.421	71.74	28.26	1.83	1.27	0.78	0.37	1.00	1.89	1.58	1.41	1.04
Agricultural & Other Chemical Products	2.896	67.83	32.17	1.24	0.93	1.76	0.20	2.37	2.02	3.93	1.18	1.02
Petroleum (Including Integrated) and Coal Products	1.039	83.28	16.72	0.07	0.61	0.75	0.09	0.85	2.40	4.30	0.11	0.46
Petroleum Refining (Including Integrated)	324	83.40	16.60	0.05	0.60	0.73	0.09	0.85	2.41	4.32	0.10	0.46
Petroleum & Coal Products, not elsewhere classified	715	71.20	28.80	1.66	0.96	1.98	0.28	1.01	1.56	2.80	0.75	0.99
Rubber & Misc. Plastics Products	8.109	70.17	29.83	1.52	1.36	1.34	0.35	2.10	3.06	3.24	1.04	2.15
Rubber Products; Plastics Footwear Hose & Belting	1.140	70.14	29.86	0.55	1.38	1.59	0.29	2.35	3.29	3.30	1.29	2.65
Misc. Plastics Products	6.969	70.22	29.78	3.72	1.32	0.79	0.51	1.55	2.54	3.11	0.47	1.01
Leather & Leather Products	2,080	73.44	26.56	1.58	2.07	0.52	0.44	2.16	2.55	1.30	1.10	1.03
Footwear, except Rubber	547	72.68	27.32	0.77	2.50	0.37	0.49	2.61	2.61	1.35	1.27	1.02
Leather & Leather Products, not elsewhere classified	1,533	75.18	24.82	3.44	1.08	0.87	0.32	1.13	2.41	1.17	0.73	1.06

ppendix 5—A (continued)

Industry	Total Number of Returns Filed	Cost of Goods Sold	Gross Margin	SELECTED OPERATING EXPENSES: Compen-sation of Officers	Rent Paid on Business Property	Repairs	Bad Debts	Interest Paid	Taxes Paid†	Amortiza-tion Deprecia-tion Depletion	Adver-tising	Pension & Other Employee Benefit Plans
		%	%	%	%	%	%	%	%	%	%	%
Stone, Clay & Glass Products	9,563	68.77	31.23	1.62	1.03	2.62	0.41	1.94	2.99	4.81	0.56	2.14
Glass Products	850	68.20	31.80	0.56	1.05	3.25	0.14	1.91	3.27	4.70	0.60	3.30
Cement, Hydraulic	45	67.21	32.79	0.64	1.10	2.49	0.38	2.92	3.00	7.59	0.44	2.23
Concrete, Gypsum & Plaster Products	5,326	69.80	30.20	2.45	0.94	2.50	0.53	2.05	2.85	5.05	0.35	1.30
Other Non-Metallic Mineral Products	3,342	68.63	31.37	2.01	1.10	2.16	0.55	1.53	2.87	3.76	0.79	1.92
Primary Metal Industries	4,636	73.57	26.43	0.50	0.53	4.08	0.15	2.03	2.41	3.83	0.19	2.59
Ferrous Metal Industries; Misc. Primary Metal Products	1,983	71.66	28.34	0.40	0.46	5.63	0.10	1.42	2.53	3.91	0.16	3.15
Non-Ferrous Metal Industries	2,653	76.83	23.17	0.67	0.64	1.44	0.24	3.08	2.19	3.69	0.23	1.62
Fabricated Metal Products	25,327	72.38	27.62	2.18	0.91	1.21	0.31	1.53	2.54	2.30	0.60	1.79
Metal Cans & Shipping Containers	124	72.69	27.31	0.37	1.21	3.46	0.40	1.35	2.56	3.55	0.62	2.47
Cutlery, Hand Tools & Hardware; Screw Machine Products, Bolts & Similar Products	3,488	65.92	34.08	2.09	0.80	1.15	0.24	1.43	2.92	2.61	1.62	1.98
Plumbing & Heating, except Electric & Warm Air	744	70.34	29.66	1.09	0.85	1.59	0.20	1.81	2.46	2.04	0.67	2.87
Fabricated Structural Metal Products	8,003	75.54	24.46	2.51	0.81	0.52	0.43	1.55	2.33	1.78	0.33	1.23
Metal Forgings & Stampings	3,150	75.10	24.90	2.59	0.82	1.67	0.18	1.36	2.61	2.42	0.24	2.09
Coating, Engraving & Allied Services	2,448	66.10	33.90	4.40	1.60	1.08	0.43	1.65	3.19	3.41	0.33	1.32
Ordnance & Accessories, except Vehicles & Guided Missiles	124	76.19	23.81	0.87	0.82	0.96	0.32	2.80	2.81	2.13	0.90	2.20
Miscellaneous Fabricated Metal Products	7,246	72.00	28.00	2.87	0.94	0.56	0.25	1.44	2.47	2.05	0.47	1.37
Machinery, except Electrical	24,879	65.96	34.04	1.54	1.03	0.85	0.32	2.82	3.05	3.81	0.70	2.20
Farm Machinery	818	68.02	31.98	0.85	0.70	1.52	0.23	2.91	2.02	1.75	0.92	2.89
Construction & Related Machy	2,080	73.37	26.63	0.86	0.68	1.01	0.19	2.43	2.31	2.75	0.56	2.14
Metal Working Machinery	7,307	67.86	32.14	3.82	0.99	0.88	0.24	1.69	3.28	2.63	0.71	2.40
Special Industry Machinery	2,349	70.49	29.51	1.97	1.01	0.70	0.29	2.06	2.66	2.31	0.89	1.93
General Industrial Machinery	2,627	69.41	30.59	1.67	1.06	0.94	0.47	1.98	2.64	2.25	0.64	2.04
Office & Computing Machines	719	50.40	49.60	0.41	1.50	0.50	0.47	5.05	4.49	8.10	0.73	2.28
Other Machinery, except Electrical	8,979	72.41	27.59	2.98	0.97	0.84	0.25	1.61	2.80	2.58	0.69	1.93
Electric & Electronic Equipment	10,800	69.55	30.45	0.90	1.05	0.69	0.44	2.81	2.86	3.34	1.05	1.99
Household Appliances	216	72.05	27.95	0.41	1.30	1.00	0.53	2.53	2.45	2.57	1.71	1.68
Radio, Television & Communications Equipment	1,796	67.44	32.56	0.99	1.55	0.67	0.47	3.77	3.04	3.82	1.16	1.75
Electronic Components & Accessories	3,881	71.83	28.17	1.13	0.81	0.38	0.47	1.99	2.89	3.03	0.83	1.13
Other Electric Equipment	4,907	68.53	31.47	0.85	0.88	0.79	0.38	2.89	2.88	3.50	0.94	2.69
Motor Vehicles & Equipment	2,203	79.66	20.34	0.21	0.47	0.99	0.17	2.47	2.18	2.79	0.61	3.94
Transportation Equipment, except Motor Vehicles	3,651	77.44	22.56	0.58	0.84	0.90	0.14	1.91	2.78	2.70	0.33	2.98
Aircraft, Guided Missiles & Parts	987	76.79	23.21	0.38	0.84	0.94	0.09	1.76	2.90	2.72	0.24	3.43
Ship & Boat Building & Repairing	1,547	80.06	19.94	1.43	0.92	0.42	0.42	2.53	2.62	1.86	0.46	1.24
Other Transportation Equipment, except Motor Vehicles	1,117	79.69	20.31	1.17	0.75	1.08	0.23	2.34	2.11	3.30	0.84	1.40
Instruments & Related Products	5,761	65.63	34.37	1.29	1.12	1.30	0.25	1.70	2.59	3.47	2.07	2.17
Scientific Instruments & Measuring Devices; Watches & Clocks	1,910	71.34	28.66	1.31	1.09	0.69	0.29	2.47	2.50	3.50	1.32	1.95
Optical, Medical & Opthalmic Goods	3,341	61.45	38.55	2.08	1.28	0.92	0.34	1.44	2.79	2.54	3.37	1.48
Photographic Equipment & Supplies	510	60.92	39.08	0.56	1.02	2.53	0.11	0.79	2.54	4.27	2.02	3.11
Misc. Manufacturing & Mfg. Not Allocable	12,677	69.70	30.30	2.56	1.22	0.66	0.45	2.77	2.52	2.13	2.06	1.18
SERVICE, TRANSPORTATION & COMMUNICATION												
Hotels & Other Lodging Places	18,236	51.44	48.56	2.19	6.67	2.56	0.55	7.76	6.03	7.58	2.17	0.56
Personal Services	38,272	52.34	47.66	6.84	4.61	1.35	0.47	1.53	4.03	4.74	1.53	1.05
Business Services	106,484	57.90	42.10	6.56	3.22	0.76	0.55	2.66	3.01	5.36	1.29	1.26
Advertising	12,061	74.51	25.49	5.17	1.82	0.16	0.46	0.62	1.49	0.97	1.80	0.97
Business Services, except Advertising	94,423	51.92	48.08	7.06	3.72	0.97	0.58	3.39	3.56	6.94	1.10	1.36
Auto Repair & Services	34,218	49.97	50.03	5.15	4.51	2.06	0.46	5.50	3.52	18.14	0.97	0.73
Misc. Repair Services	14,904	64.70	35.30	9.28	1.79	0.57	0.17	0.73	3.21	2.09	0.87	1.13
Motion Picture Production, Distribution & Services	5,252	60.29	39.71	5.07	2.35	0.30	0.49	3.31	1.78	9.88	2.87	1.63
Motion Picture Theaters	3,789	53.50	46.50	2.05	6.85	1.58	0.09	3.34	4.08	4.99	5.65	0.34
Amusement & Recreation Services, except Motion Pictures	26,071	53.37	46.63	4.01	5.37	2.27	0.29	3.87	5.36	6.66	2.21	1.04

Appendix 5—A (continued)

Industry	Total Number of Returns Filed	Cost of Goods Sold	Gross Margin	SELECTED OPERATING EXPENSES									
				Compensation of Officers	Rent Paid on Business Property	Repairs	Bad Debts	Interest Paid	Taxes Paid†	Amortization Depreciation Depletion	Advertising	Pension & Other Employee Benefit Plans
		%	%	%	%	%	%	%	%	%	%	%
Other Services	141,606	44.12	55.88	20.95	3.82	0.49	0.32	1.52	3.14	2.01	0.66	4.81
Offices of Physicians, Including Osteopathic Physicians	44,728	21.64	78.36	42.30	4.21	0.24	0.05	0.22	2.16	1.31	0.34	10.78
Offices of Dentists	12,882	32.00	68.00	35.83	4.30	0.35	0.04	0.48	2.49	1.83	0.44	7.36
Nursing & Personal Care Facilities	5,996	62.41	37.59	3.28	5.02	1.18	0.36	4.89	5.63	3.55	0.32	0.39
Medical Laboratories	1,795	56.75	43.25	6.07	3.14	0.45	0.58	1.31	3.62	2.78	0.40	1.53
Other Medical Services	10,279	51.09	48.91	11.61	3.67	0.62	1.16	3.24	3.76	2.95	0.19	2.74
Legal Services	8,330	17.12	82.88	38.13	5.32	0.22	0.13	0.42	2.68	1.54	0.04	5.91
Educational Services	7,819	48.92	51.08	8.46	6.40	1.01	0.66	2.18	4.17	3.61	3.88	1.19
Misc. Services, not elsewhere classified	49,777	60.09	39.91	8.59	2.57	0.43	0.25	1.21	3.00	1.64	0.99	1.79
Transportation & Public Utilities	80,232	61.67	38.33	0.93	2.57	0.23	0.47	6.02	6.06	10.15	0.37	2.35
Transportation	62,153	67.76	32.24	1.55	4.79	0.23	0.48	3.10	4.90	6.45	0.50	1.83
Railroad Transportation	425	67.54	32.46	0.46	9.76	0.34	1.22	4.56	9.12	7.85	0.13	0.83
Local & Interurban Passenger Transit	9,495	65.31	34.69	4.44	2.20	0.08	0.15	1.56	5.21	6.08	0.38	1.43
Trucking & Warehousing	32,459	65.68	34.32	2.28	3.17	0.16	0.26	1.92	5.04	5.22	0.22	2.15
Water Transportation	5,315	71.63	28.37	2.04	1.92	0.18	0.31	3.26	2.15	4.73	0.20	1.96
Air Transportation	4,561	65.41	34.59	0.52	5.77	0.32	0.31	3.43	2.91	9.02	1.57	3.08
Pipelines, except Natural Gas	307	80.44	19.56	0.21	0.30	0.32	0.02	3.56	1.67	5.00	0.02	0.25
Transportation Services, not elsewhere classified	9,591	74.15	25.85	2.85	2.17	0.09	0.32	3.77	2.06	4.51	0.64	0.91
Communication	9,369	51.50	48.50	0.53	1.41	0.13	0.66	6.67	6.25	14.87	0.50	4.56
Telephone, Telegraph & Other Communication Services	3,580	50.81	49.19	0.23	1.35	0.13	0.59	7.15	6.64	16.12	0.30	5.00
Radio & Television Broadcasting	5,789	56.73	43.27	2.84	1.85	0.13	1.16	3.02	3.30	5.35	2.01	1.21
Electric, Gas & Sanitary Services	8,710	61.01	38.99	0.40	0.55	0.30	0.32	9.31	7.43	11.59	0.12	1.46
Electric Services	212	54.23	45.77	0.23	0.39	0.38	0.29	11.72	8.77	14.98	0.11	1.47
Gas Production & Distribution	1,362	66.89	33.11	0.37	0.64	0.40	0.23	6.77	4.12	8.11	0.15	1.31
Water Supply & Other Sanitary Services	7,062	52.51	47.49	4.00	1.33	0.11	0.46	7.87	7.17	9.84	0.34	1.17
FINANCE, INSURANCE & REAL ESTATE												
Banking	14,534	—	—	3.63	1.51	0.36	3.37	56.36	2.07	2.45	0.80	1.24
Mutual Savings Banks	452	—	—	1.72	0.55	0.16	2.03	74.06	2.04	0.85	1.09	0.79
Bank Holding Companies	420	—	—	2.75	1.76	0.33	3.57	56.99	1.85	2.75	0.61	1.28
Banks, except Mutual Savings Banks & Bank Holding Companies	13,662	—	—	5.32	1.38	0.44	3.38	51.53	2.39	2.38	1.02	1.28
Credit Agencies other than Banks	48,597	—	—	1.77	0.86	0.29	3.50	48.10	1.53	1.37	1.19	0.58
Savings & Loan Associations	5,046	—	—	2.30	0.51	0.36	4.08	71.84	1.72	1.03	1.64	0.65
Personal Credit Institutions	4,422	—	—	1.06	2.43	0.34	5.64	18.08	2.23	2.19	2.02	0.83
Business Credit Institutions	834	—	—	1.50	1.31	0.22	3.73	44.88	1.75	4.67	0.81	0.81
Security Commodity Brokers and Services	4,867	—	—	9.59	4.43	0.21	0.62	13.69	2.87	1.22	0.69	1.72
Insurance	8,343	61.79	38.21	0.54	0.77	0.05	0.25	1.68	2.75	0.96	0.40	1.07
Life Insurance, Stock Companies	1,541	58.07	41.93	0.58	0.40	0.01	0.17	0.77	2.61	0.55	0.36	0.69
Life Insurance, Mutual Companies	158	61.74	38.26	0.18	0.51	0.03	0.03	0.85	2.73	0.88	0.19	1.50
Mutual Insurance, except Life or Marine & Certain Fire or Flood Insurance Companies	1,111	65.07	34.93	0.41	0.52	0.02	0.10	0.11	2.90	0.55	0.38	1.22
Insurance Agents, Brokers & Service	35,387	26.99	73.01	15.15	2.72	0.24	0.76	1.23	2.69	1.62	1.01	2.35
Real Estate	266,616	—	—	5.20	2.96	2.58	0.72	17.86	9.77	9.88	1.77	0.52
R.E.Operators & Lessors of Buildings	175,984	—	—	3.14	3.49	3.93	0.56	21.58	14.97	14.60	0.44	0.34
Subdividers & Developers	33,431	—	—	5.66	1.67	1.46	1.43	25.65	5.27	4.23	3.17	0.71
AGRICULTURE, FORESTRY & FISHING	53,458	76.20	23.80	3.24	1.95	1.82	0.14	3.00	2.13	3.97	0.28	0.44
Agricultural Production	37,314	77.09	22.91	2.57	2.17	1.83	0.11	3.45	2.12	4.17	0.23	0.36
Agricultural Services, Forestry & Fishing	16,144	73.36	26.64	5.35	1.25	1.75	0.22	1.57	2.15	3.33	0.43	0.69
MINING	15,732	36.26	63.74	0.66	0.41	0.67	0.09	1.26	1.51	15.27	0.05	0.56
Metal Mining	1,769	67.12	32.88	0.38	0.43	0.72	0.12	3.24	3.89	11.71	0.03	1.53
Iron Ores	585	80.74	19.26	0.40	0.79	0.56	0.06	5.95	2.55	10.44	0.00	1.07
Copper, Lead & Zinc, Gold & Silver Ores	799	62.92	37.08	0.26	0.26	0.52	0.03	1.59	4.46	12.06	0.04	1.74
Coal Mining	2,059	60.57	39.43	1.12	1.00	1.35	0.08	1.90	3.51	9.82	0.03	1.39
Oil & Gas Extraction	8,350	24.73	75.27	0.43	0.25	0.24	0.06	0.75	0.69	17.44	0.03	0.21
Crude Petroleum, Natural Gas & Natural Gas Liquids	3,915	20.30	79.70	0.18	0.10	0.06	0.03	0.41	0.49	18.53	0.01	0.11
Oil & Gas Field Services	4,435	61.81	38.19	2.51	1.48	1.80	0.31	3.59	2.35	8.36	0.24	1.06
Nonmetallic Minerals, except Fuels	3,554	62.62	37.38	1.92	0.74	2.92	0.26	2.62	2.76	9.83	0.29	1.18

6

Step 3: Strategy Formulation—Anticipating Future Environment*

You've determined your objectives, mission, and policies. You've also examined the strengths and weaknesses of your firm. The first part of strategy development is to forecast the future environment your firm will operate in. The need to do so is obvious. Few strategies work equally well regardless of prevailing business conditions. For example, a strategy including high ownership of facilities and a high debt/equity ratio will work better during times of inflation and easy money than during recession and tight money.

Unfortunately, the future has become increasingly hard to pin down. Too many key factors are simply too unpredictable. You may say, "That's always been the case." And you've got a point. A saying, attributed by some to Confucious, "To forecast is risky, especially in regards to the future." Now if the source is correct, this saying reflected thoughts almost 2,000 years ago. But now there's a difference. Today, predicting the future is even more difficult. To mention a few root causes: There are more inventions leading to more rapid product obsolescence. There's more government intervention (which is usually

*Much of this chapter is excerpted from Robert E. Linneman and John D. Kennell, "Shirt-Sleeve Approach to Long-Range Plans," *Harvard Business Review,* 55 (March-April 1977), 141–50, with permission of the publisher.

not predictable). And then there's the rate of inflation. For example, in a recent seminar a group of corporate planners were asked what they thought the rate of inflation would be in five years. The range: between 2 and 27 percent. Imagine, back in 1963, asking a similar group to predict what the rate of inflation would be in 1968. Probably the range would have been somewhere between 1 and 3 percent.

In recent years our forecasting techniques, based on traditional trend lines and relationships, have not served us well. Listen to the laments in 1974 after two especially humbling years for forecasters:

> Roderick G. Dederick, chief economist for Chicago's Northern Trust Co.: "We did not provide advance warning to our managements of the distressing situation into which the U.S. economy has drifted over the past several years."
>
> Milton W. Hudson, economist for Morgan Guaranty Trust Co.: "We've decided that economic forecasting is so deficient that we're not going to perpetuate any more confusion. There is something misleading about giving people what purport to be accurate numbers when they are really no such thing."[1]

Perhaps Paul Samuelson isolated a major problem: "I think that the greatest error in forecasting is not realizing how important are the probabilities of events other than those everyone is agreeing upon."[2]

Often the planning process involves using a single "most probable" forecast as the basis of thinking. Estimates are made of uncontrollable make-or-break variables—such as competition, industry growth, and inflation—and then a strategy is developed to achieve the company's objectives. But what happens when, because of faulty forecasting, the assumed values of one or more key variables are wrong? What seemed to be a solid strategy might prove surprisingly treacherous under these different, unplanned-for conditions. Even tactical contingency plans may fail to compensate for the faulty strategy.

As a consequence, many companies of all sizes now measure their strategies against several possible future environments, relevant to their businesses, as a formal part of their planning procedures. This chapter explains how you can use multiple futures to give you a better idea of plausible environments in which your company may be operating. Although it doesn't cover forecasting techniques, it does point out how you can integrate your forecasts, arrived at by conventional methods, in developing multiple futures. (If you're interested in improving your forecasting methods, two easy-to-get references are described in Appendix 6A.)

The overriding benefit of constructing multiple futures is already clear: It enables you, even forces you to see how a strategy might fare in the event of an unexpected (but possible) future. There are other benefits. Awareness that the future may wear "different faces" will alert you more fully to the need for a flexible strategy, and for contingency plans as well. Further, the act of committing alternative futures to paper helps clarify your assumptions and variables, and hence the logic of your arguments. Even the process of writing down assumptions and variables has benefits. After going through the exercise, the president of a small manufacturing company ($2,000,000 in sales) confessed, "You know, this is the first time I've really tried to think through—in a systematic way—all of the make-or-break variables for our major product line. And it's really got me thinking."

Formally writing out multiple futures in corporate planning also helps improve communication. There are less likely to be misunderstandings among members of the planning team. And it's a process that most executives enjoy. The president of a bank (200 employees) confided, "I've gotten more interface with my top management team in these two hours trying to hammer out alternative futures than I've had in the two and one-half years since I've been with this bank!"

Of course there are potential disadvantages as well. Too much worry about possible dangers, for instance, can lead to timidity and risk avoidance. Certainly, the safest path is seldom the most rewarding, and you're being paid to evaluate and accept risk, after all, not simply to avoid it. Since you've already set your objectives, however, you're less likely to fall into this "no hits, no runs, no errors" trap.

Another criticism might be that examining multiple futures takes too much time. It can, of course, if you let it, but it doesn't need to involve much more work than traditional forecasting. In addition, you can—and at first you probably should—design multiple futures on a shirt-sleeve basis. Finally, it could happen that all the futures you plan for turn out wrong. Even so, a technique like this will leave your company better prepared to deal with the unexpected.

Like any procedure, this one can be misused, but on the whole its advantages appear to outweigh its disadvantages. A moment's reflection reveals that multiple future planning is intuitive. Informally we do this in arriving at decisions that we make daily. Usually we'll come up with a most-probable-case forecast. Then we'll develop a plan that we think will work best in this "environment." But we don't stop there. We say to ourselves, "But what if this environment doesn't come true? What will be the results?" Intuitively, we measure our plans against several possible future environments.

Following is a step-by-step procedure for incorporating the concept of multiple futures into strategy planning. Although designed with smaller companies in mind, larger companies that want to keep planning simplified will find it equally useful.

Let's assume that you have established your objectives, mission, and policies, and have conducted the situation analysis as well. You're now ready to start the following process: First, determine the factors relevant to your business that you are sure will occur within your planning time frame—these are your assumptions. Second, list the key uncontrollable variables that could have make-or-break consequences for your company. Third, assign a range of reasonable values to each key variable. Finally, develop at least two but no more than three plausible futures that your firm could find itself operating in. One of these futures should be the most probable case, and the other(s) should represent the most plausible (worst case and/or best case) futures. When these are completed, the planning team develops a strategy for the most-probable-case future, and measures it—adjusting it for responsiveness, when possible—against the other future(s) the company might face. A more detailed step-by-step approach follows.

STATING ASSUMPTIONS RELEVANT TO YOUR BUSINESS

Assumptions are factors you can forecast with almost complete certainty. Calculated natural resources (in some cases) or the number of sixty-five-year-olds five years from now (in all cases) are examples. Or it may be that members of your planning team are *sure* that some things will happen. If that be the case, consider them assumptions. There is no sense changing these values and designing multiple futures around changes. No one will consider the alternatives realistic.

Other projections, such as the rate of economic growth, are unpredictable and should be classified as variables. Variables differ from assumptions in that assumptions must be thought to be accurate and conclusive; a high probability of occurrence is not enough. A test: If some members of your planning team doubt its value, consider it a variable.

At first thought, you may feel that your business is so unpredictable that there's nothing you can consider an assumption. In your case you may be right. After you've given it some consideration, you still may not be able to identify any assumptions. Then you'll just have more variables to deal with. More than likely, however, you'll have the same experience as one president who claimed, "We have no assumptions in our business." After an hour of careful reflection, he and his planning team came up with eight.

Don't minimize the importance that demographics may have on your firm. For example, the president of a wholesaling firm handling costume jewelry remarked that changing demographics would not affect her firm because its products were sold to all age groups. After completing her review, however, she realized that their long-range plans would have to take account of the changing distribution of numbers within age groups.

For your convenience, Appendix 6B is a "Fast Fact File." Here you'll find, among other factors, a graphic illustration of age distributions until the year 1985. All of the numbers of people in the age groups are certain and may be considered assumptions, except for those age groups affected by the birth rate after 1977.

CASE EXAMPLE

To help explain how to develop multiple futures, a case example will be given after each step. The Acme case will be used throughout.

Having set objectives, mission, and policies (Chap. 4) and conducted the situation analysis (Chap. 5), the planning team started to develop future plausible operating environments for their firm. They made the following assumptions:

- *Demographics.* During the next five years, the number of twenty-five-to-forty-four-year-olds (the age group most likely to buy budget low-price desks) will increase from 65 million to 72 million, approximately a 10 percent increase.
- *Education level of customers.* The education level of the target market will have increased; there will be more people attending evening schools, "re-treading," etc., causing the need for more home offices.

- *Housing prices.* Housing prices will continue to rise.
- *Government regulation.* There will be more governmental regulation—even at the consumer level—which will require better home record-keeping.
- *Channels of distribution.* Mass merchandisers will continue to dominate sales to consumer markets. There will be a continuing trend to fewer, but larger, wholesalers and dealer-office supply houses.
- *Steel prices in relation to general price level.* In times of rapid growth steel prices will rise at a greater rate than general price level because of lack of steel mill capacity.

LISTING KEY VARIABLES

After you have defined your assumptions, you need to identify the variables that will be important to your business in the future. Try to use key variables that are commonly predicted and monitored, such as GNP and the rate of inflation. Easily identifiable vital signs facilitate forecasting and simplify control.

Carefully review "Fast Fact File" (Appendix 6B). Here historical trends are given of variables that often have major impact on businesses. Some of these variables may have make-or-break potential for your firm. If not, at least they may give you insights into the variables that will.

If time and resources permit, you may wish to broaden your viewpoint by scanning future-oriented periodicals, such as *Futures* and *The Futurist,* in addition to your normal fare of business and general periodicals. Of course, there are also a number of proprietary services available, such as the Arthur D. Little Impact Service, the National Planning Association Economic Projections Series, Predicasts, the Futures Group Scout Service, and the Stanford Research Institute Business Intelligence Program.

You can keep the planning task on a shirt-sleeve basis by limiting key variables to no more than four or five by using the following guidelines:

- Omit variables having a low probability of occurrence and a low potential impact. On the other hand, include those with low probabilities but high impact.

- Consider the timeliness of the variable. Because the future is so unpredictable, it is more important to include an event that is likely to happen or have an impact in the next few years than one that may not happen or be insignificant until near the end of the planning horizon.
- Omit disastrous events. Events that would cause total disaster—such as a major nuclear war—should not be considered seriously.
- Aggregate when possible. For example, the factors responsible for economic growth include, to name a few, expenditures on consumer, investment, and government goods. If only the economic growth rate is relevant, just use it as the representative variable for your analysis. A food processor was exasperated because he had too many variables: drought, insects, floods—all of which affected supply. Then he realized he could aggregate all of these variables into one: available supply.
- Separate dependent from independent variables. Check for interdependence. Is the value of one variable based upon the value of another? If so, then remove the dependent variable. Keep a separate list of dependent variables for use in helping to describe the multiple futures.

You may be one of the few (very few) that has a hard time coming up with any make-or-break variables. If so, better take another look. One president of a small company that manufactures a specialty maintenance product for industrial companies was in such a "predicament." His market was in the northeastern part of the United States, and he was happy to say that his product was not affected by recessions and that he had no competition. Upon closer reflection, however, he realized that his sales were vulnerable to the possible growth of maintenance contractors. And, for the first time, he became consciously aware that the continued migration of manufacturers to the sunbelt would have an effect on his market potential.

CASE EXAMPLE

The planning team at Acme decided that *retail sales, steel prices,* and *availability of raw materials* are the key variables that have the greatest impact on its operations. More specifically:

- *Retail sales.* Traditionally, sales of budget low-price steel desks have varied directly with retail sales. Beyond that, retail sales are a general measure of prosperity. Since the target market consists of apartment dwellers or "first home" buyers, when retail sales are down (in slow growth times), compact home office furniture will obtain a larger share of the home office furniture market.
- *Steel prices.* Other things being equal, the demand for budget low-price steel desks will vary directly with the price of steel up to a certain point. Steel price increases will cause the commercial market to trade down. Prices beyond a certain point, however, would cause the commercial as well as the consumer market to switch to budget office furniture made from other materials.
- *Availability of raw materials.* Ability to supply demand for budget low-price steel disks will vary directly with availability of steel and energy (oil).

The planning team identified two dependent variables:

- *Loyalty of key customers:* Loyalty of customers will depend upon reliability of supplies (delivery and quality).
- *Household formations:* Other things being equal, household formations will vary with retail sales (retail sales being considered as a measure of prosperity).

ASSIGNING REASONABLE VALUES TO EACH KEY VARIABLE

Pick a reasonable range within which each variable may vary, and divide the range into two or three sets of values—a "most probable case" and the extremes. What is "reasonable," of course, can only be determined by common sense. However, reject values so extreme that they seem absurd. Although it is generally recommended that *three sets of values* be estimated for each variable, in some instances two may suffice.

An example for the Acme case is shown in Table 6-1. Here only two sets of values are given because, for simplicity, only two plausible operating environments (the most probable case and the worst case) will be developed.

To forecast the values of these key variables, you can follow the same forecasting procedures you've been using in the past. The only difference is that you're now trying to predict the extremes as well as the most-probable-case forecast. To maintain objectivity, you may want to seek the opinions of trade association officials and staff. Or, if relationships permit, customers and suppliers. Or even consultants who are experts in your field.

Table 6-1 Possible Future Environments for Acme Metalworking Company

Key Variable	*Most Probable Case*	*"Worst" Case*
Retail sales	Real growth of 5% a year steady growth	"Boom and bust" times, the net result a stagnant roller-coaster economy
Steel prices	Same increase as general price level	6% a year higher than general price level
Availability of raw materials	Same	Periodic shortages of oil due to severe winters; inadequate supplies of steel because of "boom" times

DESCRIBING PLAUSIBLE FUTURES IN WHICH YOUR COMPANY MAY OPERATE

The end result is the description of possible futures in which you may be operating. Do this by selecting a value for each key variable; estimating the resulting interactions between key variables, dependent variables, and assumptions; and writing a brief description of the future under this set of conditions.

You'll find the following suggestions helpful.

- First take your most-probable-case values of each variable and put together the most-probable-case future. This you normally do intuitively. Only now, you are putting down this picture of the future in written statements. The written statements are necessary for two major reasons: You can better link together (describe) the effects of variables (for example, increased competition and increased inflation); and you'll improve communication among members of your planning team.

- Write from the viewpoint of someone standing in the future (at the end of your time frame) describing "present" conditions. Your description should point out potential problems and opportunities facing firms in your industry. Keep in mind that you are describing a setting in which your firm may be operating. As a consequence, for now keep your firm—and its potential actions—out of the portrayed future. Once you've put together these alternative settings, then you can go about seeing what courses of action your firm should take.
- Limit yourself to one or two paragraphs. Use concrete terms and classifications, and don't worry about the elegance of your sentence construction. Simple clarity is much more important. You'll probable be surprised at how easy it is to put together a story line after you've merely listed assumptions and variables. In fact, in some cases listing them may be all that is necessary.
- Besides the most probable case, describe at least one, but not more than two, alternative futures. You may wish to use only one other alternative future. Most companies that develop only two futures develop the second one for the downside. If you develop two alternative futures, the third should be for optimistic conditions. Regardless of whether you develop two or three, make sure that the alternative futures (other than the most probable case) have a moderately high probability of occurrence, or else no one will pay serious attention to them.
- Make sure that the multiple futures are significantly distinct from each other. In fact, it has been recommended that you develop "deadly enemies" futures ("deadly enemy" futures refer to those in extreme contrast to the most probable case. In this sense the best case future can be a "deadly enemy").[3] After all, you're trying to find out what will happen if you follow one strategy and a much different environment should occur. Almost identical alternative futures lead to almost identical strategies, defeating the purpose of the analysis.

- Keep the length of each multiple future roughly even. People tend to give more credulence to a longer description.
- For your "deadly enemy" futures (other than the most probable case), make sure that the combined variable mix makes sense. For example, low double-digit inflation, rapid economic growth, and severe oil shortage by themselves might seem plausible, but their joint occurrence does not. To keep from overlooking plausible combinations of key variables, examine all possibilities.

CASE EXAMPLE

Most-Probable-Case Future for Acme: Moderate Growth*

During the past five years the economy has experienced a moderate growth. In general, the period can be characterized by stability and relatively good times.

Household formations have increased at 10 percent annually during this period. The members of these new households are more sophisticated than those of previous generations. Their educational levels are higher, and they are continuing their education by taking more evening courses. This, coupled with the increasing need for more accurate home records (especially income tax), has created a brisk demand for budget low-price home office equipment.

Housing costs have continued their dramatic increases. Because most of the new households are made up of apartment dwellers or first-home buyers, they have had to settle for limited space. Consequently, they prefer more compact types of budget low-price home office equipment and, since often this furniture is an integral part of a room (other than an office), have sought styles and colors that blend in with their surroundings.

The increase in steel prices has been the same as the increase in the general price level. The prices of steel desks have not increased, relatively. Consequently, budget low-price steel desks have not lost their competitive position.

*(Note that in both of Acme's hypothesized futures some aspects—the assumptions—are the same. Also, the style of writing is from a person projecting himself or herself five years into the future and describing conditions for that date as well as the five years leading up to that time. To make the futures seem more real, certain hypothesized conditions are stated as fact. For example, "Three years ago the winter was . . .")

Raw materials, both steel and energy, have been available in adequate supplies. Suppliers have not experienced any difficulties in fulfilling demand. Key customer loyalty remains high.

Worst-Case Future for Acme: "Roller-Coaster"

The economy has experienced "boom or bust" times over the past five years. There have been economic recoveries, but these were quickly aborted by prolonged recessions. As a result, economic growth has been at a standstill.

Household formations have not increased at the rate demographics might suggest. More young people remain at home or in "communes," postponing marriage until better times. Many people are trying to upgrade their skills and are pursuing evening courses and, this, together with the increasing need for more accurate home records, has helped the market. Still, the purchase of desks can be postponed, and many hard-pressed families have done just that.

Housing costs have continued their dramatic increases. Because most of the new households are made up of apartment dwellers or first-home buyers, they have had to settle for limited space. Consequently, they prefer more compact types of budget low-price home office equipment and, since often this furniture is an integral part of a room (other than an office), have sought styles and colors that blend in with their surroundings.

The increase in steel prices, in times of recovery, has been higher than the general price level, making budget low-price steel desks less competitive with wood and other materials.

Three years ago the winter was extremely severe. Fuel shortages forced many plant shut-downs. Then in the following year there was an exceptional recovery—although short in duration. Because of low inventory levels in both of these years, many manufacturers could not meet the demands of their customers. These two experiences caused mass merchandisers to seek out back-up sources of supply, and in several instances to acquire production facilities.

You may disagree with these multiple futures. Fine. And that's an advantage of using this method. It lays everything out in the open, which is what you want. You'll have better communication among members of your planning team. But note how much easier it would be to visualize an effective strategy, for example, for the most-probable-case future as described above than if you had merely stated the most probable case of a certain level of retail sales, steel prices and availability of raw materials.

The above discussion and example were for a company with a single-product line. What if you are a diversified company and have product lines that are affected by key variables which vary from product line to product line? In such a case, you may find it necessary to construct separate futures for those product lines which are affected by different key variables. If some of the key variables are the same, use identical values (from one product line future to the next) for these variables.

GETTING THE JOB DONE

For the initial meeting, try to get away for an entire day. Have some members of the planning team responsible for reporting on past trends. Discuss these. Then have someone talk about the future. You may even wish to bring in an outsider for this part of your meeting. Decide at the meeting—on a preliminary basis—on both your assumptions and your make-or-break variables.

Assign a task force to check into these assumptions and forecast plausible ranges for the key variables. Determining such ranges is almost identical to conventional forecasting, except now you're projecting ranges as well as the most probable case. Because of the similarity, you may wish to use the same forecasting techniques you have in the past.

While the task force is projecting ranges for key variables, also have it come up with a tentative industry forecast for the coming year. Such a forecast will be necessary while developing strategies, for you want to make sure that your long-range plans can be integrated with short-range plans. For this you'll have to have at least a rough idea of what next year will be like. It may be that in developing alternative futures you'll want marketing to take the lead. But make sure you get involvement from all of the members of the planning team. This is *not* to be viewed as solely marketing's job.

Have the task force send its findings to the planning team within a set period of time (depending on the complexity of what they have to do and the amount of available time).

Schedule a one-day meeting to discuss the task force's findings and to hammer out the two to three plausible descriptions of what the future for your company might be like. If possible, hold the meeting away from the office.

Constructing multiple futures need not be a lengthy, burdensome procedure, especially since it fits in so readily to the conventional planning and forecasting process. It's most successful, however, under the circumstances summarized below.[4]

Multiple futures should be an integral part of the planning—not only for strategy development, but also in the formal contingency planning. How to develop contingency plans will be covered in Chapter 8.

Unless top management is highly sophisticated in quantitative terms, the projections should stick mainly to qualitative descriptions.

If you use consultants use them only for methodology or for forecasts of industry conditions. It's worth repeating: Don't have them take the lead in the developing of multiple futures.

At the outset, it's probably best to keep the future horizons to five years. Much further may seem to be "blue sky" for members of your planning team. Develop two to three scenarios, and don't get bogged down in expository prose.

Most important, your planning team—as a unit—should be deeply involved in determining assumptions and key variables. It's not marketing's or finance's job, to be done in isolation and then presented to the planning team. Inputs will be needed from manufacturing, personnel, and so forth in order to come up with "realistic" futures. Besides, the thought process is a great learning experience. One executive, who has used this procedure for a number of years, remarked that "multiple futures designed by others may or may not be helpful, but they're always meaningful to those people who are involved in developing them." In one company when the newly formed planning team formally developed alternative futures for the first time, they discovered that, much to their shock, even the most optimistic future for their company was a bleak one. Having been involved in developing these futures, they were able to accept them as realistic. Furthermore, this planning team accepted the fact that drastic changes had to be made.

Of course, managerial involvement is essential to successful planning. This has been well documented. An executive of a major oil company emphasized the necessity of involvement by remarking,

"The principal benefit of our formal planning procedure is not a plan, as such, but rather it is the framework that the system provides for involving all levels of management and the great variety of their individual expertise, in the decisions about what the corporation should be trying to do and why."

APPENDIX 6—A Supplemental Readings

SPYROS MAKRIDAKIS and STEVEN C. WHEELWRIGHT, "Forecasting: Issues and Challenges for Marketing Management," *Journal of Marketing,* 41, No. 4 (October 1977), 24–38. A concise explanation of forecasting techniques. Describes their relative effectiveness for particular situations.

STEVEN C. WHEELWRIGHT and DARRAL G. CLARKE, "Corporate Forecasting: Promise and Reality," *Harvard Business Review,* 54, No. 6 (November-December 1976), 40 ff. Practical suggestions—with emphasis on "people problems"—as to developing the "best" system for forecasting. Based on the findings of a survey of small-, medium-, and large-sized companies.

APPENDIX 6—B Fast Fact File

Here's a collection of historical trends of key variables that impact on many businesses. Some may have make-or-break potential to your firm. Even if none apply, they may provide insight into factors that will.

With the exception of demographics, the future values of these variables are at best tenuous. However, an historical perspective may help you forecast what the plausible future values might be.

CONTENTS

- Employment
- Corporations
- Individual Business Tax Returns
- Motor Vehicle Registrations
- Steel Production
- Energy: Consumption—Net Trade
- Merchandise Exports and Imports

International Statistics

- Gross National Product and Population
- Trends in Output
- Currency Exchange Rates

GROSS NATIONAL PRODUCT

Gross National Product (GNP) is the market value of all final output of goods and services produced by the United States economy, before deduction of depreciation charges for capital goods. GNP covers both public and private output produced by all factors whose owners reside in the United States. Perhaps the greatest use of GNP growth rate is that it provides an overall indication as to general prosperity; i.e., consumer and industrial spending, capital availability, and credit risks.

Table 6B-1 Growth Rate of Gross National Product (in constant dollars), 1909–78

Year	% Growth	Year	% Growth	Year	% Growth	Year	% Growth
1909–10	2.8	1926–27	.0	1943–44	7.2	1960–61	2.0
1910–11	2.6	1927–28	.6	1944–45	– 1.7	1961–62	6.6
1911–12	5.7	1928–29	6.7	1945–46	11.9	1962–63	4.0
1912–13	.9	1929–30	– 9.8	1946–47	– .9	1963–64	5.5
1913–14	– 4.3	1930–31	– 7.6	1947–48	4.5	1964–65	6.3
1914–15	– .8	1931–32	–14.7	1948–49	.1	1965–66	6.5
1915–16	7.9	1932–33	– 1.8	1949–50	– 9.6	1966–67	2.6
1916–17	.7	1933–34	9.1	1950–51	7.9	1967–68	4.7
1917–18	12.3	1934–35	9.9	1951–52	3.1	1968–69	2.6
1918–19	– 3.5	1935–36	13.9	1952–53	4.5	1969–70	– .6
1919–20	– 4.3	1936–37	5.3	1953–54	– 1.3	1970–71	3.0
1920–21	– 8.6	1937–38	– 5.0	1954–55	7.6	1971–72	5.7
1921–22	15.8	1938–39	8.6	1955–56	1.9	1972–73	5.5
1922–23	12.1	1939–40	8.5	1956–57	1.4	1973–74	–1.4
1923–24	– .2	1940–41	16.1	1957–58	– 1.1	1974–75	–1.3
1924–25	8.4	1941–42	12.9	1958–59	6.4	1975–76	5.7
1925–26	5.9	1942–43	13.2	1959–60	2.5	1976–77	4.9
						1977–78	3.9[a]

Sources: For 1909–1969, *Historical Statistics of the U.S. from Colonial Times to 1970,* Series F31; for 1970–78, U.S. Department of Commerce, Bureau of Economic Analysis.

Comments: The sixty-nine-year average growth of GNP is 3.3. Ask yourself: What is going to cause the GNP growth rate to be higher in the next five years? Keep in mind: A greater percentage of our labor force is moving to the service industries, and it is generally agreed that it's harder to realize productivity gains in this sector.

[a]First two quarters of 1978.

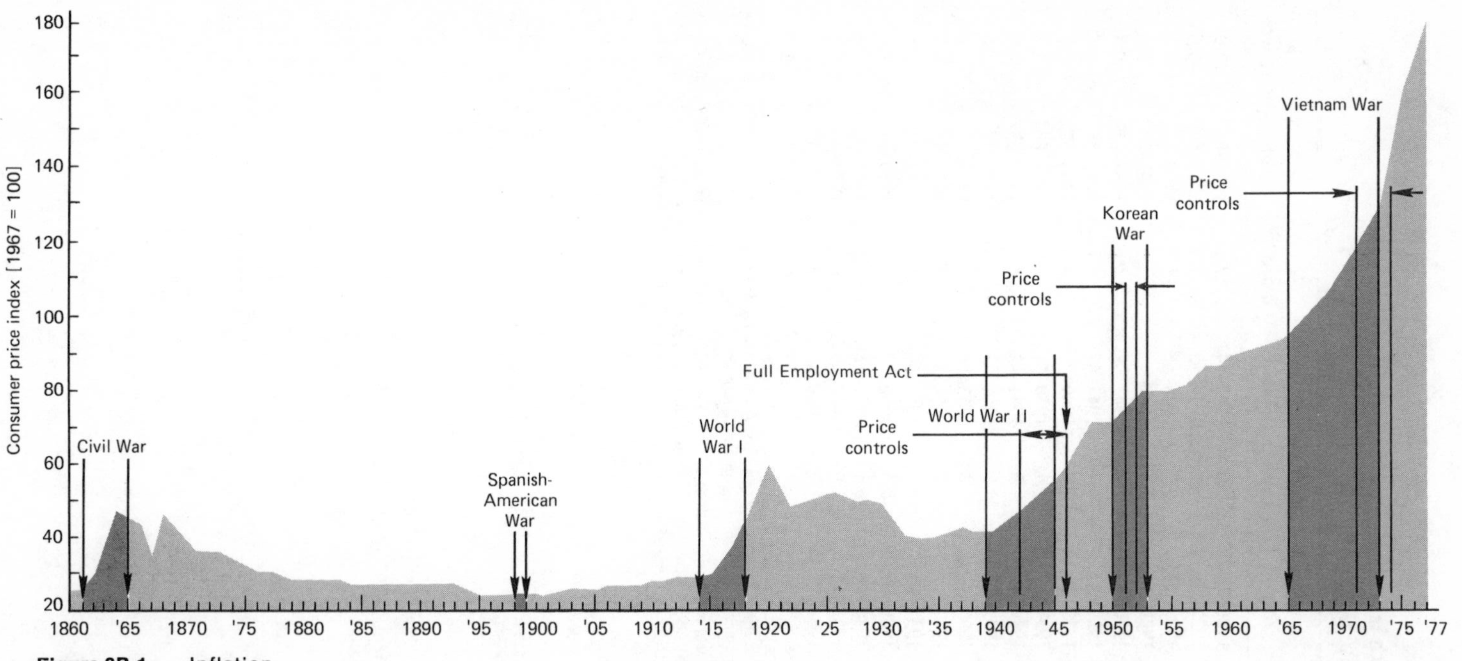

Figure 6B-1 Inflation

INFLATION

Reprinted from the May 22, 1978 issue of *Business Week* by special permission,

Comments: Inflation has persisted since the early 1940s, and since 1970 has increased dramatically. If the rate of inflation affects your business, ask yourself: What forces will likely affect the rate of inflation, and will the rate likely increase, decrease or stay the same? Although no one seems to know *for sure* the causes or cures of inflation, it is generally agreed that the government's deficit spending is a prime contributor. Also ask yourself: What is the possibility of a balanced budget within the next few years? Keep in mind: with an inflation rate of 7 percent, in 10 years it will require 2 dollars to purchase the same amount that 1 dollar will buy today.

PRIME INTEREST RATES

Table 6B-2 Prime Interest Rates, New York City, 1929–78

Year	*Average Rate*	*Year*	*Average Rate*	*Year*	*Average Rate*	*Year*	*Average Rate*
1929	5.76	1941	1.80	1953	3.16	1966	5.84
1930	4.75	1942	1.50	1954	3.06	1967	5.73
1931	3.87	1943	1.50	1955	3.16	1968	6.45
1932	3.62	1944	1.50	1956	3.71	1969	8.03
1933	3.43	1945	2.00	1957	4.10	1970	8.22
1934	1.50	1946	1.05	1958	4.12	1971	6.01
1935	1.76	1947	1.80	1959	4.50	1972	5.57
1936	1.50	1948	1.85	1960	4.79	1973	8.06
1937	1.50	1949	2.37	1961	4.50	1974	11.12
1938	1.69	1950	1.75	1962	4.50	1975	8.37
1939	1.50	1951	2.39	1963	4.50	1976	7.12
1940	1.50	1952	3.00	1964	4.50	1977	6.82
				1965	4.83	1978	8.04

Sources: For 1929–40, U.S. Board of Governors of the Federal Reserve System; for 1941–70, *Banking and Monetary Statistics.* Federal Reserve System; for 1971–76, *Statistical Abstract of the U.S.*, 1977; for 1977–78, Federal Reserve Bank of Philadelphia.

Comments: The prime rate has risen during the past fifty years, certainly reflecting the loss of monetary values due to inflation. Keep in mind: Interest rates will probably vary directly with the rate of inflation.

Table 6B-3. U.S. Population and Percent Increase, 1800–1976

Year	*Number (millions)*	*Percent Increase*
1800	5.3	35.1
1810	7.2	36.4
1820	9.6	33.1
1830	12.8	33.5
1840	17.0	32.7
1850	23.1	35.9
1860	31.4	35.6
1870	39.8	26.6
1880	50.1	26.0
1890	62.9	25.5
1900	75.9	20.7
1910	91.9	21.0
1920	105.7	14.9
1930	122.7	16.1
1940	131.6	7.2
1950	151.3	14.5
1960	179.3	18.5
1970	203.2	13.3
1971	207.1	1.1
1972	208.8	.8
1973	210.4	.8
1974	211.9	.7
1975	213.6	.8
1976	215.1	.7

Source: *Statistical Abstract of The U.S.,* 1977.

Comments: If the annual percentage increase holds at 0.7, by the year 2000 there will be 259 million people in the United States, a 20 percent increase. In contrast between 1950 and 1975 there was a 41 percent increase. Ask yourself: Will this slower rate of population growth affect my business?

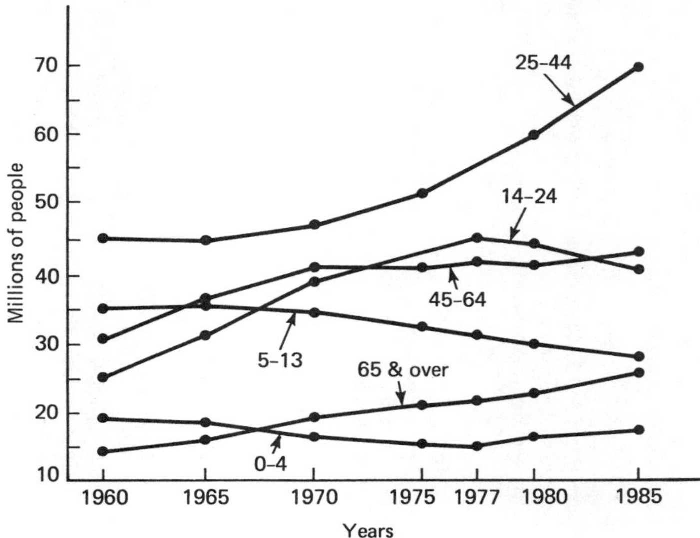

Figure 6B-2. Population by Age Group

Sources: For 1960–70, *Historical Statistics of the U.S. From Colonial Times to 1970,* Series A, Nos. 29 to 42; for 1970–85, *Population Estimates and Projections,* Series P-25, Nos. 704, 721, U.S. Department of Commerce, Bureau of the Census.

Comments: Note how the numbers of people in certain age groups are changing; especially 5–13, 14–24, 25–44 and 65 and over. Ask yourself: Will these shifts affect my business?

Table 6B-4 Population in 116 Largest Metropolitan Areas, 1975

Rank 1975	*Standard Metropolitan Statistical Area*	*1970 Population*	*1975 Estimate*	*Rank 1975*	*Standard Metropolitan Statistical Area*	*1970 Population*	*1975 Estimate*
1	New York, N.Y.-N.J.	9,973,716	9,635,200	57	Akron, Ohio	679,239	668,200
2	Chicago, Ill.	6,977,611	6,982,900	58	Worcester-Fitchburg-Leominster,		
3	Los Angeles-Long Beach, Calif.	7,041,980	6,944,900		Mass.[a]	637,037	648,100
4	Philadelphia, Pa.-N.J.	4,824,110	4,797,200	59	Syracuse, N.Y.	636,596	647,800
5	Detroit, Mich.	4,435,051	4,444,200	60	Gary-Hammond-E. Chicago, Ind.	633,367	640,400
6	Boston-Lowell-Brockton-Lawrence-			61	Northeast Pennsylvania, Pa.	621,882	636,900
	Haverhill, Mass.-N.H.	3,848,593	3,914,600	62	Allentown-Bethlehem-Easton,		
7	San Francisco-Oakland, Calif.	3,107,355	3,128,800		Pa.-N.J.	594,382	621,500
8	Washington, D.C.-Md.-Va.	2,910,111	3,016,200	63	Springfield-Chicopee-Holyoke,		
9	Nassau-Suffolk, N.Y.	2,555,868	2,622,000		Mass.[a]	583,031	597,400
10	Dallas-Fort Worth, Tex.	2,378,353	2,552,800	64	Charlotte-Gastonia, N.C.	557,785	594,500
11	St. Louis, Mo.-Ill.	2,410,602	2,369,400	65	New Brunswick-Perth Amboy-		
12	Pittsburgh, Pa.	2,401,362	2,315,900		Sayreville, N.J.	583,813	589,600
13	Houston, Tex.	1,999,316	2,297,300	66	Tulsa, Okla.	549,154	585,800
14	Baltimore, Md.	2,071,016	2,136,900	67	Orlando, Fla.	453,270	535,200
15	Minneapolis-St. Paul, Minn.-Wis.	1,965,391	2,027,500	68	Jersey City, N.J.	607,839	582,800
16	Newark, N.J.	2,057,468	1,995,900	69	Richmond, Va.	547,542	581,500
17	Cleveland, Ohio	2,063,729	1,975,400	70	Omaha, Nebr.-Iowa	542,646	572,800
18	Atlanta, Ga.	1,595,517	1,806,100	71	Grand Rapids, Mich.	539,225	567,600
19	Anaheim-Sta. Ana-			72	Youngstown-Warren, Ohio	537,124	548,500
	Garden Grove, Calif.	1,421,233	1,710,200	73	Greenville-Spartanburg, S.C.	473,454	526,300
20	San Diego, Calif.	1,357,854	1,587,500	74	Flint, Mich.	508,664	520,100
21	Miami, Fla.	1,267,792	1,438,600	75	Wilmington, Del.-N.J.-Md.	499,493	517,200
22	Milwaukee, Wis.	1,403,884	1,426,400	76	Long Branch-Asbury Park, N.J.	461,849	486,700
23	Seattle-Everett, Wash.	1,424,605	1,411,700	77	Raleigh-Durham, N.C.	419,254	473,200
24	Denver-Boulder, Colo.	1,239,477	1,404,300	78	New Bedford-Fall River, Mass.[a]	444,301	463,800
25	Cincinnati, Ohio-Ky.-Ind.	1,387,207	1,384,500	79	West Palm Beach-Boca Raton, Fla.	348,993	460,100
26	Tampa-St. Petersburg, Fla.	1,088,549	1,365,400	80	Paterson-Clifton-Passaic, N.J.	460,782	452,700
27	Buffalo, N.Y.	1,349,211	1,327,200	81	Lansing-East Lansing, Mich.	424,271	447,000
28	Kansas City, Mo.-Kans.	1,273,926	1,287,100	82	Fresno, Calif.	413,329	445,600
29	Riverside-San Bernardino-			83	Tucson, Ariz.	351,667	441,200
	Ontario, Calif.	1,141,307	1,223,400	84	Oxnard-Simi Valley-Ventura, Calif.	378,497	438,100

30	Phoenix, Ariz.	971,228	1,217,500
31	San Jose, Calif.	1,065,313	1,173,400
32	Indianapolis, Ind.	1,111,352	1,147,400
33	New Orleans, La.	1,046,470	1,094,400
34	Portland, Oreg.–Wash.	1,007,130	1,081,700
35	Columbus, Ohio	1,017,847	1,077,000
36	Hartford–New Britain–Bristol, Conn.[a]	1,035,195	1,059,800
37	San Antonio, Tex.	888,179	977,200
38	Rochester, N.Y.	961,516	971,200
39	Louisville, Ky.–Ind.	867,330	891,700
40	Sacramento, Calif.	803,793	880,100
41	Memphis, Tenn.–Ark.–Miss.	834,103	873,200
42	Fort Lauderdale–Hollywood, Fla.	620,100	862,500
43	Providence–Warwick–Pawtucket, R.I.[a]	855,495	851,100
44	Dayton, Ohio	852,531	836,900
45	Albany–Schenectady–Troy, N.Y.	777,977	799,000
46	Bridgeport–Stamford–Norwalk–Danbury, Conn.[a]	792,814	793,900
47	Birmingham, Ala.	767,230	793,000
48	Salt Lake City–Ogden, Utah	705,458	783,800
49	Toledo, Ohio–Mich.	762,658	781,400
50	Norfolk–Virginia Beach–Portsmouth, Va.–N.C.	732,600	772,600
51	Greensboro–Winston Salem–High Point, N.C.	724,129	765,000
52	New Haven–West Haven–Waterbury–Meriden, Conn.[a]	744,948	760,900
53	Nashville–Davidson, Tenn.	699,271	753,100
54	Oklahoma City, Okla.	699,092	752,900
55	Honolulu, Hawaii	630,528	704,500
56	Jacksonville, Fla.	621,827	700,600

85	Knoxville, Tenn.	409,409	436,100
86	Harrisburg, Pa.	410,505	426,300
87	El Paso, Tex.	359,291	414,700
88	Baton Rouge, La.	375,628	411,300
89	Tacoma, Wash.	412,344	409,800
90	Canton, Ohio	393,789	408,300
91	Mobile, Ala.	376,690	401,600
92	Johnson City–Kingsport–Bristol, Tenn.–Va.	373,591	398,900
93	Austin, Tex.	323,158	294,800
94	Chattanooga, Tenn.–Ga.	370,857	393,000
95	Albuquerque, N. Mex.	333,266	387,700
96	Wichita, Kans.	389,352	382,500
97	Fort Wayne, Ind.	361,984	374,600
98	Charleston–N. Charleston, S.C.	336,125	371,600
99	Columbia, S.C.	322,880	370,700
100	Davenport–Rock I.–Moline, Iowa–Ill.	362,638	369,300
101	Little Rock–N. Little Rock, Ark.	323,296	367,300
102	Newport News–Hampton, Va.	333,140	351,800
103	Peoria, Ill.	341,979	351,100
104	Beaumont–Port Arthur–Orange, Tex.	347,568	349,500
105	York, Pa.	329,540	347,400
106	Shreveport, La.	333,826	345,700
107	Bakersfield, Calif.	330,234	343,700
108	Lancaster, Pa.	320,079	341,300
109	Utica–Rome, N.Y.	340,670	334,900
110	Las Vegas, Nev.	273,288	332,500
111	Des Moines, Iowa	313,562	331,300
112	Trenton, N.J.	304,116	320,500
113	Madison, Wis.	290,272	309,900
114	Reading, Pa.	296,382	305,100
115	Spokane, Wash.	287,487	304,900
116	Binghamton, N.Y.–Pa.	302,672	303,100

[a]New England County Metropolitan Area.

Source: *Population Estimates,* Series P-26, U.S. Department of Commerce, Bureau of the Census.

Comments: Note that the largest twenty metropolitan areas contained almost one-third of the population in the United States.

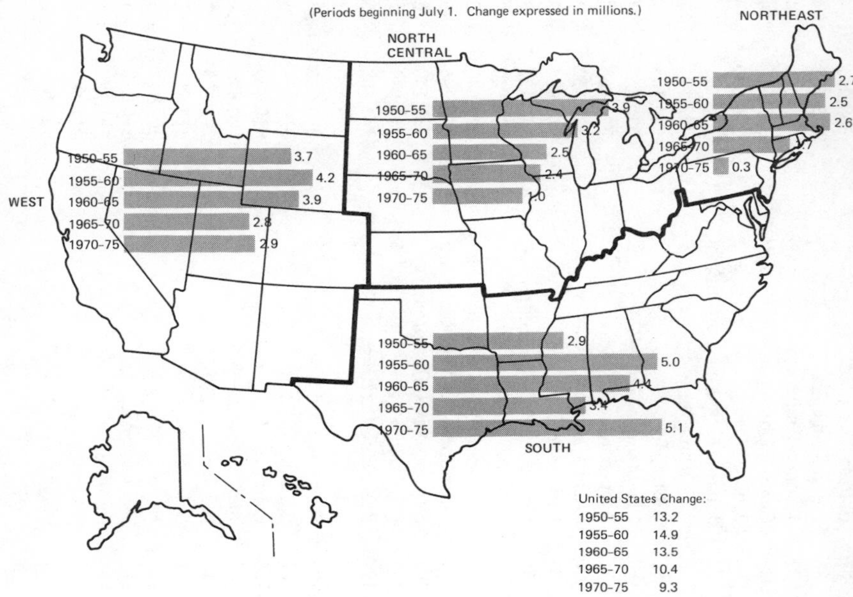

Figure 6B-3. Population Shifts: Population changes for five-year periods by region, 1950 to 1975

Source: *Population Estimates and Projections,* Series P-25, No. 640, U.S. Department of Commerce, Bureau of the Census.

Comments: Ask yourself: Are these population movements having an impact on my business? If so, then: Will these movements be likely to continue? Some authorities claim that the shifts in population should slow down in the 1980s when the sunbelt begins to experience urban blight and its related problems which are so familiar to the older, established cities of the northeast and north central areas.

Table 6B-5 New Privately and Publicly Owned Housing Units Started, 1965–77

		Region							
Year	*Total*	*Northeast*		*North Central*		*South*		*West*	
		Number[a]	*% of Total*	*Number*[a]	*% of Total*	*Number*[a]	*% of Total*	*Number*[a]	*% of Total*
1965	1,509.7	281.3	19	368.7	24	588.6	39	271.1	18
1966	1,195.8	215.6	18	297.3	25	482.9	40	200.0	17
1967	1,321.9	223.5	17	343.9	26	531.5	40	223.0	17
1968	1,545.4	236.4	15	377.0	25	633.7	41	298.3	19
1969	1,499.5	212.9	14	356.6	24	602.9	40	327.2	22
1970	1,469.0	224.1	15	301.4	21	628.9	43	314.5	21
1971	2,084.5	271.0	13	439.9	21	883.9	43	489.8	23
1972	2,378.5	334.1	14	445.3	19	1,067.5	45	531.5	22
1973	2,057.5	278.4	14	442.2	21	905.7	44	431.2	21
1974	1,352.5	183.4	14	319.8	24	560.8	41	288.5	21
1975	1,171.4	149.9	13	295.4	25	448.3	38	277.7	24
1976	1,547.6	169.5	11	400.7	26	574.9	37	402.5	26
1977	1,989.8	201.6	10	465.0	23	784.5	40	538.7	27

Source: *Housing Starts,* June 1978, U.S. Department of Commerce, Bureau of the Census.

[a]In thousands of units. Because of rounding, detail may not add to total.

Comments: Notice how the population changes are reflected in housing starts. (See Figure 6B-3.)

Table 6B-6 Degrees Conferred, 1900–1977

Year	*All Degrees*	*Bachelor's or First Professional*	*Master's or Second Professional*	*Doctor's or Equivalent*
1900	29,375	27,410	1,583	382
1910	39,755	37,199	2,113	443
1920	53,516	48,622	4,279	615
1930	139,752	122,484	14,969	2,299
1940	216,521	186,500	26,731	3,290
1950	496,874	432,058	58,183	6,633
1960	476,704	389,183	77,692	9,829
1965	663,622	530,003	117,152	16,467
1970	1,065,391	827,234	208,291	29,866
1975	1,305,382	978,849	292,450	34,083
1977[a]	1,399,300	1,041,800	322,200	35,300

[a]Projected.

Sources: For 1900–1970, *Historical Abstract of the U.S. From Colonial Times to 1970,* Series H751–765; for 1975–1977, National Center for Education Statistics.

Comments: Given the large number of college degrees, the "bulge" in population in the twenty-five-to-forty-four-year-old bracket, and slow population growth may lead to a large number of young people who will not be able to reach their career aspirations. If this does happen, it will most certainly have an impact on values, life styles, and subsequent product and service needs.

CONSUMER INSTALLMENT DEBT

Table 6B-7 Rates of Consumer Installment Debt to Disposable Personal Income, 1947–77.

Year	*Disposable Personal Income (in millions of dollars)*	*Consumer Installment Debt (in millions of dollars)*	*% of Installment Debt to Disposable Personal Income*
1947	168,387	6,695	3.9
1950	205,511	14,703	7.1
1955	273,413	28,906	10.5
1960	349,370	42,968	12.2
1965	472,157	70,893	15.0
1970	685,935	102,064	14.8
1975	1,086,700	164,955	15.1
1977	1,303,000	216,572	16.6

Sources: Disposable Personal Income for 1947–70, *National Income Products Accounts,* U.S. Department of Commerce; for 1975–77 *Survey of Current Business,* U.S. Department of Commerce. Consumer Installment Debt for 1947–75, *U.S. Business Statistics,* 1977, U.S. Department of Commerce, Bureau of Economic Analysis; for 1977, Board of Governors of the Federal Reserve System.

Comments: Disposable personal income is the income remaining to persons after the deduction from personal income of personal tax and nontax payments to general government.*

As defined by the Board of Governors of the Federal Reserve System, short- and intermediate-term consumer credit includes credit used to finance the purchase of commodities and services for personal consumption or to refinance debt originally incurred for such purposes. Consumer credit does not include real estate mortgages and insurance policy loans.

Consumer installment debt represents all consumer credit that is scheduled to be repaid in two or more payments. Revolving credit, budget, and coupon accounts are treated as installment credit rather than as charge accounts because they provide for scheduled repayment on a periodic basis.

Consumer installment debt includes the following: automobile paper representing credit extended for the purchase of new or used automobiles; other consumer goods paper representing credit extended for home appliances, furniture, jewelry, mobile homes, and boats; repair and modernization loans to finance the maintenance and improvement of homes; personal loans including all installment loans not covered in the previous categories that are made by financial institutions to individuals for consumer purposes.†

Since 1950, the percent of installment debt (of disposable income) has more than doubled. Many authorities claim that the percentage figure cannot rise much above its present level.

**Historical Statistics of the U.S. from Colonial Times to 1970,* Series F6–9.

†*Ibid,* Series X551–560.

Table 6-B8 Employment Status of the Noninstitutional Population 16 Years and Over, 1950–77

	Total Labor Force			
	Employed		*Unemployed*	
Year	*Number (000)*	*Percent of Population*	*Number (000)*	*Percent of Labor Force*
1950	63,858	59.9	3,288	5.3
1955	68,072	60.4	2,852	4.4
1960	72,142	60.2	3,852	5.5
1965	77,178	59.7	3,366	4.5
1970	85,903	61.3	4,088	4.9
1975	94,793	61.8	7,830	8.5
1977	99,534	62.8	6,855	7.0

Source: *Employment and Earnings,* U.S. Department of Labor, Bureau of Labor Statistics.

Table 6B-9 Percentage of Women in the Labor Force, by Age Group

	Percentage of Total Labor Force (Employed) Comprised by Women			
Year	*All Age Groups*	*Ages 20–24*	*Ages 25–34*	*All Other Age Groups*
1950	28.8	4.2	5.6	19.0
1955	30.2	3.6	6.0	20.6
1960	32.1	3.6	5.8	22.7
1965	33.9	4.4	5.6	23.9
1970	36.7	5.7	6.6	24.4
1975	39.1	6.4	10.0	22.7
1976	39.7	6.5	9.5	23.7
1977	41.0	6.8	10.1	24.1

Sources: For 1950 and 1955, *Historical Statistics of the U.S. from Colonial Times to 1970* Series D 29–41; for 1960–76 *Statistical Abstract of the U.S.,* 1977; for 1977, *Special Labor Force Report 212,* Bureau of Labor Statistics.

Comments: Two major trends should be noted: (1) The increase in the unemployment rate and (2) the increase in the percentage of women in the work force is mainly comprised of those women in the lower age groups. It is highly likely that they will remain in the labor force, and this trend will be reflected in family life styles, creating demands for different products and services.

Table 6B-10 Size of U.S. Corporations Based on Assets 1955–56 to 1975–76

Tax Year	*Total*	*Asset Zero or Not Reported*	*Under 25,000*	*25,000–100,000*	*100,000–500,000*	*500,000–1,000,000*	*1,000,000–10,000,000*	*10,000,000 100,000,000*	*100,000,000 250,000,000*	*250,000,000 500,000,000*	*500,000,000 1,000,000,000*	*1,000,000,000 & Over*
1955–56	746,762	N/A	185,260	245,614	220,833	39,301	47,647	7,080	607			420[a]
1960–61	1,068,525	N/A	292,905	283,724	317,323	82,697	84,572	6,575	436	167	70	56
1965–66	1,423,980	N/A	429,617	354,342	406,669	108,054	115,544	8,739	589	216	131	79
1970–71	1,665,452	N/A	451,933	390,490	516,862	141,139	152,013	11,509	825	332	177	172
1971–72	1,733,299	N/A	458,872	406,416	543,875	147,535	162,528	12,477	856	358	198	184
1972–73	1,812,723	N/A	459,241	421,110	578,420	155,253	181,870	15,032	989	376	223	209
1973–74	1,904,670	N/A	466,030	434,946	612,813	165,694	205,703	17,400	1,130	451		503[a]
1974–75	1,965,342	62,456	1,078,690[a]		568,784	118,476	113,654	20,079	1,973			1,230[ab]
1975–76	2,021,207	99,310	1,081,075[a]		577,753	122,426	116,199	21,019	2,118			1,307[abc]

Note: All industries included; based on IRS returns.

Sources: For 1955–56 to 1974–75, *Statistics of Income,* Corporate Income Tax Returns, Department of the Treasury, Internal Revenue Service; for 1975–76 *Statistics of Income,* Preliminary 1977.

[a] Grouped together

[b] Consolidated returns only

[c] Estimated

N/A = Not available

INDIVIDUAL BUSINESS TAX RETURNS (OTHER THAN CORPORATE)

Table 6B-11 Individual Tax Returns 1955–56 to 1974–75

Tax Year	*Total*	*Business and Professional*	*Farm*	*Partnership*	*Small Business Corporation*
1955–56	10,768,215	8,972,677	*a*	1,795,538	*a*
1960–61	10,591,056	8,708,292	*a*	1,882,764	*a*
1965–66	10,795,697	5,907,667	3,008,840	1,879,190	*a*
1969–70	11,651,609	6,159,985	3,026,530	2,005,006	460,088
1970–71	N/A[b]	N/A	N/A	N/A	N/A
1971–72	12,208,377	6,688,300	2,810,358	2,213,436	496,283
1972–73	12,635,169	6,916,393	2,865,851	2,340,448	512,477
1973–74	N/A[b]	N/A	N/A	N/A	N/A
1974–75	13,068,471	7,242,542	2,755,041	2,472,626	598,262

Note: Includes all taxable and nontaxable returns regardless of profit and loss.

[a] Farms and Small Businesses included in Business and Professional figures.

[b] Figures available only in standard metropolitan areas.

Sources: For 1955–56 to 1972–73, *Statistics of Income,* Department of the Treasury, Internal Revenue Service; for 1973–74 and 1974–75, *1975 Supplement.*

Definitions: Business and Professional: sole proprietors. Farm: unincorporated enterprises; self-employed. Partnership: proprietors; may include more than two partners. Small Business: those businesses with ten or fewer stockholders; most likely owners and developers who wish to be taxed as individuals.

Table 6B-12 Motor Vehicle Registrations, 1976 (000)

1950	49,300	1967	96,905	1972	118,797
1955	62,689	1968	100,898	1973	125,654
1960	73,858	1969	105,096	1974	129,934
1965	90,358	1970	108,418	1975	132,950
1966	93,950	1971	112,986	1976	137,287

Table 6B-13 Motor Vehicle Registrations by State, 1976

State	*Registrations (000)*	*% of Total*	*State*	*Registrations (000)*	*% of Total*
Ala.	2,590	1.9	Mo.	2,924	2.1
Alaska	255	0.2	Mont.	620	0.5
Arizona	1,491	1.1	Nebr.	1,218	0.9
Ark.	1,327	1.0	Nev.	476	0.3
Calif.	14,102	10.3	N.H.	504	0.4
Colo.	1,994	1.4	N.J.	4,312	3.1
Conn.	2,009	1.5	N. Mex.	863	0.6
Del.	360	0.3	N.Y.	7,758	5.6
D.C.	265	0.2	N.C.	3,837	2.8
Fla.	5,603	4.1	N. Dak.	569	0.4
Ga.	3,263	2.4	Ohio	7,469	5.4
Hawaii	483	0.4	Okla.	2,181	1.6
Idaho	681	0.5	Oreg.	1,678	1.2
Ill.	6,542	4.8	Pa.	7,979	5.8
Ind.	3,382	2.5	R.I.	576	0.4
Iowa	2,157	1.6	S.C.	1,877	1.4
Kans.	1,848	1.3	S. Dak.	549	0.4
Ky.	2,350	1.7	Tenn.	2,858	2.1
La.	2,277	1.7	Tex.	8,674	6.3
Me.	680	0.5	Utah	881	0.6
Md.	2,508	1.8	Vt.	294	0.2
Mass.	3,192	2.3	Va.	3,398	2.5
Mich.	5,723	4.2	Wash.	2,666	1.9
Minn.	2,576	1.9	W. Va.	1,003	0.7
Miss.	1,424	1.0	Wis.	2,683	1.9
			Wyo.	358	0.3

Source: *Statistical Abstract of The U.S.*, 1977.

Comments: Out of the fifty states and the District of Columbia, eight states (California, Florida, Illinois, Michigan, New York, Ohio, Pennsylvania and Texas) contain 48 percent of all registered motor vehicle licenses.

Table 6B-14 Steel Production, Imports, Exports, and Apparent Supply, 1967–77

Year	*Domestic Production*	*Imports*	*Exports*	*Apparent Supply*	*Imports as % of Supply*
1967	83,897,340	11,454,502	1,684,921	93,666,921	12.2
1968	91,855,894	17,959,886	2,169,783	107,645,997	16.7
1969	93,876,871	14,034,287	5,229,337	102,681,821	13.7
1970	90,798,126	13,364,474	7,052,614	97,109,986	13.8
1971	87,037,772	18,303,959	2,827,377	102,514,354	17.9
1972	91,805,000	17,680,687	2,872,687	106,613,000	16.6
1973	111,430,497	15,149,682	4,052,451	122,527,728	12.4
1974	109,471,569	15,970,038	5,833,148	119,608,459	13.4
1975	79,956,827	12,012,442	2,953,127	89,016,142	13.5
1976	89,446,581	14,284,605	2,654,006	101,077,180	14.1
1977	91,147,267	19,306,612	2,003,101	108,450,778	17.8

Source: American Iron and Steel Institute.

Comments: Comparing years 1967-69 with 1975-77, there was a decline in the domestic production of steel. On the other hand, using the same time spans, there was an increase of imported steel while domestic exports decreased.

Table 6B-15 (1) Domestic Energy Consumption by Primary Energy Type, 1950–77 (in trillions of BTUs)

Year	*Coal*[a]	*Natural Gas*[b]	*Petroleum*[c]	*Hydropower*	*Nuclear Power*	*Geothermal*	*Total Gross Energy Consumption*
1950	12,913	6,150	13,489	1,371			33,923
1955	11,540	9,232	17,524	1,370			39,666
1960	10,140	12,699	20,067	1,614	5		44,525
1965	11,908	16,098	23,241	2,027	39		53,313
1970	12,698	22,029	29,537	2,614	232	11	67,121
1971	12,043	22,469	30,570	2,827	406	11	68,326
1972	12,423	22,698	32,966	2,909	577	33	71,606
1973	13,294	22,512	34,851	2,978	885	43	74,563
1974	12,889	21,732	33,468	3,276	1,215	54	72,634
1975	12,814	19,948	32,742	3,186	1,839	69	70,598
1976	13,748	20,344	35,086	3,042	2,037	78	74,335
1977[d]	14,117	19,613	36,956	2,397	2,675	78	75,836

Source: Bureau of Mines and Energy Information Administration.

Comments: Between 1974 and 1977, the domestic consumption of coal increased by only 1,228 trillion BTUs. On the other hand, the domestic consumption of petroleum increased by 3,488 trillion BTUs.

[a] Includes anthracite, bituminous coal, lignite, and net imports of coke.

[b] Excludes natural gas liquids. Prior to 1971, consumption includes adjustments.

[c] Includes domestically produced crude oil, natural gas liquids, and condensate, plus imported crude oil and products.

[d] Preliminary.

Table 6B-15 (2) Net Trade in Mineral Fuel, 1947–77 (in trillions of BTUs)

Year	*Coal*	*Petroleum*[a]	*Natural Gas*	*Total*
1947	2,007	– 10	19	2,016
1950	756	– 1,223	27	– 440
1955	1,484	– 1,956	21	– 451
1960	1,037	– 3,544	– 149	– 2,656
1965	1,413	– 4,971	– 444	– 4,002
1970	1,990	– 6,841	– 774	– 5,625
1971	1,566	– 7,943	– 881	– 7,258
1972	1,544	– 9,648	– 967	– 9,071
1973	1,466	– 12,983	– 976	– 12,493
1974	1,544	– 12,585	– 903	– 11,944
1975	1,771	– 12,411	– 899	– 11,539
1976	1,529	– 15,188	– 917	– 14,576
1977[b]	1,351	– 18,110	– 959	– 17,718

Source: Bureau of Mines and Energy Information Administration.

Comments: Between 1974 and 1977 (inclusive), U.S. imports of petroleum have increased by 44 percent.

[a] Includes natural gas liquids.

[b] Preliminary.

Table 6B-16 Value of Merchandise, Gold, and Silver Exports and Imports, 1920–77 (in millions of dollars)

Year	*Exports*	*Imports*	*Excess of Exports (+) or Imports (−)*
1920	8,664	5,784	+ 2,880
1930	4,013	3,500	+ 513
1940	4,030	7,433	− 3,403
1950	10,816	9,125	+ 1,691
1960	20,603	15,046	+ 5,557
1970	43,265	40,189	+ 3,076
1971	43,300	45,600	− 2,300
1972	49,400	55,800	− 6,400
1973	71,400	70,500	+ 900
1974	98,300	103,700	− 5,400
1975	107,100	98,000	+ 9,100
1976	114,694	124,047	− 9,353
1977	120,585	151,644	−31,059

Sources: For 1920–70, *Historical Statistics of The U.S. From Colonial Times to 1970*, Series U187–200; for 1971–75, *Statistical Abstract of the U.S.*, 1977; for 1976–77, Bureau of Economic Analysis.

Comments: Traditionally (since the Civil War) the U.S. has had a favorable balance of trade. However, since 1971 U.S. has experienced a chronic balance of trade deficit.

Table 6B-17 Gross National Product: World Regions and Nations 1975

	GNP Total ($ millions)	GNP Per Capita (dollars)	Population Mid-1975 (millions)
Western Europe	1,487,540	3,440	
Austria	31,290	4,273	7.5
Belgium	53,290	5,443	9.8
Denmark	29,740	5,877	5.1
Finland	19,330	4,161	4.7
France	303,560	5,737	52.9
Germany (Fed. Rep.)	379,900	6,144	61.8
Greece	17,440	1,927	9.1
Iceland	940	4,200	0.2
Ireland	7,410	2,367	3.1
Italy	159,720	2,862	55.8
Luxembourg	1,940	5,389	0.4
Malta	380	1,152	0.3
Netherlands	67,770	4,965	13.7
Norway	23,330	5,818	4.0
Portugal	11,680	1,333	8.8
Spain	73,780	2,080	35.5
Sweden	60,910	7,428	8.2
Switzerland	44,640	6,975	6.4

	GNP Total ($ millions)	GNP Per Capita (dollars)	Population Mid-1975 (millions)
Kuwait	13,900	13,900	1.0
Lebanon	3,700	1,289	2.9
Qatar	1,900	21,111	0.1
Saudi Arabia	31,000	5,536	5.6
Syria	4,000	544	7.4
Turkey	24,050	614	39.2
United Arab Emirates	7,300	33,182	0.2
East Asia	597,920	1,156	
China (Taiwan)	14,400	900	16.0
Hong Kong	6,430	1,471	4.4
Indonesia	28,000	215	130.1
Japan	483,500	4,358	111.0
Korea (South)	18,700	551	34.0
Malaysia	9,000	761	11.8
Philippines	14,950	352	42.5
Singapore	5,660	2,516	2.3
Thailand	14,120	334	42.3
Oceania	87,920	3,357	
Australia	73,280	5,424	13.5

United Kingdom	200,490	3,583	56.0	New Zealand	12,940	4,188	3.1
Africa (Excluding Egypt)	149,230	1,520		*Latin America*	290,340	956	
Algeria	12,500	745	16.8	Argentina	39,810	1,569	25.4
Ethiopia	2,770	99	28.0	Brazil	97,810	913	107.1
Ghana	3,700	375	9.9	Chile	8,340	814	10.3
Ivory Coast	2,930	599	4.9	Columbia	12,740	515	24.7
Kenya	2,800	209	13.4	Dominican Republic	3,200	703	4.7
Libya	11,900	4,877	2.4	Ecuador	4,160	618	6.7
Morocco	7,760	448	17.8	Jamaica	2,420	1,192	2.0
Nigeria	26,000	413	62.9	Mexico	64,360	1,070	60.2
Rhodesia	3,210	500	6.4	Panama	1,780	1,066	1.7
South Africa	34,500	1,288	26.4	Peru	12,100	764	15.8
Sudan	4,090	230	17.8	Uruguay	3,280	1,072	3.1
Tanzania	2,260	149	15.2	Venezuela	27,300	2,277	12.0
Tunisia	3,570	619	5.8	*North America*	1,661,550	6,730	
Uganda	1,840	159	11.6	Canada	145,250	6,363	22.8
Zaire	3,890	156	24.9	UNITED STATES	1,516,300	7,098	213.6
Zambia	2,510	512	4.9	*Communist Countries*			
South Asia	121,990	133		Cuba	7,100	755	9.4
Bangladesh	10,240	133	76.8	Czechoslovakia	54,630	3,691	14.8
India	94,220	158	598.3	Germany (Dem. Rep.)	60,400	3,574	16.9
Pakistan	10,360	147	70.3	Hungary	25,460	2,425	10.5
Sri Lanka	2,930	209	14.0	Poland	85,490	2,514	34.0
Near East	175,320	1,592		Romania	46,810	2,208	21.2
Egypt	11,400	306	37.2	USSR	786,700	3,088	254.5
Iran	50,000	1,514	33.0	Vietnam	4,500	102	44.0
Israel	11,850	3,516	3.4	Yugoslavia	35,200	1,650	21.3

Source: Department of State, Special Report No. 33, May 1977.

INTERNATIONAL—TRENDS IN OUTPUT OF SELECTED COUNTRIES

Table 6B-18 Trends in Output per Employed Civilian, 1950–75

	Real Gross Domestic Product per Employed Civilian (Average Annual Percent Change)		
Country	*1950–75*	*1950–67*	*1967–75*
United States	1.7	2.4	0.4
Canada	2.2	2.6	1.4
France	4.4	4.7	3.8
Germany	4.8	5.2	4.0
Japan	7.2	7.4	6.9
United Kingdom	2.2	2.4	2.0

Source: *Productivity and The Economy,* Bulletin No. 1926, U.S. Department of Labor, Bureau of Labor Statistics, 1977.

Table 6B-19 Trends in Manufacturing Productivity, 1950–75

	Output per Employee-Hour (Average Annual Percent Change)		
	1950–75	*1950–67*	*1967–75*
United States	2.6	2.7	2.1
Canada	4.1	4.1	3.6
France	5.3	4.9	4.6
Germany	6.0	6.2	5.2
Japan	9.2	8.6	8.2
United Kingdom	3.4	3.0	3.2

Source: *Productivity and The Economy,* Bulletin No. 1926, U.S. Department of Labor, Bureau of Labor Statistics, 1977.

Comments: The U.S. has experienced slower growth rates for both "Trends in Output per Employed Civilian" and "Trends in Manufacturing Productivity" than any of the other compared industrial countries.

INTERNATIONAL—CURRENCY EXCHANGE RATES

Table 6B-20 Exchange Rates for Selected Currencies, 1950–78

Year	*United Kingdom (pound)*	*Canada (dollar)*	*Netherlands (guilder)*	*West Germany (mark)*	*Switzerland (franc)*	*France (franc)*	*Belgium (franc)*	*Japan (yen)*	*Italy (lira)*
1950	280.07	91.47	26.25	23.84	23.14	28.58	1.99	NA	.1601
1960	280.76	103.12	26.51	23.98	23.15	20.39	2.00	.2778	.1610
1970	239.59	95.80	27.65	27.42	23.20	18.09	2.01	.2792	.1595
1975	222.16	98.30	39.63	40.73	38.74	23.35	2.73	.3371	.1533
1976	180.48	101.41	37.85	39.74	40.01	20.94	2.59	.3374	.1204
1977	174.62	94.11	40.78	43.12	41.79	20.74	2.79	.3739	.1134
1978[a]	197.25	87.87	47.08	51.15	63.11	23.36	3.23	.5398	.1214

[a]1978 figures are closing day figures, August 16, 1978.

Source: Board of Governors of the Federal Reserve System, *Federal Reserve Bulletin*.

7

Step 3 (Continued): Strategy Formulation— Guidelines for Strategic Action

Strategies enable you to move from where you are today (as revealed by the situation analysis) to where you wish to be (as indicated by your objectives). They are the general courses of action you follow within the parameters set by mission and policies, in order to achieve certain levels of profitability, growth, or whatever your objectives might be.

Because no company can do everything it wants, strategy selection represents practical choices. There are always limitations of some sort, whether of time, money, or available resources. Strategies are the channeling of company efforts, a putting forth of strength where it will do the most good.

Figure 7-1 illustrates how the strategy evolves. Note that objectives, mission, and policies specify the overall requirements. The growth and competitive actions (strategy) you choose to meet these overall requirements depend heavily on your knowledge of your company (situation analysis) and of future external environments.

Naturally, the greater your knowledge about various strategies, and the conditions under which they're most effective, the more likely you'll be able to select the best strategy for your firm. In this chapter

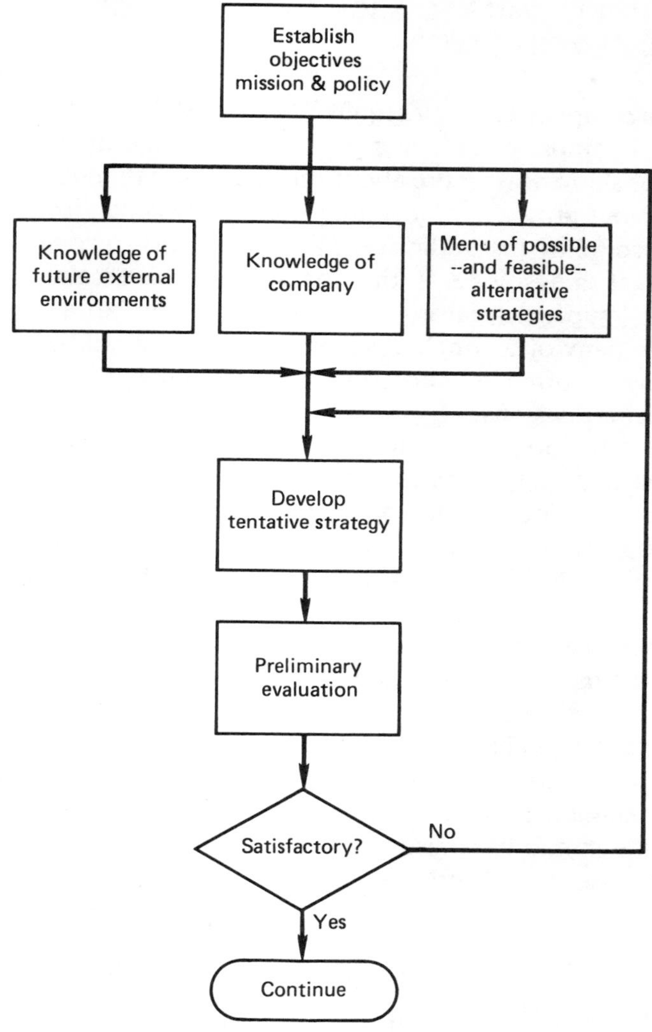

Figure 7-1. The Evolution of the Strategic Plan

a number of types of strategies and guidelines for their use are given. The guidelines are general rules of thumb that apply to smaller, growing companies. Because of your company's special circumstances, some might not hold true for you. If you don't follow one or more of these guidelines, however, make sure you have a good reason for violating the general rule.

RECOGNIZING LIMITS TO GROWTH AS DICTATED BY MANAGEMENT STYLE

As a company grows, it requires different skills of its management. In a small company the owner controls every step of the operation, and he (or she) knows more about the mechanics than anyone else. If the company grows, he inevitably becomes a supervisor who must delegate some of his authority. He has to work through others in order to get things done. In the final state of this escalation he must become a "super delegator," such as the president of a highly diversified company or a conglomerate. Here he must delegate authority to managers, often without fully understanding the intricacies of their various divisions.

Often the president either cannot or does not wish to make the transition from one stage to the next. This poses a real limit to the firm's growth. There's only so much one person can do. Furthermore, good people want responsibilities and challenges. If they're not given opportunities they'll go elsewhere, leaving the corporation with weak people.

When the company reaches a certain size, the functional area managers must also become effective delegators. And as the company grows, lower echelon managers must also possess this management skill. (Chapter 13 gives pointers on how to improve delegation skills.)

Now this does not mean that top management *must* delegate. After all, this is a personal choice. But any unwillingness—or inability—to delegate should be considered in developing your strategy. In fact, it may be a reason to modify objectives.

IDENTIFYING BASIC STRENGTHS AND BUILDING UPON THEM

Identify what your company does well. This may be harder to do than it seems. Often firms operate under fixed attitudes inherited from the past and assume that what they are most accustomed to doing is what they're best at. Use your situation analysis to counter these natural biases. It will help you identify where the firm already has or could develop an advantage over its competition.

Such an analysis requires objectivity. You may find it helpful to rate your company's strengths as if you were an outsider—an outsider who is interested in acquiring a company in your industry. Always ask: What are our core strengths? Overall, basic strengths divide into those of the market and those of technical skills. Consider an example of the former. Hallmark Cards, Inc., having a well-recognized and respected trade name—plus a distribution system of 6,000 independent dealers—capitalized on these market strengths. Hallmark expanded its product line into noncard items which could be sold through its distribution system. New products included crystal, pewter, and jewelry products.[1]

But just because customers value your name for one product does not necessarily mean they will hold your other products in high regard. Sears, for example, had sold appliances to the middle- and upper-middle classes for years. It decided it could sell its wealthier clientele clothes as well. The customers were already in the store, after all, and had demonstrated considerable loyalty to the brand name. Sears consequently upgraded the quality and price of its clothing, only to find that the better-heeled customers continued to pass through these departments (en route to the appliances) without buying anything. They still purchased their refrigerators from Sears—and their clothes from department stores and specialty shops. The Sears name on a washing machine was simply not the same, at least in the minds of the customers, as the Sears label on a man's suit. It was a costly mistake in strategy, and the direct result of Sears's failure to gauge the attitudes and values of its customers. It's the customer who determines the market, not the seller.

The second area of core strengths is in technical skills. For technology to be a source of strength, however, it must be a proven skill rather than knowledge of theory. For example, United States universities failed when they took on government contracts to solve urban problems. The universities were long on theory but short on practical expertise; they simply did not grasp how things get done in politics.

The technology must also be sufficiently distinct for your company to make its product a leader with your target market. It's best to stay out of areas where customers do not—or cannot be "taught" to—appreciate your excellence. Xerox found this out during its unsuccessful foray into the computer industry.

Besides asking, "What are our basic strengths?" you must also ask, "What makes us subject to 'precarious exposure?'" There are three major sources. The first can be described as "rigor mortis," which sets in when existent power centers protect their positions by fighting every major change that is proposed. The usual ground for resistance is that change involves difficulties too great to overcome. Innovation, however, is essential. The wars of tomorrow will not be fought on the battlefields of yesterday. The massive guns of Manila, for instance, could have blown the Japanese Imperial Navy out of the water in 1941. Enemies had always attacked Manila from the sea. But the Japanese approached from inland, a direction in which the guns could not fire.

United States involvement in Vietnam offers a more painful example. The American army operated with the same strategy that had proved so successful in World War II and the Korean War. Moreover, it was aided by extraordinary advances in the technology of warfare. But conventional strategy failed anyway, for at least three major reasons: A large element of South Vietnam's population remained indifferent to the outcome; the tropical terrain was less hospitable than the forests and fields of Europe or the bare hills of South Korea; South Vietnam's extensive borders proved impossible to defend against guerilla infiltration.

Company after company has failed for a similar reason—clinging to the past and failing to innovate. Take the Baldwin Locomotive Works. When the diesel engine was introduced, Baldwin chose to make improvements in their steam engines—such as reducing the de-scaling time—rather than to produce their own diesel. As a result, they produced the finest steam engine in the world; but at that moment of time no improvements could make the steam engine competitive with the diesel. The company folded.

It's hard to shake methods that have been successful. But always ask yourself whether these methods will be successful in the environments of tomorrow.

The second source of "precarious exposure" stems from failing to see a future that has (in effect) already happened. Many things cannot be predicted with certainty, such as wars, the rate of inflation, competition, and so forth. But some things can, such as the number of eighteen-year-olds living in the United States by 1985. Their declining number could have been predicted as far back as 1968. Surprisingly, in the 60s (and even in some cases until the mid-70s) management in many colleges and universities overlooked—or ignored—this vital information. As a consequence, many universities are now plagued with problems created by overbuilding, overstaffing, and the like.

Take a close look at the environment that is relevant to your business. If you can gather any information, demographic or otherwise, that partially "creates" the future, don't ignore its implications.

The third source of "precarious exposure" simply involves being the wrong size. The Boston Consulting Group has pointed out that economies of scale govern the costs of production and/or marketing in many industries. In such industries costs usually decline 20 percent to 30 percent with every doubling of volume.

Business Week reported the following case history:

> One of Boston Consulting's first efforts at applying learning curve theory to all costs—the experience curve had not even been named then—was with Norton Co. of Worcester, Mass., back in 1965. Norton was having trouble making money in a particular market for pressure-sensitive tapes that was dominated by 3M Co.
>
> Norton had successfully cut costs, Henderson recalls, but still was unable to make a dent in the market share. It soon became clear that Norton, in effect, was chasing a competitor down the cost curve, and that so long as 3M followed pricing and growth strategies to maximize market share, it was a fruitless struggle.
>
> Thus Norton, a leading abrasives maker and an important producer of some kinds of tapes, concluded that it could not compete against such a broad range of products in so many markets, says its president, Robert Cushman. The company decided to concentrate instead in selected areas of strengths.[2]

When there are economies of scale in production and/or marketing, and when there is little brand preference, firms that cannot gain enough market share to be cost competitive should get out of that business. It is always better to be a major producer for a small market segment than a small producer (relative to others) in a large market segment. In other words, try to be the dominant producer.

USING THE OPPORTUNITY CHART

Figure 7-2 presents four sectors you should examine in developing your strategy, numbered in the order they should be investigated.

Let's take a look at each of these sectors. The opportunities suggested by "present products/present markets" would involve

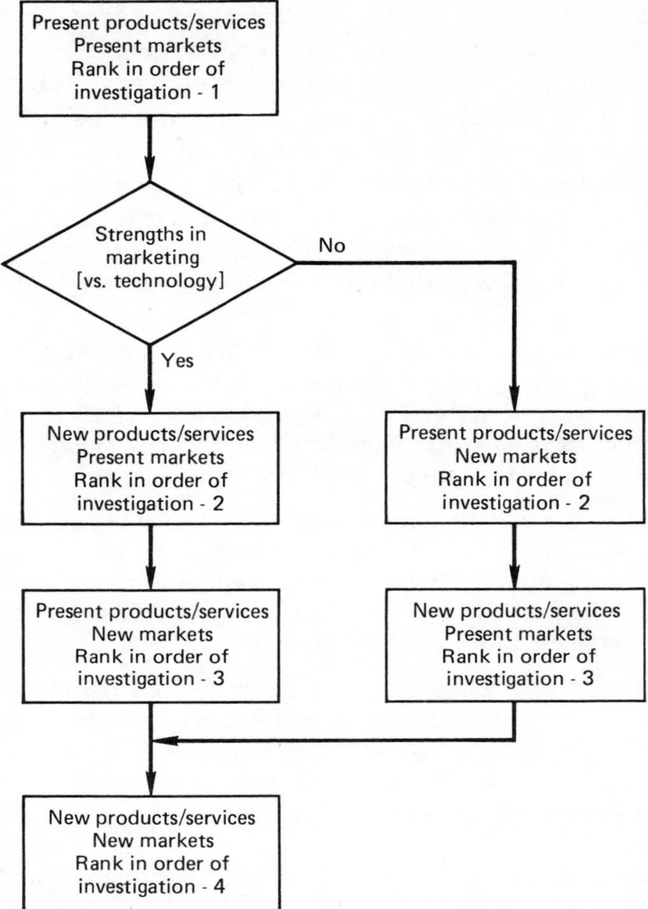

Figure 7-2. The Opportunity Chart

selling essentially the same products (requiring the same manufacturing technology) to the same markets (using the same marketing skills). For example, a manufacturer of automobile mufflers for domestic cars (selling to the after-market) might increase its product line to include mufflers for foreign cars.

Opportunities in the "new products/present markets" sector would involve using present channels of distribution to reach present customers, but making more than model changes or line extensions in the product. Often, though not always, this requires new manufacturing technology. For example, the muffler manufacturer might begin producing silicone lubricants for sale to after-market distributors.

Opportunities in the "present products/new markets" sector often require using different channels of distribution to serve new markets for products similar to those already produced. For example, the muffler manufacturer might begin selling to automobile manufacturers.

Opportunities in the "new products/new markets" sector involve expansion requiring both new manufacturing technology and different marketing skills. For example, the muffler manufacturer acquires a firm that manufactures recreational tents.

In examining your possibilities, start first with present products/present markets. If you can't satisfy growth and sales here, move on. If your core strengths are in technology, then see if you can increase sales and profitability by selling present products and/or services to new markets. Conversely, if your core strengths are in marketing, make new products/services to your present markets your second order of investigation. The last sector that you should examine is in new products/services to new markets, because here it's a new ball game.

Naturally, present products/present markets, new products/present markets, and present products/new markets sometimes overlap. It's hard to distinguish which should belong where. And sometimes a company is equally strong in marketing and technology. In that case it doesn't matter which of these sectors it examines first.

Company after company has found that the areas that offer most profitability and growth are those that they know best. Interpace, which had experienced almost no earnings increase in over six years—and only an unexciting return on investment—decided its best course of action was to concentrate on one product line and de-emphasize the firm's other businesses.[3] Singer almost met its Waterloo because of diversification.[4] Perhaps Daroff Industries (Botany) did.

Possibly a company straying from Sector 1 would be doing nothing more than (in the words of Ellis Parker Butler) gathering "goat-feathers."

> Goat-feathers are the feathers a man picks and sticks all over his hide to make himself look like the village goat.... [They] are the distractions, sidelines, and deflections that take a man's attention from his own business and keep him from getting ahead.... Even a cow does better if she sticks close to the business of eating grass and chewing the cud. When a cow strays from plain milk-producing methods and begins climbing trees and turning somersaults, she may be more picturesque, but she is gathering nothing but goat-feathers.[5]

Now this doesn't mean that you won't wind up finding your greatest opportunity in new products/new markets. But you should only undertake this investigation after you have examined the other three sectors. (Even if you have met your sales and profit objectives you may wish to examine other possibilities because you might uncover even greater opportunities. But caution: Make sure that you have examined potential opportunities in present products/present markets first. That's where there is less risk.)

Below is a compendium of options for increasing sales and profits in each of the four sectors. These lists are not all inclusive; they are meant to help trigger ideas about possible strategies you could implement to help meet your objectives.

Your situational analysis—if properly carried out at the functional and corporate level—will serve as a valuable guide in determining the practicality of the various suggestions.

Examining Present Products/Present Markets

Begin with an eye to improving efficiencies in your present operation. The situation analysis will have revealed weaknesses and opportunities. Correcting these weaknesses and taking advantage of the opportunities may not be the complete answer, but good management practices usually dictate that these improvements should be made.

Manufacturing. Consider boosting productivity by improving short-interval scheduling; using standard operating procedures; modernizing plant to reduce labor; obtaining better space and machinery utilization (are multiple shifts a possibility?); subcontracting limited runs; performing preventative maintenance; improving energy conservation programs. How about relocation to increase your proximity to raw materials and/or customers? Or shipping fabricated parts to assembly points closer to customers?

Look at instigating (or improving) value analysis; changing your materials mix; improving quality control. You might also consider centralized purchasing and utilizing purchase commitment reporting. Can you take better advantage of vendors' warehousing? Can you reduce materials handling or improve inventory control? Speed up your inventory turnover ratio?

Finance. In looking for financial improvements, consider the possibility of investing idle assets; of a more prompt collection of accounts receivables and depositing of cash. Analyze float. Make an analysis of slow-pay and delinquent accounts. Reexamine your guidelines for accounts receivables. On the other hand, are you taking advantage of discounts for quantity purchases? Prompt payment?

Examine your long- and short-term financing. Consider renegotiation of loans. Consider additional sources. See whether you can improve your capital equipment, budgeting, evaluation, and post audit programs.

Personnel. How efficiently are you using your personnel? Could you be subcontracting labor, such as plant maintenance? (Conversely, what would be the cost of hiring employees for the job?) Can you eliminate overtime by double shifts or make use of part-time labor or consultants? Look at ways of reducing turnover. Or perhaps you should suggest relocation to areas where labor is less expensive. And there may be other benefits. Some companies have found that people in rural communities seem to be more productive. The president of a small manufacturing company, using mostly semiskilled labor, claimed, "Not only will they work for less, but they have a better sense of direction." He went on to explain that workers in the metropolitan area (where his plant used to be located) approached their jobs with the attitude, "How much can I get from the company with as little effort as possible?" In the rural community where he is now located the attitude of employees is, "How quickly and efficiently can these tasks be accomplished?"

Can you improve the screening and interviewing of applicants? Set up better means of employee indoctrination? Consider training to improve manpower performance (skills and/or leadership) or to provide future manpower requirements. Think about instituting profit improvement programs, suggestion systems, or work simplification teams. What about profit-sharing plans?

Marketing. Closely look at increasing present customers' rate of usage. Since your present customers are probably your real core of advantage, this is probably your easiest way to increase sales and profits for your company. Is it feasible to attract competitors' customers, present nonusers, and/or additional geographic segments? What about modifying the marketing mix? You may have to do so to carry out the above. Or, changing market conditions might have made certain parts of your marketing mix obsolete. Or sometime back, some element of the mix might have been ill conceived. For example, a marketing consulting firm uncovered the fact that a client's annual $3,000,000 advertising budget was virtually creating no impact —nor had it done so from the start.

Perhaps you can intensify availability by increasing outlets or making a "harder push" in selected locations. Consider changing channels of distribution. Switch to a direct sales force, or conversely, change to manufacturers' representatives or wholesalers or a franchise system. Or a combination of channels.

Can you improve the efficiency of your present sales force? Consider allocating effort to market potential; creating new methods of customer contact, such as consultative selling or offering technical and profit-building assistance; using special salesmen to develop new accounts; boosting advertising and direct mail to help avoid "cold calls."

In general, look at devising new and/or more efficient methods of promotion (i.e., start using direct mail, coupon, samples, etc.) and at reallocating expenditures (i.e., discontinue advertising and spend more money on direct sales contacts). Can you improve your advertising by using other media, revising copy, changing intensity or frequency?

Can you increase the efficiency of your physical distribution system by using contract carriers, or developing your own trucking system, or using public warehouses, or consolidating to several central distribution points, or drop shipping?

How about improving your present products by developing new product features. Perhaps you can:

- Adapt (to other ideas, developments)
- Modify (change color, motion, sound, odor, form, shape)
- Magnify (stronger, longer, thicker, extra value)
- Minify (smaller, shorter, lighter)
- Substitute (other patterns, layout, sequence, components)
- Rearrange (other patterns, layout, sequence, components)
- Reverse (inside out)
- Combine (blend, alloy, assortment, ensemble, combine units, purposes, appeals, ideas).[6]

Concerning the product line, can the number of products be reduced? Or perhaps you should expand the product line by developing additional models and sizes and/or quality variations (good, better, and best).

Check your pricing policies. Can you increase sales through lower prices (market penetration)? Or can you increase profitability per unit through higher prices to hard-core markets (market skimming)? If products are sold to the same target market, are prices set to maximize profits on the whole line? Or if products are sold to different target markets and exposed to different levels of competition, are your prices for each product set according to market opportunity?

Take a look at unbundling, eliminating "freebies," and at leader pricing. Would it be to your advantage to use quantity, seasonal, cash, or functional discounts? How about advertising or trade-in allowances? Rebates?

Check to make sure you are avoiding "decreases in prices" due to inflation. Can you price at time of shipment instead of time of sale? Can you get indirect price changes by reducing freight allowances? By tightening credit? Are you using price sheets so your catalogs are adaptable? What about using escalation clauses and surcharges? One coupon redemption company uses an eighteen-month contract. However, their fees are adjusted monthly according to the consumer price index. They claim that the eighteen-month contract term is just about right because by the end of the period some clients become increasingly aware of the amount of the surcharge add on. When the new contract is written, the company raises the new contract price at a figure slightly less than the previous base price plus the surcharge. Customers perceive they're getting reduced rates, and this helps maintain, and improve, good customer relations.

Examining Present Products/New Markets

Once you've examined improving your present approaches, take a look at the possibility of selling your present products to new markets (assuming your core strength is in your product/service technology). Consider making product and/or package size modifications to cater to new segments—larger packages or an economy size for heavy users, for example, or smaller packages for occasional users. Or repositioning the product line to cater to slightly different market segments. Woolworth, for example, opened Woolco discount stores and Kresge opened K Mart.

You may wish to use new methods of promotion (to reach a new target market) such as direct mail, catalogs, or manufacturers representatives. Or use entirely new channels of distribution such as export agents to tap international markets, or private labeling. How about changing your present channel of distribution—from selective to intensive, for instance?

Review different pricing policies. Seasonal (time-basis) pricing can accommodate off-season customers (airlines encourage new segments to travel by off-peak travel rate reductions), or slack-time customers (matinees at theaters). Or consider place-basis pricing: reduction in pricing according to locations such as practiced by theaters and ballparks.

Examining New Products/Present Markets

You might gain better utilization of your sales force and/or channels of distribution by increasing volume through new products. (Recall the Hallmark example earlier in this chapter, where the company successfully marketed crystal, pewter, and jewelry products through existing channels of distribution.)

Can you take advantage of brand extension, capitalizing on customer good will through the use of a well-respected brand name? The teen magazine, *Musicale,* for example, started marketing clothing to teenagers who were familiar with the magazine. Such a strategy might necessitate increasing advertising and direct mail to help promote your company and/or brand name and product awareness. Or perhaps the use of missionary salesmen.

Examining New Products/New Markets

In general, pursuing Sector 4 is most likely to pay off when your firm possesses a large share of the market. Additional market shares may be costly. Or, there may be government restrictions against monopoly. It's also valuable when you are seeking to balance your portfolio.[7] For example, you may wish to enter a new industry less susceptible to inflation, to reduce cyclical effects, to better utilize—or improve—cash flow, and, of course, to improve growth and profits.

As a general rule, make sure that the industry you're entering has high potential value added. There should be a relatively large spread between what you pay for raw materials, semifabricated materials, and parts and what you sell your product for. For example, see Figure 7-3, which shows the value added for two imaginary companies. In Company A there is $0.65 value added, and in Company B only $0.20. If the price of materials increased by 10 percent, Company B would have to pass these costs on to the purchaser. Yet this may not be possible. For example, what if competitors can offer substitute products that are unaffected by the cost increases? Company A is safer. Because of the relatively high value added, and the "experience curve," the firm may be able to absorb some of the cost increases. The advantage of being in an industry with relatively high value added is particularly great in inflationary times.

		Company A	Company B
	Selling Price	1.00	1.00
Value Added	Profit	.05	.05
	Expenses (selling Administrative, labor)	.60	.15
	Cost of raw materials, semi fabricated materials, parts	.35	.80

Figure 7-3 Value Added Example

There are three methods of entering Sector 4.

- *Vertical integration*—acquiring a company either closer to raw materials (backward) or closer to the consumer (forward). An example of forward vertical integration is a manufacturer's acquisition of a wholesaler. Consider vertical integration when you are in a high-growth industry, when your best growth is in the channel or supply end of the industry, when you possess a large market share, and/or when there are long-linked technologies.

- *Concentric diversification*—using technological skills to produce new products that will appeal to new customers, and/or using marketing skills to sell to new customers through new channels of distribution. Concentric diversification may be advisable if the firm has a competitive edge in technology or marketing in this new field. For example, many aerospace contractors developed advanced technological skills which they subsequently used to help develop consumer products. But, of course, make sure the technology is specific (not theoretical) and/or that the market values your excellence.

- *Conglomerate diversification*—acquiring a firm totally unrelated to your present operation and where there are no synergisms present from vertical integration or concentric diversification. In conglomerate diversification, therefore, you lack technological and marketing skills in the industry. Consider expanding into another industry (and this holds true for concentric diversification, as well) only if it has high growth potential. Moreover, it should not be dominated by competitors nor be easy for other companies to enter and gain a competitive footing. There is no point in developing a market only to find it "stolen" by competitors when the payoff is just around the corner.

Expanding into the Four Sectors: Internally, Joint Development, Acquisition, or Merger?

Generally speaking, consider joint development, acquisition, or merger when speed is essential, when major patents are held by other firms, when you lack manufacturing (or service) and/or marketing skills, and/or if you lack financial strength to successfully build and maintain the market. Since you normally have to pay a premium to acquire a firm, acquisitions usually have a greater immediate impact (adverse) on return on investment than internal growth investments. Growth investments, however, are likely to take longer to generate a positive cash flow than acquisitions.

A special caution concerning acquisitions. Studies of unsuccessful acquisitions point out that the root cause will likely be among the following:

- The companies were too anxious to close the deal.
- The parent company failed to develop and apply rigorous criteria for acquisition. It failed to develop and use checklists.
- A lack of understanding on the part of the parent company of the industry's conditions of the acquired firm.
- A lack of thorough investigation of the acquired firm's reasons for selling, potential synergisms, and managerial and financial needs necessary for a successful merger.
- The acquisition was never adequately integrated with the overall corporate strategy.

- Despite the acquisition, top managers in the acquired firm were unwilling to change their organization's strategy. On the other hand, too often the present company made major changes in the acquired firm's strategies, tactics, and management without an accurate assessment as to the company's strengths and weaknesses.
- The head of the acquired firm did not have a specific, long-term contact in the parent firm to whom he should report.[8]

QUESTIONS OF SCALE

An important question to ask is, "Will the proposed change be worth the trouble?" A small program may prove successful—but will such a success make a significant difference to your firm? Too many small programs are likely to overextend managerial expertise.

No one has expounded on this problem better than Peter Drucker:

> I have been reading for years the acceptance speeches of Nobel prize winners. Again and again one hears them say, "What started me on the work that led to this achievement was a chance remark by a teacher who said, 'Why don't you try something where the results really make a difference?' "[9]

If it won't make a major difference, you can't afford the time and effort.

Minimizing Limitations (and Capitalizing on Advantages) of Scalability and Size

Consider scalability. Every cook knows that some recipes cannot be doubled. The same is true in business. The success of many small firms, for instance, stems from the customized service they afford their clients. When these firms grow beyond a certain size it is unlikely that they can give clients the service that made the firms successful in the first place. Or it may be that some skills are "unique" to certain individuals and are not duplicable. A small, extremely successful truck rental firm was considering expansion; their proposed strategy was essentially one of continuation. Their core strengths were in the two partners who were extremely shrewd in buying used equipment at bargain prices and who possessed ingenious mechanical skills enabling them to fix up and modify the equipment so it would be serviceable. These two partners were actually overextended, however, and it was highly unlikely that they could hire, motivate, and supervise people who possessed the same qualities that they did. This does not mean that this firm should not try to expand, but to do so by extending their present method of operation would appear to be folly.

Look for the crumbs. There are always segments of the market that larger companies do not find attractive. Seek these out. A company that did so with success is Carpenter Technology. Afraid of takeovers and threatened by rising steel imports, Carpenter attempted to save itself by diversifying. It was a bad idea. So Carpenter did an about-face.

Almost solely restricting its production to specialty metals, which is what it had always done best, Carpenter became the only steel company whose primary business was specialty metals (98 percent of its business). Its 1977 sales were $326 million—which was miniscule compared to the corporate giants—but with an 8.8 percent net and a 16.7 percent return on total capital. That was tops in the industry.

Carpenter concentrated on service. Unlike most other companies, which depended on independent warehouses, Carpenter distributed its products through twenty-two warehouses of its own. It did so for a reason: Much of its success stemmed from the attention it gave to its customers' needs. In short, Carpenter found a niche that held little interest for the industry giants, and filled it admirably.[10]

Don't try to be a mass marketer. Instead, cater to the needs of a specific segment of the market. If possible, position yourself uniquely. At all costs avoid head-on clashes in promotion and distribution with large companies. They simply have more resources than you do. They can buy better distribution facilities, they can afford better "brains" to develop promotion programs, and they can hire more—and better—salesmen.

Coming to Grips with the "Precarious Exposure" of Size

There are three ways to deal with the problem of being the wrong size. First, change what you do. A small chemical company, for example, unable to compete with larger established firms, might switch to consultative selling. That's the approach Quaker Chemical Corporation takes. Although the company takes pride in offering quality products, its main threat is an aggressive sales program. The company's salesmen present themselves and attempt to gain a reputation as consulting engineers. They strive to understand the customers' total operation and then point out how Quaker's products can help solve their problems. And to this end they are usually quite successful. In fact, it was reported that in one case a plant manager believed that the Quaker salesmen knew more about the plant than anyone else—including the plant's own employees.[11]

Second, acquire what you need. Consider acquisition or merger. A company that needs an expanded distribution system for its product, for instance, might look at a company that already has such a system.

Finally, if you cannot change what you do or gain what you need through merger and acquisition, consider selling it, either all or in part. General Electric followed this course when it sold its computer mainframe business to Honeywell.

Don't Invite Competition when You Can Avoid Doing So. It boosts one's ego to give success stories at trade conventions and the like, but such publicity may awaken sleeping giants.

Withdraw when the Large Companies Become Your Direct Competitors. Perhaps you've staked out a market segment that large competitors neglected until now. It may have grown to the point where they find it attractive. Regardless of why they attack, retreat unless you have a competitive advantage in the field. Remember that only in the movies does the outgunned small-time rancher beat the monied interests stacked against him, and it takes a sentimental script to help him do it.

React Quickly. One advantage of the small company is its ability to respond swiftly to opportunities in the market. Keep your organization flexible, your management prepared to capitalize on market developments as they occur. Similarly, be ready to shed in a hurry any products or services that are no longer profitable.

In spite of all the caveats about being inconspicuous, retreating, and being ready to shed unprofitable products, you should have an offensive strategy. Such a strategy is more motivating, and you can be energetic and positive without being noisy or "heady."

PRUNING YOUR PRODUCT LINE

Many companies, both large and small, suffer from having too many unprofitable products. The 80–20 principle is usually in effect: 80 percent of profits come from 20 percent of products. If this is true in your firm, consider shrinking the line. Benefits include less investment in direct labor and a smaller inventory. Then you may need less machinery and may save space. But most important of all, you save time.[12] Executives generally agree that they have so many things to do that there is never enough time to really do things right. As one corporate president put it, "We're not 'farming' now as well as we know how." And this is typical because too often management has to spend too much time trying to keep unprofitable products from falling further behind. Yet if unprofitable products can be eliminated, management can give fuller attention to the products and strategies that will really get the company somewhere. And the payoffs are reflected on the P. & L. statement. Studies show that high growth–high profit companies are usually those where the president cuts losses. And quickly.[13]

Getting rid of the losers can be difficult. There is always the hope that some day the product will become a winner. Or there is sentiment attached to the product. Or pride. For example, the president may have recommended its addition, and it is difficult (and maybe dangerous) to confront him (or her) with the advantages of dropping it. And he may find it painful to admit he was wrong, not only to his subordinates and the board of directors, but also to himself. For this reason, often new management is able to turn a sluggish company around because they aren't burdened with emotional ties and promptly shed unprofitable products (and customers and personnel).

Of course, in some cases loss leaders must be retained to round out the product line. But often the need for them is imaginary, based more on emotional than economic grounds.

FOLLOWING STRATEGIC GUIDELINES DICTATED BY THE PRODUCT LIFE CYCLE (PLC)

Determining Product Strategies

Products have life cycles. Like people, they go through stages of precommercialization (fetus), introduction (birth and early years), growth (adolescence), maturity (middle age), and decline (old age and death). (See Fig. 7-4.) The time length of the PLC varies from product to product. Some have very short life cycles (such as the Hula Hoop) while others are greatly extended (autos). As a general rule, products spend most of their "lives" in the mature stage of the PLC. The vast majority of products on the market today are in their mature stage.

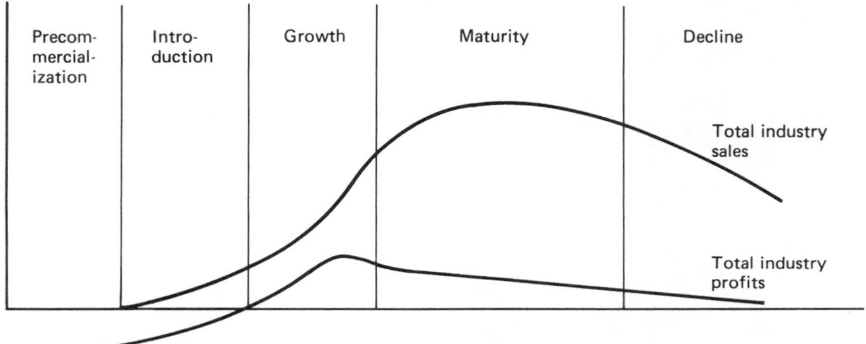

Figure 7-4 Product Life Cycle Chart

It's important to recognize that the PLC refers to the product category as a whole—industry-wide. You may be introducing a product that is new to your company, but that, industry-wide, is in the mature stage of its life cycle. In such a case you have a dual task: gaining trade and consumer/user acceptance while competing with companies who already have established marketing and production processes.

The correct strategy depends upon the product's stage in the PLC (Fig. 7-5). You may wish to be a maverick, and perhaps you have a good reason for doing so. After all, many companies have gained notable success by being different. But make sure it is a well-thought-out choice.

Figure 7-5 indicates that the "correct" strategy changes from one stage to the next. For example, greater emphasis should be placed on economics of production when the product is in the mature stage than during stages of introduction, growth, and decline. Then, marketing expenditures would be much more important in introduction, growth, and maturity than in decline. For example, it is reported that Scott Paper spends very little on promotion for Cut-Rite wax paper (a product in the decline stage).

Fox's Hypotheses About Appropriate Business Strategies over the Product Life Cycle

	Functional Focus	*R&D*	*Production*	*Marketing*	*Physical Distribution*	*Personnel*	*Finance*	*Management Accounting*	*Other*	*Customers*	*Competition*
Precom-mercial-ization	Coordination of R&D and other functions	Reliability tests Release blueprints	Production de-sign Process planning Purchasing dept. lines up vendors & subcontrac-tors	Test marketing Detailed market-ing plan	Plan shipping schedules, mixed carloads Rent warehouse space, trucks	Recruit for new activities Negotiate opera-tional changes with unions	LC plan for cash flows, profits, investments, subsidiaries	Payout planning: full costs revenues Determine opti-mum lengths of LC stages thru present-value method	Final legal clear-ances (regula-tory hurdles, patents) Appoint LC co-ordinator	Panels & other test respondents	Neglects op-portunity or is working on similar idea
Intro-duction	Engineering: debugging in R&D produc-tion, and field	Technical corrections (Engineer changes)	Subcontracting Centralize pilot plants; test va-rious processes; develop stand-ards.	Induce trial; fill pipelines; sales agents or com-missioned sales-men; publicity	Plan a logistics system	Staff and train middle manage-ment Stock options for executives	Accounting defi-cit; high net cash outflow Authorize large production facilities	Help develop production & distribution standards Prepare sales aids like sales man-agement port-folio		Innovators and some early adopters	(Monopoly) Disparagement of innovation Legal & extra-legal inter-ference
Growth	Production	Start successor product	Centralize produc-tion Phase out subcon-tractors Expedite vendors output; long runs	Channel commit-ment Band emphasis Salaried sales force Reduce price if necessary	Expedite deliv-eries Shift to owned facilities	Add suitable per-sonnel for plant Many gievances Heavy overtime	Very high profits, net cash outflow still rising Sell equities	Short-term analyses based on return per scare resource		Early adopters & early majority	(Oligopoly) A few imitate, improve, or cut prices
Maturity	Marketing and logistics	Develop minor variants Reduce costs thru value analysis Originate major adaptions to start new cycle	Many short runs Decentralize Import parts, low-priced models Routinization Cost reduction	Short-term pro-motions Salaried salesmen Coorperative ad-vertising Forward integra-tion Routine market-ing research: panels, audits	Reduce costs and raise customer service level Control finished goods inventory	Transfers, ad-vancements; incentives for efficiency, safety, and so on Suggestion system	Decline profit rate but in-creasing net cash inflow	Analyze dif-ferential costs/ revenue Spearhead cost reduction, value analysis, and efficiency drives	Pressure for resale price maintenance Price cuts bring price wars; possible price collusion	Early adopters, early & late majority, some laggards; first discontinued by late majority	(Monopoly com-petition) First shakeout; yet many rivals
Decline	Finance	Withdraw all R&D from initial version	Revert to subcon-tracting; sim-plify production line Careful inventory control; buy foreign or competitive goods; stock spare parts	Revert to com-mission basis; withdraw most promotional support Raise price Selective distri-bution Careful phase-out, considering entire channel	Reduce inventory and services	Find new slots Encourage early retirement	Administer sys-tem. retrench-ment Sell unneeded equipment Export the machinery	Analyze escapable costs Pinpoint remain-ing outlays	Accurate sales forecast very important	Mainly laggards	(Oligopoly) After 2nd shake-out, only few rivals

Figure 7-5

Source: Harold W. Fox, "A Framework for Functional Coordination," *Atlanta Economic Review,* Vol. 23, No. 6 (November–December, 1973), 8–11. Reprinted with permission of author and publisher.

Examine your products. What stage of the PLC are they in? Is the cycle moving fast or slowly? If the majority of your products are approaching their period of decline, you had better introduce some new ones now. The decline stage usually means both lower volume and lower profits (see Fig. 7-4).

USING THE MARKET ATTRACTIVENESS/COMPANY STRENGTHS MATRIX

It's common sense that a company should be active in those markets that offer it the greatest opportunities. In essence, your company should follow the strategic direction dictated by your relative strengths compared to the product's (or service's) market attractiveness. The trick is how to determine this.

In general, the process is as follows: First, determine the market attractiveness of the business (products or services). Second, estimate what it takes to be successful in the business. Third, rate your company's strengths. Fourth, place the ratings on a market attractiveness/company strengths matrix. And fifth, follow the strategy indicated by the position of the matrix.

If your company is a single-industry firm, you would first determine the basic strategic direction for your company. Then, if you have several major product categories, you might also wish to subsequently examine each of the product categories (treating each of the categories as a business) using the same procedure.

On the other hand, if your company is diversified and has product categories that are sold to different classes of customers, use different trade channels, require different production facilities, and are affected by different market forces (economic and competitive), then you will have to plan as a diversified company. In such a case you'll have to group your product lines according to strategic business units (SBUs). A SBU comprises those products that are similar in nature; that is, products that may use the same production facilities and marketing channels and are affected by similar economic and competitive forces. For example, if you have two dissimilar businesses (a manufacturer of desks which sells to education institutions and a manufacturer of tents which sells through sporting goods wholesalers), then you'd have to rate each of these SBUs separately. An example of how a diversified company uses the matrix for strategic planning is found in Appendix 7A.

Here, in detail is how you can use the market attractiveness/ company strengths matrix.

Step 1. Determining the Market Attractiveness of the Business

Using the list below to provide insights, determine market attractiveness factors that you consider most appropriate for the business being evaluated. Naturally there are other factors that are more important to your industry.

- *Growth.* Of course there are more opportunities in a growing business. What is the outlook for the future? Where is the business on the PLC?
- *Competition.* Is the business dominated by powerful competitors? Is there excess capacity in the industry?
- *Investment requirements.* What is the critical mass (learning time, capital, patents) required for success? Can new competitors enter freely?
- *Profits.* What is the profit potential? High profits can serve as a double-edged sword. Unless you are protected, sooner or later you'll have competition.
- *Amount of value added.* High-value-added industries are desirable. Low-value-added businesses, on the other hand, may find themselves trapped by rising costs they cannot pass on.
- *Inflation.* Is the business particularly vulnerable to inflation?
- *Energy dependency.* Is the business highly dependent upon one source of energy? What is the ratio of energy costs/value added?
- *Reciprocity.* Is this a business where sales to potential customers is highly dependent on the volume of the purchases from these potential customers?
- *Bargaining power of customers.* A business that is dominated by powerful customers will likely keep profits at a minimum.
- *Regulatory climate.* Is the business under heavy government regulation? Is the regulatory climate likely to change?

- *Cyclicality.* Is the business highly cyclical? If so, can you handle the excess capacity during "down times?"
- *Customer financials.* Are customers "current," or must you carry them?

After you select the market factors that you consider the most important, rate the business as to its attractiveness: high, medium, or low. There are no absolutes. For example, what might seem like high market attractiveness to your firm might be rated a low market attractiveness by another firm. Differences in ratings are especially noticeable between firms of different sizes. A small firm might rate a small market as being extremely attractive while a larger firm might view it as being not worthy of consideration because of limited potential.

Step 2. Estimating the Success Requirements of the Business

Develop a list of factors necessary to succeed in the business. Assume that if someone has asked you, "What characteristics does a firm have to have to be successful in this business?" What would you include in this list?

The following are some characteristics you might wish to include. This list is hardly inclusive, yet it will provide you with insights.

- *Nature of production.* Is mass production required? Does production demand high-technology, or is "junk shop" production satisfactory?
- *R & D requirements.* What is the level of technology required for initial success? For continued success?
- *Sales requirements.* Is a direct sales force necessary? Or are middlemen available who can provide effective distribution?
- *Advertising requirements.* Is mass advertising needed to prepare the product's entry into the market? Will it be needed after the product establishes itself, or later on in its life cycle?
- *Distribution and service requirements.* What is the importance of plant and warehouse locations? Is it necessary to have technical representatives or service centers?
- *Initial investment requirements.* How much capital is required (in R & D, production, marketing) to launch the product successfully?
- *Continued investment requirements.* How much capital will it take to keep the product a success after it enters the market?

- *Access to raw materials.* Is the availability of raw materials likely to be a problem?
- *Access to customers.* Are customers likely to start to manufacture their own? Is reciprocity a factor to be considered?

Analysis of these factors should produce a key success requirement list. For example, the key success requirements for a firm selling to the military weapons system might be:

- "A strong research and development capability;
- A commitment to using project management systems;
- A strong field marketing effort closely tied in with customer organizations;
- An ability to deal effectively with a relatively few knowledgeable customers;
- An ability to identify and track emerging technological and market opportunities over long periods leading to consummation of sales;
- Willingness to commit substantial company resources to study and prepare bids on government proposals."[14]

Or, for a firm selling to the mass markets in a consumer-oriented industry:

- "Standardization of product line components;
- High volume production runs;
- Highly dispersed marketing and service centers;
- Low technology;
- Development of a recognized brand name."[15]

Step 3. Rating your Company's Strengths

The situation analysis should make it easy for you to put together a list of the company's strengths. Match these in a point-by-point fashion against the list of success factors selected from Step 2. Be sure to take into consideration both your company's absolute strengths and how your company stacks up against your competitors. Rate your company's strengths according to high, medium, or low.

Step 4. Placing Ratings on the Market Attractiveness/Company Strengths Matrix

Match the rating given for market attractiveness (Step 1) with that for company strengths (Step 3). In Figure 7-6 the intersection of the two bars (*high* market attractiveness and *high* company strengths) falls in the upper left-hand corner.

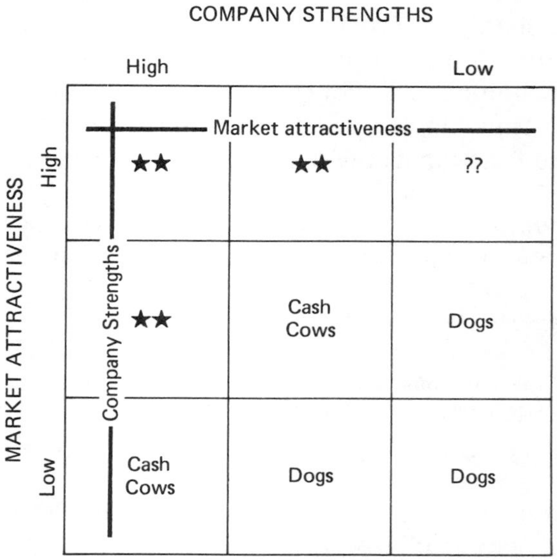

COMPANY STRENGTHS

MARKET ATTRACTIVENESS	High		Low
High	★★	★★	??
	★★	Cash Cows	Dogs
Low	Cash Cows	Dogs	Dogs

Market attractiveness

Company Strengths

Figure 7-6. Market Attractiveness/Company Strengths Matrix

The matrix offers a graphic demonstration of company strengths compared to market opportunity. This position suggests strategic actions (discussed in Step 5). Since placement on the grid is a matter of individual judgement, there will be differing viewpoints. The resulting discussion will be extremely worthwhile. In fact, this is one of the advantages of matrix planning. It provides a structured format for analysis, thus enabling better communications. But, of course, eventually your planning team must arrive at a consensus about its position.

Step 5. Following the Strategy Indicated by Position on the Matrix

The position on the matrix suggests the strategic posture you should take: stars, invest/grow; cash cows, earn/protect; dogs, harvest/divest; and question marks, either invest/grow or harvest/divest. Examine each of these postures more fully.

Cash Cows (Earn/Protect). The overall strategy should be to make investments only to hold your position and maintain cash flows. Although the growth rate is low, you have high business strengths. This business should be providing you with good earnings and cash flow (a low-growth market provides good cash flow because you're usually not spending much money for expansion). But recognize that major growth opportunities will have to come from another business.

Indicated functional area strategies are as follows:

- *Manufacturing.* Increase efficiency in production; cut back R & D on product improvements but spend R & D money to increase production efficiency.
- *Marketing.* Hold or slightly decrease market share to maximize cash flow and earnings; trim product line; price to maximize cash flow and earnings; and make only highly selective investments in promotion or new product additions.
- *Personnel.* Get the organization lean; reward operating efficiency.

Stars (Invest/Grow). The overall strategy should be to invest to improve your excellent position and opportunity. Although your earnings should be high, because you're expanding, cash flow may be a problem.

Indicated functional area strategies are as follows:

- *Manufacturing.* Build capacity; invest to achieve cost reductions with volume; spend on R & D to improve products and product line.
- *Marketing.* Invest to increase market share; increase product line; price and invest in promotion to build market share.
- *Finance.* Extend credit and investments.
- *Personnel.* Plan for expansion; train and assure backups; reward personnel for achieving growth.

Dogs (Harvest/Divest). An unpromising future. You should seek other business opportunities. The overall strategy should be to manage for near-term cash or divest and/or shut down. Investing in businesses that lack both market attractiveness and company strengths may keep them afloat for a while, but the best courses of action are to make your investments in other areas while getting as much cash from this business as possible, or to cut losses and find an interested buyer.

Expect low earnings with little or negative cash flow. Indicated functional area strategies are as follows:

- *Manufacturing.* Make maintenance investments only; avoid R & D expenditures unless they have immediate short-term payoffs; consider subcontracting to free plant capacity for other uses.
- *Marketing.* Give up market share for profits; drastically reduce product line; price higher to maximize earnings and cash flow; spend promotion dollars only to improve short-term profits.
- *Finance.* Aggressively reduce working capital and investments; tighten credit.
- *Personnel.* Cut back to a skeleton force; reward personnel for efficiency.

Question Marks. The overall strategy should be to invest aggressively or withdraw. If you consider it feasible (and desirable) to build your company strengths, then you should follow the strategic direction of invest/grow. If this is not feasible (or desirable), however, then follow the strategic direction of harvest/divest.

If you chose to invest/grow, expect low earnings, a negative cash flow, and at a relatively high risk. Your functional area strategies would be similar to those for stars.

If you withdraw, then the functional area strategies would be similar to those for dogs (harvest/divest).

USING THE MARKET ATTRACTIVENESS/COMPANY STRENGTHS VENTURE MATRIX TO HELP EVALUATE NEW BUSINESSES

Follow the same procedure (Steps 1–5) for each new business you're considering. Match the rating given for market attractiveness in Step 1 with that of company strengths from Step 5. Then place the ratings on the venture matrix Figure 7-7. Note that the venture matrix is different from the market attractiveness/company strengths matrix

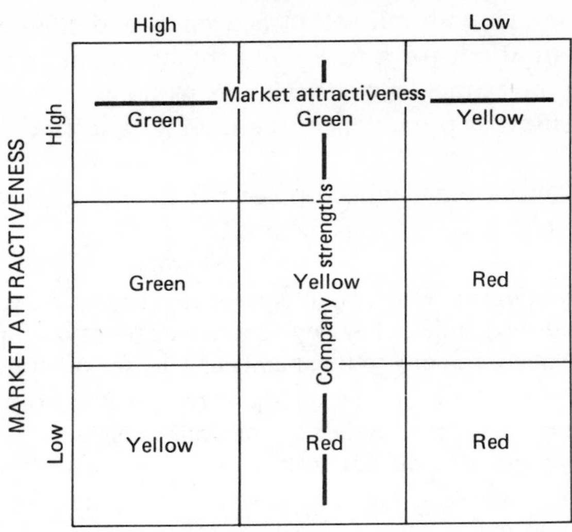

Figure 7-7. Venture Matrix

in that each square has a color. This converts the matrix into what General Electric calls the "Spotlight Theory."[16] Green indicates "go" situations; red, "discontinue"; yellow means "caution"—since the venture is risky and calls for extensive investigation. In the illustration in Figure 7-6 company strengths are only medium, but market attractiveness is high. It's a go situation.

Obviously, for reasons of time, you can't evaluate all possible future opportunities in detailed manner. Instead, work each potential venture through the five steps in a highly simplified manner. Then, if the "fit" looks good, go through the five steps again in greater detail. In this way you may go through the steps three or four times for "successful" candidates, but you've eliminated unpromising ventures almost right away. Overall, you'll save time.

These guidelines will help you find effective and appropriate strategies. But how do you put all this together to get the job done? That's covered in the next chapter.

APPENDIX 7—A: An Example of How a Diversified Company Uses the "Matrix Approach" for Strategic Planning

JAMES W. McSWINEY, CHAIRMAN:

We have just completed the best year in our history and we feel this performance was brought about as the result of intensive planning and implementation of programs initiated in 1970-71. So, today we would like to recap:

- Where we have been;
- Where we are today; and
- Where we expect to go.

Warren Batts, our President, will discuss how we have gone about our job, the results to date and how we stack up against those with whom we are normally compared. This should help you evaluate the probability of achieving our plans for the next 5 years which W. W. Wommack, Vice Chairman in charge of strategy, will cover.

Now, to set the framework, I would like to discuss briefly what was going on in the 1970–71 period:

The earnings of Forest Products companies, in general, were severely depressed. In addition, we decided Mead was capable of much better performance. An in-depth assessment found that:

Mead Executive Management Presentations to Paper & Forest Products Analysts at the Princeton Club, New York, N.Y., February 8, 1977. Reprinted with permission.

- We should streamline the company.
- We needed to translate into performance our strategic planning concept which was to operate in areas where we were leaders or could achieve leadership; or otherwise generate cash and redeploy assets. And, to carry this out—
- We needed to strengthen our management team.

Further, we found we had as a resource some $200 million of excellent investments made in 1970–71. However, these investments would take some time before reaching their potential. We also felt we had a sound group of base businesses from which to proceed.

To sharpen our focus, management and the Board of Directors set some longer range financial goals which Bill Wommack will talk about later. Also we set up two straightforward goals:

- *Short Term*—To be in the *upper half* of those companies against which we are normally compared.
- *Long Term*—To be in the *upper quartile* of those companies against which we are normally compared.

I think you will find Warren's presentation demonstrates that we accomplished what we set out to do—*and then some.*

1972–1976
WARREN L. BATTS, PRESIDENT

As the first step toward achieving Mead's corporate goals, Mr. McSwiney assigned Bill Wommack full-time responsibility for developing a new strategic philosophy, a planning system, and then a strategy for each of Mead's businesses. The strategic concept he developed was straightforward and very effective. We have used it for the past five years.

The concept is to:

- Obtain market leadership in markets we serve; or
- If market leadership is not possible, redeploy our assets to markets where leadership potential exists.

We are convinced that being a leader is the key to achieving the best performance in comparison to that of our competitors.

This concept can be translated into a matrix with the market segment growth rate on the vertical axis and market share on the horizontal axis (Figure 7A-1). Each quadrant represents a different type of business and requires a different strategy.

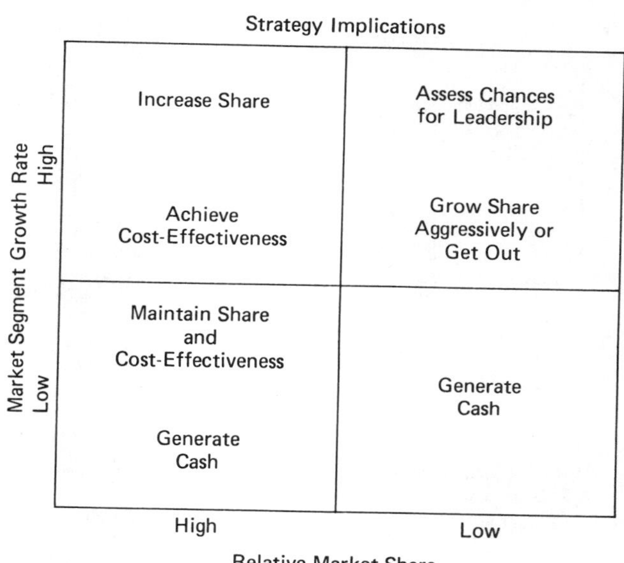

Figure 7A-1

Starting with the upper right-hand quadrant:

- For a business in a high-growth market with a low-market share, we assess our chances for leadership, and either grow our share aggressively or get out.
- In a high-growth market with a high-market share, we grow our share as rapidly as we can and invest to become the most cost effective producer.
- In a low-growth market with a high-market share, we maintain our market share and cost effectiveness. We also generate cash for the balance of the company.
- In a low-growth market with low-market share, we operate to generate cash—we have generally found this means we get out.

We classify our businesses on the same matrix with the axis calibrated—with market segment on the vertical axis and relative market share on the horizontal axis (Figure 7A-2). We consider a high growth market to be one that is growing by at least 10% in real terms.

To us, relative market share is what counts. We consider a leadership position exists when a business has a market share that is at least 1.5 times the share of its next largest competitor, as shown in Figure 7A-2 by the vertical line at 1.5.

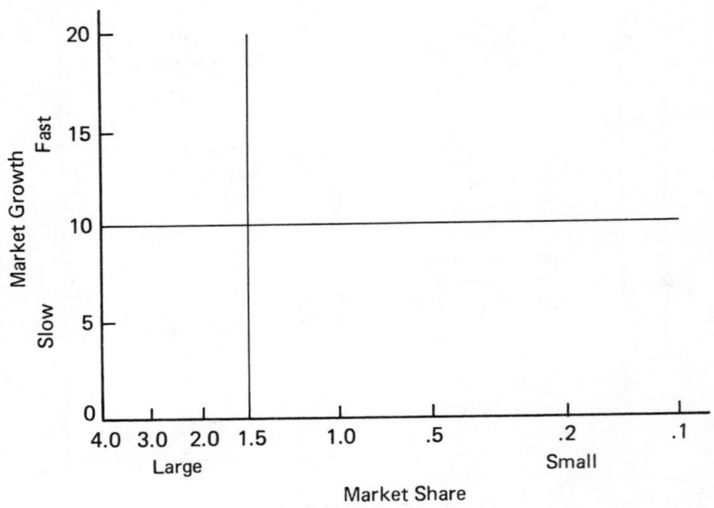

Figure 7A-2

In 1972, when we classified our businesses on this matrix, we found many were competing in low-growth segments with low-market share. We decided that by 1977 we should eliminate those low-growth and low-market share businesses and allocate capital to the balance so that they could attain greater market share and grow larger.

To implement this strategy we concentrated on three factors during the last 5 years:

- People Management,
- Capital Allocation, and
- Asset Management.

People Management

To achieve the goals Mr. McSwiney had set for the company meant we simply could not execute our strategies in a half-hearted way; nor, could we be satisfied with just trying harder. We had to change the way our managers managed; plus we all had to operate in a more highly focused manner.

We started with formal in-house training programs for some 300 Mead managers. We knew that even though we understood what we wanted to do, it would not be carried out unless key managers truly understood the new strategic philosophy, and how to use the underlying analytical techniques. The first seminar covered our new Financial and Strategic planning concepts, including:

- Market segmentation;
- Financial analysis; and
- Integration of Marketing and Finance.

Later we found that our managers required help in coping with new levels of inflation. These seminars covered:

- The nature of inflationary environment;
- Analytical techniques to determine how inflation impacts on the elements of a business; and
- Tactics for coping with these impacts.

But even when managers understood what we were trying to do, some were unable to accept the discipline required. We had to reorganize several businesses and change a number of managers. Five of our 6 operating group vice presidents were changed, as well as 19 of our 24 division presidents. Fortunately, the talent to effect these changes was largely in-house. However, we did bring in a few people from the outside who had outstanding track records.

While we reduced employment from 32 thousand people in 1972 to 26 thousand in 1976, we concentrated on improving productivity. As a result, sales per employee have nearly doubled during this period (Figure 7A-3).

In addition, we also brought on board talented young people at all levels to prepare for Mead's future growth. Today, for example, exempt personnel are, on average, 2 years younger, and 10% more have college degrees.

With our managers trained in the new strategy and reorganized to be more effective, we brought about new management focus by what we emphasized. We used a highly disciplined process:

- To develop specific policies;
- To thrash out and resolve issues as they arose; and
- Most important, to keep us all focused on executing our strategies and improving our performance.

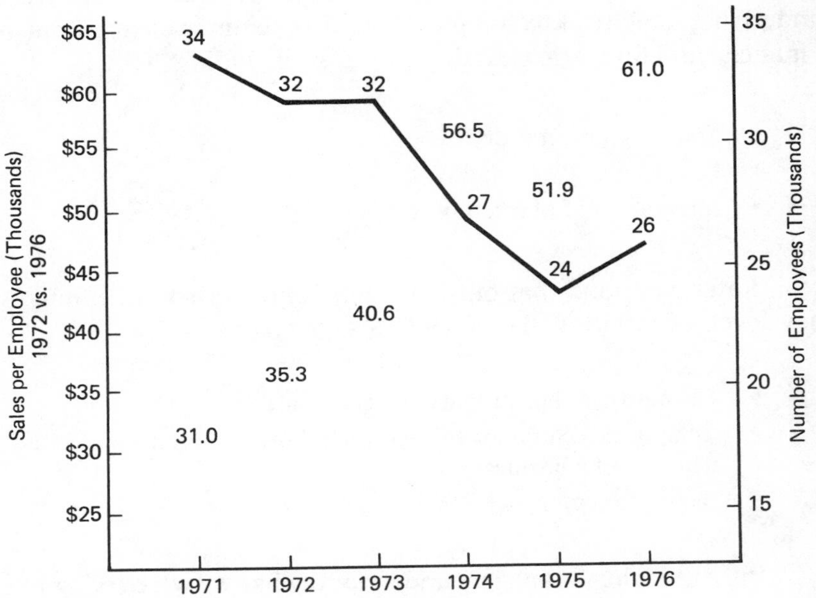

Figure 7A-3

Capital Allocation

We have given people management a good deal of attention, but probably the single most important change in the management of the company is the way we allocate capital today:

- We don't divvy up our capital funds on some pro-rata basis;
- Nor, do we automatically approve projects that meet some hurdle rate.
- Instead, we fund strategies according to our market share/market growth concept.

After we had classified our businesses in 1972, our first step was to dispose of fifteen businesses where it was not practical to become a leader (Table 7A-1). They were essentially the low-growth, low-market share businesses. This step generated $80 million in cash, plus it saved $25 million we would have had to invest if we'd kept them. Especially important, these actions immediately improved our mix of businesses and the total return from our assets.

Table 7A-1 Divestitures, 1972–1976 (dollars in millions)

Business	*Cash Realized*
Industrial products group	
Golden Foundry	$ 6.9
Anniston Soil Pipe	5.1
Woodward & Chattanooga Coke	7.1
Roane Electric & Woodward Electric	6.4
National Cement	7.0
Woodward Blast Furnace	6.9
Longview Lime	5.2
Mead products group	
Mead Educational Services	6.2
SE&M Vernon	5.3
Virginal	15.9
Other	8.0
Subtotal	$ 80.0
Estimated on-going capital requirements	25.0
Total	$105.0

In addition, in the past 5 years, we have funded our strategies with substantial capital investments (Table 7A-2). Some were to improve cost effectiveness and some were to grow higher potential businesses even faster.

Table 7A-2 Capital Expenditures, Mead & Mead's Share of Affiliates 1972–1976 (millions)

	$200			$154		
	150		$ 98	30	$ 92	$105
Mead's share of affiliates	100	$ 66 26	$ 21	124	29	29 76
Mead	50	40	77		63	
		1972	1973	1974	1975	1976

Including our share of affiliates, we invested $516 million to improve and grow the company (Table 7A-3). Here are some examples. The major project:

- In 1972—was the Escanaba Pulp Mill;
- In 1973—the Archer Creek Foundry;
- In 1974—the expansion of Stanley Furniture;
- In 1975—the Stevenson Corrugating Medium Mill; and
- In 1976—modernization of a linerboard mill.

Table 7A-3

Major Capital Expenditure Projects	*Total Capital Expenditures (millions)*
1972	
Escanaba —pulp mill	
Northwood—Bulkley Valley acquisition	
BCFP —plywood mill	
BCFP —Mackenzie expansion	$ 66
1973	
Archer Creek—foundry	
Covington —container plant	
Fairless Hills —packaging plant	
Brunswick —McCormick saw mill	$ 98
1974	
Stanley—plant expansion	
BCFP —Mackenzie & Tilbury saw mills	$155
1975	
Stevenson —corrugating mill	
Chillicothe —carbonless	
Lewisburg —container plant	
BCFP —Boston bar saw mill	
Brunswick —Pearson saw mill	
Georgia Kraft—saw mill	$ 92
1976	
Georgia Kraft—Rome modernization	
Containers —Amarillo	
Packaging —merchandising facility	$105
Total	$516

Asset Management

Next, we put increased emphasis on managing our assets. We consider Return on Net Assets (Table 7A-4) the true measure of operating performance. In order to focus attention to this measurement, we tied each general manager's compensation to a balance between his business unit's earnings and its net assets.

One result was that we increased our net asset turnover from 1.4 in 1972 to 1.6 today. This was an improvement of 14%. Mead probably achieves one of the best scores in this area of all the companies with whom we're normally compared.

Table 7A-4

Return on net assets
Net earnings + Interest Expense Net of Taxes

÷

Total assets − Current Liabilities + Current Maturities of Long-Term Liabilities

This improvement is demonstrated by the reduction of non-cash working capital from $150 million at the end of 1971 to $69 million at the end of 1976, while sales were increasing (Figure 7A-4).

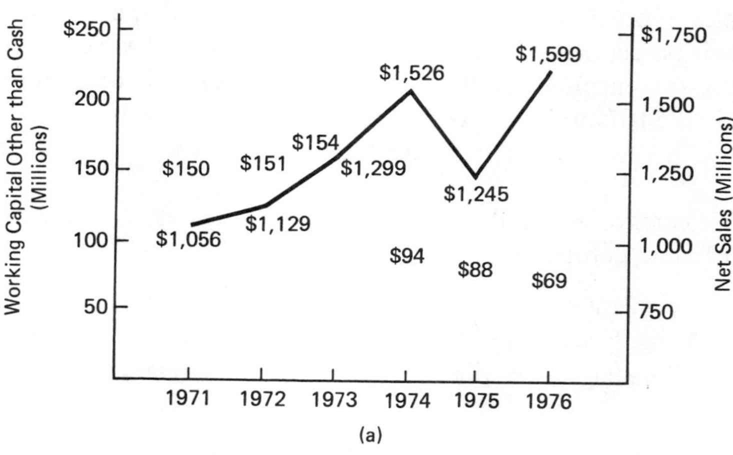

Figure 7A-4

I might add that during the same period cash increased from $41 million to $152 million, adding substantially to our liquidity (Figure 7A-5).

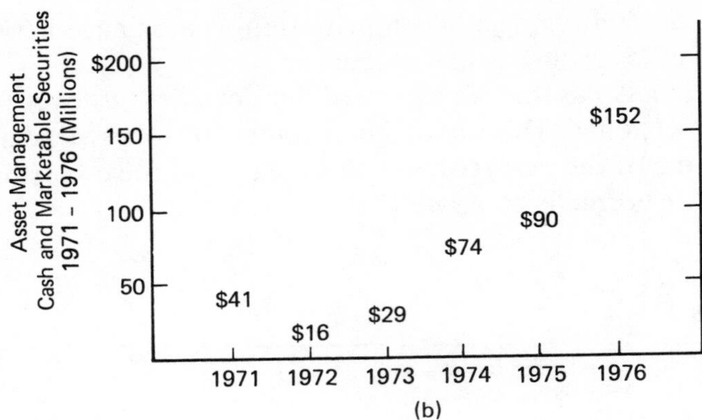

Figure 7A-5

Results

We've talked about our strategic concept, and how we implemented our strategies and improved our operations. Now let's review our financial results:

In 1972 our sales totaled $1.1 billion. By 1976 sales totaled $1.6 billion. This was a 9% compound growth rate, even though we had disposed of businesses having sales of $180 million. It is worth noting that sales of our Forest Products category increased at a 15% rate, so that their percentage of the total rose to 56% (Table 7A-5).

Pre-tax earnings during this period increased from about $39 million to $167 million, or a 34% compound growth rate. Again, earnings in our Forest Products Category increased sixfold (Table 7A-6).

We categorized and managed these businesses from a strategic point of view as follows:

- Poor businesses;
- Those businesses which had good strategies in place in 1972; and
- Those businesses which needed a change in strategy.

Examining these categories demonstrates how we improved our results by:

- Shifting assets;
- Improving performance; and
- Carefully investing.

Table 7A-5 Sales by Lines of Business (millions)

	1972 *Amount*	*%*	*1976* *Amount*	*%*
Forest products	$ 561.4	45.5	$ 985	55.8
Paper				
Paperboard				
Pulp				
Lumber				
Distribution	357.4	29	481.2	27.3
Paper products				
Industrial supplies				
School and office products				
Industrial products	252.4	20.5	229.9	13.0
Castings				
Coal				
Pipe and gaskets				
Interiors	56.1	4.5	56.8	3.2
Other	6.0	.5	11.8	.7
Subtotal	1,233.3	100.0	1,765.4	100.0
Affiliate eliminations	(104.5)		(166.1)	
Total	$1,128.8		$1,599.3	

Table 7A-6 Earnings by Lines of Business (millions)

	1972 *Amount*	*%*	*1976* *Amount*	*%*
Forest products	$21.8	56.3	$120.8	72.2
Paper				
Paperboard				
Pulp				
Lumber				
Distribution	5.0	12.9	22.4	13.4
Paper products				
Industrial supplies				
School and office products				
Industrial products	9.2	23.8	24.1	14.4
Castings				
Coal				
Pipe and gaskets				
Interiors	3.8	9.8	—	—
Other	(1.1)	(2.8)	(.1)	—
Total	$38.7	100.0	$167.2	100.0

As noted in Table 7A-7, we changed our asset mix substantially by disposing of most of our poor businesses. We reduced them from

13% to about 2% of our assets. Then we reinvested most of the cash in those businesses which had good strategies in place. That increased their proportion of our assets to over 53%.

Table 7A-7

Category	Asset Mix 1972	Asset Mix 1976	RONA 1972	RONA 1976
Poor businesses	13.2%	2.1%	2.4%	4.2%
No change	38.5%	53.4%	8.8%	9.6%
Change	48.3%	44.5%	2.8%	11.8%
	100 %	100 %		
Total corporate			4.7%	10.4%

Next, by changing the strategies of those businesses that were not performing to their potential, we improved the return on their assets from 2.8% to 11.8%. It was the improvement in this category that contributed most to increasing our total corporate Return on Net Assets from 4.7% in 1972 to 10.4% in 1976.

We continually review our businesses, and, as Bill Wommack will cover later, we will reclassify a business and change its strategy when it's prudent to do so.

Earnings after taxes were up from $26 million in 1972 to about $89 million in 1976. And primary earnings per share were up from $.72 to $3.61—a compound growth rate of 50%. The impact of the strikes we took in 1975 to correct our pension plans is reflected in Table 7A-8.

What counts is our performance relative to that of our competitors. There are 15 Forest Products companies with whom we are most frequently compared. In Table 7A-9 they are not ranked but simply listed in alphabetical order.

Using Value Line data, Table 7A-10 shows how we compared in 1972, on the basis of total capital invested. We were not satisfied with our position in twelfth place on the list. Value Line *estimates* as of November 12, 1976 (Table 7A-11) show that we moved to sixth place. We had achieved our short term goal to be in the upper half of those companies with whom we are normally compared. When the *final* figures are in, we may well be in the upper quartile.

We believe this change in relative performance is the best overall measure of the improvements Mead's management has made in the last 5 years.

Table 7A-8 Primary Earnings Per Share, 1968–1976

	1968	1969	1970	1971	1972	1973	1974	1975	1976
$4.00									$3.61
3.50							$3.27		
3.00								$2.62[b]	
2.50								$2.05	
2.00						$1.77			
1.50	$1.12	$1.15							
1.00				$.61	$.72[a]				
.50			$.47						

[a] Before extraordinary items
[b] Strike to correct pension plan

Table 7A-9 15 Forest Products Companies (sales $500 MM)

1. Boise Cascade
2. Champion
3. Crown Zellerbach
4. Georgia Pacific
5. Great Northern Nekoosa
6. Hammermill
7. International Paper
8. Kimberly Clark
9. Mead
10. Potlatch
11. St. Regis
12. Scott
13. Union Camp
14. Westvaco
15. Weyerhaeuser

I believe we now have the fundamentals for long term success firmly in place—both in the physical sense of good businesses serving

Table 7A-10 1972 Actual Performance
15 Forest Products Companies (sales $500MM)

Company	*ROTC %*
1. Weyerhaeuser	9.4
2. Georgia Pacific	9.2
3. Union Camp	9.0
4. Kimberly Clark	8.3
5. International Paper	7.1
6. Scott	6.4
7. Potlatch	6.3
8. Champion	5.9
9. Crown Zellerbach	5.9
10. Great Northern Nekoosa	5.9
11. St. Regis	5.7
12. Mead	5.0
13.	4.0
14.	3.7
15.	2.5

Source: Value Line

Table 7A-11 1976 Estimated Performance of 15 Forest Products Companies (sales $500 MM)

Company	*ROTC (%)*
1. Union Camp	14.5
2. Georgia Pacific	12.0
3. International Paper	11.5
4. Kimberly Clark	11.5
5. Great Northern Nekoosa	11.0
6. Mead	11.0
7.	11.0
8.	9.5
9.	9.5
10.	9.0
11.	8.5
12.	8.0
13.	7.5
14.	7.5
15.	7.5

Source: Value Line, 11/12/76

growing markets—and in the management sense of realistic objectives, sound strategies—and the internal discipline to carry them out.

Much of the improvement since 1972 has been the result of having a principal officer of the company devote full time to strategy. More and more companies are adopting the market share/market growth concept—which Bill Wommack helped pioneer. As some of you know, he is chairman of the strategic planning institute, whose membership, composed of some of our major corporations, is developing advanced strategic management principles.

1977–1981
WILLIAM W. WOMMACK, VICE CHAIRMAN

Warren has outlined how we have gone about change over the past 5 years—I'll cover:

- Our financial goals;
- Resources we have to work with;
- Where we expect to invest these resources; and
- How we expect the Company to look in 1981.

We have translated our long-term goal of being in the upper quartile of those companies against which we are compared into specific numbers. We recognize that as markets, competitors and external factors such as the rate of inflation change—these numbers may have to be revised. Currently, these are the targets we are shooting for:

Financial Goals	
Return on Net Assets	12%
Sustainable Growth Rate	10%
Debt to Equity Ratio	50%
Dividend Payout	±30%
Return on Equity	17%

These financial goals will produce a 17% return on equity. However, as you know, Return on Equity will vary as the actual debt/equity ratio moves around the 50% figure.

These goals are also designed to support a dividend which increases on a regular basis, a policy we have followed since 1972, and one which we think will be increasingly important to our shareowners.

As we move into the next 5 years, our first group of resources are the investments we have already made but which have not yet achieved their full potential. 1977 will be the first year that we will get a material return from Stevenson.

Prior Capital Expenditures

Stevenson	$ 65
Stanley	12
Medium Castings Facility	12
Chillicothe (Carbonless)	24
Total	$113

Our next group of resources are the investments we plan to make in the future. Based on a 50% debt/equity ratio, Mead's financial resources, including our share of affiliates, may well support a $1 billion program over the next five years. We have in hand a base plan which covers about $700 million of that $1 billion. The balance should fall in place as we move through the next year or two.

Our strategy is to fund:

- Growth of our higher potential businesses;
- Improvement of the cost effectiveness of our base businesses; and
- Maintenance and environmental requirements.

All three will contribute to increasing our Return on Net Assets.

We plan to invest roughly $120 million in our growth businesses (Table 7A-12).

Table 7A-12* Planned Capital Expenditures, Major Growth 1977–1981 (millions)

Castings	
Containers	
Products	
Paperboard (Stevenson)	
Advanced systems	
Total	$120

*Detailed expenditures confidential

We plan to spend about $440 million in order to improve our cost effectiveness (Table 7A-13).

Table 7A-13 Planned Capital Expenditures, Major Cost Effectiveness 1977–1981 (millions)

Area	
Paper	$168
Pulp and forest products	112
Linerboard	78
Other	82
Total	$440

One large part of this is our $125 million program, the Chillicothe, Ohio complex. Specific projects in this program are:

- Improvement of the pulp mill thruput;
- A new turbine generator to reduce our energy costs; and
- Precision sheeters to increase productivity.

In the third category we have the remaining $130 million which includes expenditures shown in Table 7A-14.

Table 7A-14* Capital Expenditures, 1977–1981 (millions)

—Maintain operations	
—Conserve energy	
—Meet 1983 standards	
Total	$130

*Detailed expenditures confidential

As a result of these expenditures, we expect to improve our position on the market share/market growth matrix with more of our businesses getting bigger and moving to the left, indicating growth and stronger market share positions.

Today, 61.5% of our net assets are employed in businesses which are meeting our Return on Net Assets goals. Strategies for this group of businesses are okay. In the businesses comprising the other 38.5% of our assets, we are making new changes in strategy. We plan to increase the RONA on these businesses from 5% to 9% over the next 5-year period (Table 7A-15).

Table 7A-15

	Asset Mix		*RONA*	
	1976	*1981*	*1976*	*1981*
	%		%	
No change in strategy	61.5	59.0	13.1	13.3
Change in strategy	38.5	41.0	5.1	9.2
Total	100	100	10.4	12.3
Objective				12.0

Remember, in the prior five-year period, we increased RONA in the businesses in which we changed strategies from about 3% to 12%. The $700 million in capital expenditures will be a major factor in improving the returns of these businesses. We plan to increase our Return on Net Assets from the current level of 10.4% to 12.3%.

A key point as we fund our strategies is that we intend to take maximum advantage of opportunities to invest capital in existing facilities where we have good incremental returns. Overall, we believe we will achieve the objective of a 12% Return on Net Assets by 1981.

As mentioned earlier, given our 50% debt to equity goal, our financial resources should support another $200–300 million of internal or external growth. External growth would be in businesses closely related to our current businesses and would be in growing markets where we believe our goal of market leadership is achieveable.

As you review this, it becomes clear we have plans to make good investments over the next five years which will increase our corporate Asset Base from approximately $1 billion to $1½ billion, exclusive of affiliates (Table 7A-16).

Obviously the key question is: "Will we achieve our goals?" We believe performance over the past five years has demonstrated a dedication to sound strategic planning and firm discipline to execute. This gives us a very high level of confidence.

SUMMARY

In summary, I think the 1972–1976 period was one of great progress for Mead. I believe we can be counted on to continue our relative and absolute performance improvements through the 1977–1981 period.

Table 7A-16 Net Assets, Excludes Affiliates 1977–1981 (millions)

$2,000					
1,800					
1,600					1,449
1,400			1,215	1,327	
1,200	1,052	1,124			
1,000					
800					
600					
400					
200					
	1977	1978	1979	1980	1981

8

Step 3 (Continued): Strategy Formulation—Putting It All Together

Now it's time to decide what longer-range course of action your firm should follow. You'll also want to make sure that it's workable in the shorter range—like next year. You do comprehensive planning intuitively. But make the process explicit by putting together a rough operational plan while you're developing the strategic plan. There's no need for the operational plan to be worked out in great detail. All you want to do for now is to make sure that it has a reasonable chance of coming off.

You can see how this process is necessary. When you've finished developing the longer-range plan, you've also got a pretty good idea as to what you'll be doing next year. In this way the strategic plan will not be "pie in the sky."

The search for effective strategies, like all steps in planning, can be frustrating and unrewarding unless you approach it in a disciplined fashion. Here are steps that will help reduce the frustration level. And they'll increase your odds for finding a suitable strategy.

SETTING TIME LIMITS FOR STRATEGY DEVELOPMENT

Failure to work by a schedule will provide only another dismal proof of Parkinson's First Law: "Work expands to fill the time allowed for it." Not only will the job drag on endlessly, but new and viable strategies are less likely to develop from it. By default, you may well be left with the strategy already in operation.

Also specify what resources are available for expansion (new facilities, increased promotion activity, stepped up R & D expenditures, and the like) and/or diversification. (Could you afford to acquire a firm? If so, what's your top limit?) These facts are readily available from finance's situational analysis.

REVIEWING PREVIOUS STEPS

In order that the planning team keep them firmly in mind, review the corporate objectives, mission, and policies; the situation analysis; and the analysis of environment. In brief, objectives determine what the firm intends to accomplish; mission and policies help keep the search within reasonable bounds; the situation analysis provides agreement about company strengths and weaknesses; the analysis of the environment depicts plausible future environments.

RATING THE PRESENT BUSINESS(ES) ON THE MARKET OPPORTUNITY/COMPANY STRENGTH MATRIX

An explanation of how to utilize the matrix was given in Chapter 7. Now position your company (or if necessary, products/services) where you believe it will be five years from now on the matrix. As the basis of this rating, use the most-probable-case future, the conclusions of the situation analysis, and the estimation of the results following your present strategy.

GAP ANALYSIS

A common sense rule of search states: "Know as much as possible about what it is you are looking for." To make sure that you do, perform gap analysis; that is, decide what kind of shortcomings you'd have if you continue your present strategy.

Since you know the specific objectives of the firm as well as its risk posture, and you have already constructed the most-probable-case future, you can figure out where the gaps are likely to be. Have your planning team come up with pro forma P&L and balance sheets. But don't worry about a high degree of precision—all you're after is a general indication. Highlight your findings in a chart (see Table 8-1). You may know that your present strategy is woefully inadequate, but change seems to be more acceptable if everyone on the planning team agrees on where you'll be liable to wind up if you continue following your present strategy. For the same reason, also make a gap analysis for the next year.

A question that often comes up is, "While putting together our plans, what kind of dollars should we be working with? Current or inflated dollars?" Of course, in deciding on your strategic plan you'll take into consideration possible impacts of inflation. But as far as making tentative projections, keep things simple by working with current dollars. Later on, in Chapter 9, you'll be shown how to make adjustments for inflation. But generally it's easier at this stage to use current dollars.

Table 8-1

Key Areas	*Five-Year Objectives*	*"Most-Probable" Case Forecasts*	*"Most-Probable" Case Gaps*
Earnings			
Sales			
•			
•			
•			
Return on investment			

Naturally you'll want to design your strategy for the most-probable-case future. But you'll also want to consider how effective this strategy would be in the worst-case future since you may wish to modify the strategy so that you'll have an escape hatch. At any rate, you should give the worst-case future consideration during strategy development.

It may be that you don't have any gaps. At this point the planning team may decide that the objectives are high enough and it's perfectly desirable to continue following the same strategy. If so, skip "creative hypothesizing.'' Or the planning team may decide that, although there aren't any gaps, the objectives should be set higher to have more ''stretch.''

But, more likely, gaps will be a way of life.

CREATIVE HYPOTHESIZING

Plugging these gaps is going to take some real creativity. Your search will be easier, however, if you start with the strictest requirement so you are working within a more narrowly defined area. For example, suppose that you have gaps in earnings, sales, and return on investment, but the largest gap is in earnings. Focus your search for strategies that would increase earnings. It makes sense to examine the largest expenditures (or sources of revenues) first. And, whenever possible, avoid making major commitments in ''search time.'' Rather, try to get an indication as to whether the strategy seems plausible. If so, then do a bit more investigating. Does it still seem feasible? If so, then conduct another mini-investigation. And so on.

While doing creative hypothesizing, lean heavily on the results of the situation analysis. If the job has been done right, you'll have an accurate—and commonly agreed upon—understanding of your firm's points of leverage and vulnerabilities. This agreed-upon knowledge will serve to help fast screen various options.

Expand from strengths (using situational guidelines, of course). Use the opportunity chart, being sure to examine present products/present markets first. In some cases it may be obvious that by following a strategy of market penetration in Sector 1 you will not meet your objectives. For instance, you may be seeking products that would tend to offset the highly cyclical sales of your present products. In such a case you know you're going to have to find your solutions in another sector. You might as well move to the most likely sector first. But then, after you find your solution, come back to Sector 1 to see where you can tighten up your present operations.

Besides the compendium of strategies given in Chapter 7, you may get ideas as to how to bridge the gap—particularly for increasing earnings return on investment (R-O-I) and—from a close examination of what is commonly called ''the du Pont Chart'' (Fig. 8-1). The du Pont Chart doesn't point out anything that you don't already know, but it does offer a structure that may help jog your insights.

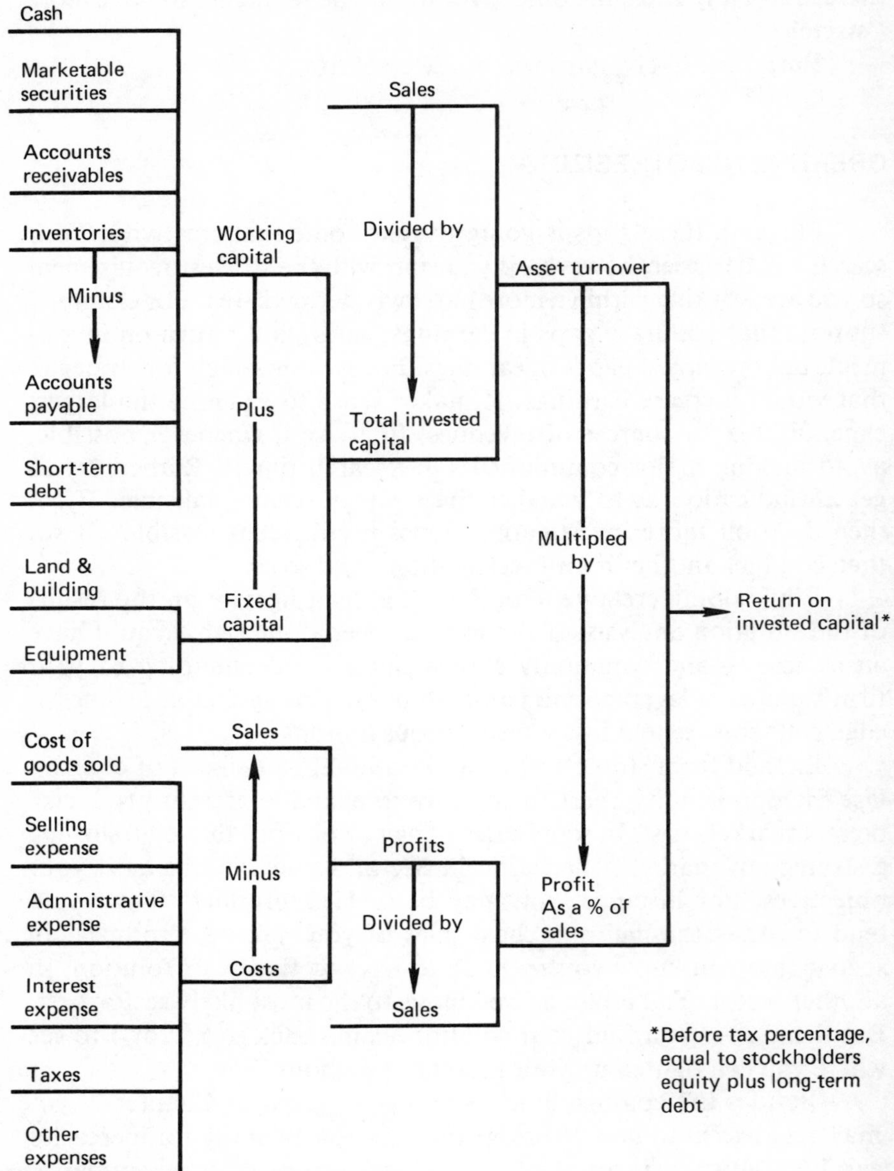

Figure 8-1. The du Pont Chart

Essentially the chart points out the factors that have impact on R-O-I. The obvious is that if you want to increase R-O-I, you must increase earnings and/or decrease assets. Closer examination, however, may give that necessary creative spark as to how this might be accomplished. Below are a few examples of the kinds of actions you might consider while taking a look at each one of the chart's items, beginning with utilization of assets.

Current Assets

If your firm is typical, more than half your assets will be in current assets. Furthermore, most smaller businesses must depend heavily on short-term bank loans and trade credit since they have a relatively limited access to long-term capital markets.

You can check to see how your ratio of current assets to current debt compares to industry averages by checking with Dun and Bradstreet's "Key Business Ratios" (Appendix 4B). This will give you a general indication. But regardless of how they compare, still take a hard look at your utilization of cash and marketable securities, inventories, and accounts receivable.

Cash and Marketable Securities. Cash and those marketable securities that return less than the firm's cost of capital reduce earnings. Although these liquid assets do decrease the riskiness of your corporation, they also increase working capital needs and act as a drag on R-O-I. Perhaps your firm has been taking too conservative an approach, and you can release some funds for expansion.

Make sure that cash and marketable securities are at the proper level. Consider the following factors: You should have enough cash to conduct your ordinary business; a reserve to cushion against errors in forecasting (the stability of your industry will be a chief influence here); and enough cash to take advantage of possible "good buys." You may be able to get some industry standards on ratios of cash and marketable securities from your association or from Dun and Bradstreet publications.

Also examine your use of float. Any dollars you can pick up here are "free."

Inventories. You can get some insights as to whether or not your inventories are in line by checking the "Key Business Ratios."

If your firm is a manufacturing firm, you probably have three types of inventories: raw material, work in process, and finished goods. Examine each for ways to reduce costs. For example, it may be to your advantage to trade off a higher initial cost for raw materials (including freight) in order to increase the reliability of supply and/or decrease the time in transit. This, of course, would decrease the costs of carrying larger stocks of raw materials.

Work-in-process inventories might be reduced by improving manufacturing processes to speed up production, or by buying component parts.

Finished goods inventory might be reduced by a more accurate determination of the optimum inventory level. Then, a closer examination may reveal that finished goods inventory could be reduced by switching methods of transportation, centralizing warehousing, or shifting to different channels of distribution. Increasing dating, of course, would merely transfer the cash required for inventories to that required for accounts receivables. But it still reduces storage costs.

Perhaps vertical integration would offer some major savings in inventory reduction.

Accounts Receivables. The volume of your accounts receivables is affected by two basic elements: the total amount of credit extended and your average collection period. These, in turn, are affected by four factors: standards (to whom will you extend credit?); time (what's your credit period? thirty days? sixty days?); discounts (1 percent if paid within ten days?); and collection/enforcement (what's your firm's policy concerning accounts receivables overdue?) Closely examine each of these. Do they conform to industry averages? Then ask yourself: Do industry averages really reflect the times? Naturally, in a sellers' market terms can be tightened. Then: How do your credit costs compare with the "Key Business Ratios"?

Fixed Assets

Take a look at fixed assets. How do your fixed asset ratios stack up with industry averages? (Again, check "Key Business Ratios.") This may give you some rough indication as to how extensively you should examine this area.

Do you have any underutilization of facilities that might give you a cost advantage in expansion in one of the four sectors?

Are you making any new capital expenditures that can be postponed without affecting your objectives? Bear in mind that usually production wants a new plant and machinery. The operation looks better and, as a result, so does the vice-president of manufacturing. But perhaps running another shift with the old facilities—even with all of its attendant problems of breakdowns and less efficient utilization of labor—might be the most profitable. The same general principle applies to other functional areas: Accounting wants a new computer to get away from some of the inconveniences of time sharing; marketing wants more modern branch offices to enhance the prestige of the sales force. And so on. But will they really pay off or will they serve as a brake on R-O-I? On the other side, keep in mind that the biggest problem with capital expenditures is timing over the business cycle. Not only are delivery times longer in a boom period, perhaps causing shortages of capacity, but financing becomes more expensive.

Again, you can increase your R-O-I by leasing, but remember, as pointed out in Chapter 4, this may merely be "gamesmanship," hiding the true condition.

The other side of the du Pont chart is increasing net income. This can be done by reducing costs or by increasing sales.

Reducing Costs

In trying to reduce costs, take a look at interest expense, depreciation, taxes, operating expenses, and costs of goods sold. Check the "Cost of Doing Business Ratios" (Appendix 5A). You will be able to get more detailed and up-to-date industry averages from your association and/or from Dun and Bradstreet. Do so. Note that such averages will be helpful for deciding the attractiveness of new business ventures as well as evaluating your present effectiveness in your present industry.

Interest Expense. Perhaps you're in much better financial condition now than when your intermediate-term loan was negotiated and your line of credit established. Maybe you can now do better rate-wise and with required compensating balances. Also, are you getting full utilization from trade credit? Then, possibly you can get funds at a lower rate by the use of factoring and/or field warehousing and, at the same time, increase your credit line. You may be able to gain some insights as to what's feasible here by checking with Dun and Bradstreet's "Cost of Doing Business Ratios."

Most smaller businesses can borrow short-term funds at a cheaper rate than intermediate loans. However, depending strictly on short-term funds can have serious—or perhaps even fatal—consequences in the event of a credit crunch. Sometimes leasing assets, rather than buying them, is attractive to smaller firms, especially those not in the maximum tax bracket (of course, the qualification on leasing still stands).

Depreciation. In many industries (especially those requiring heavy fixed assets), R-O-I is very sensitive to depreciation. Are your writeoffs (for shareholder reporting, not taxes) realistic? They may be too accelerated, thus not accurately reflecting the R-O-I; on the other hand, they may be too low. What are industry averages? (Check "Cost of Doing Business Ratios.") Understand that because of differences of depreciation, industry averages on R-O-I (and earnings) can be deceiving. Newer companies are less likely to have assets that are written off and thus would be more likely to show a much lower R-O-I than older companies, which may have already depreciated their productive plant.

Taxes. You may have a tax loss that will expire in several years, and you feel that there's no way that you'll be able to make it up in your present scope of business. The tax loss might be the cost reducer you need to make diversification, a merger, or an acquisition feasible.

On a more mundane side, when was the last time you checked the "parity" of your real estate taxes? Renegotiation may be able to save several mills. Sometimes just the threat of moving may help to reduce assessments, or at least keep them from being raised. Or perhaps now is the time you should seriously consider relocation.

Again, how do your taxes compare with industry averages in "Cost of Doing Business Ratios"?

Operating Expenses. The "Cost of Doing Business Ratios" gives percentages for selected line expenses. If you find you're out of line in one or several of these, you may wish to give them very close scrutiny.

But, in general, ask yourself if you're using the right channel to reach your customers. Perhaps market conditions have changed, and now you'll save money by going direct. Or, conversely, perhaps now's the time to switch to industrial distributors or manufacturers' representatives. Make the 80-20 principle be your bible—weed out those unprofitable salesmen, channels, advertising expenditures.

Administration costs have a way of inching up. Can you pool secretaries? What about your current information needs? Is too much time being spent gathering and assembling data no longer needed? Would you save money by using time sharing or service agencies rather than ownership or doing it yourself?

Cost of Goods Sold. You can get some indication of how much your purchasing of materials and/or manufacturing costs are in line by checking costs of goods sold in the "Cost of Doing Business Ratios." Usually one of the biggest savings in manufacturing costs can be made through proper short-interval scheduling of personnel. Take a typical example. A production worker finishes his task and goes to his foreman and asks him what he should be doing. But the foreman is extremely busy—or he gets a call from his supervisor—and so he tells the worker to go help another person. The worker does, and soon the two of them finish the job. They look for the foreman, but the foreman is with the supervisor and may not return for several hours. And so on. Experience has shown that *efficient* short-interval scheduling can often cut manpower requirements.

Increasing Sales

Increasing sales is another option for increasing net income. How much you can reasonably expect to gain depends heavily on whether your market is growing, static, or declining.

A Growing Market. Naturally, it is easiest to increase sales in a growing market. Competitors may be struggling to supply demands; buyers will be looking for backup sources of supply; and new customers —who probably have no fixed product allegiance—are swelling the ranks of purchasers.

Figure 8-2 gives you an idea how much of a market growing at 20 percent per year you'll need to capture to meet your objectives.[1] Now the figure points out a rather obvious fact: If the market growth rate is equal to your desired growth rate, all you need to do is to maintain your market share. And, if the market is growing faster than your desired growth rate, you don't even need to maintain your market share in order to meet your growth objectives. For example, if your market share is 10 percent, and the market is growing at the rate of 20 percent a year, in Year 1 you need only 5 percent of the new growth

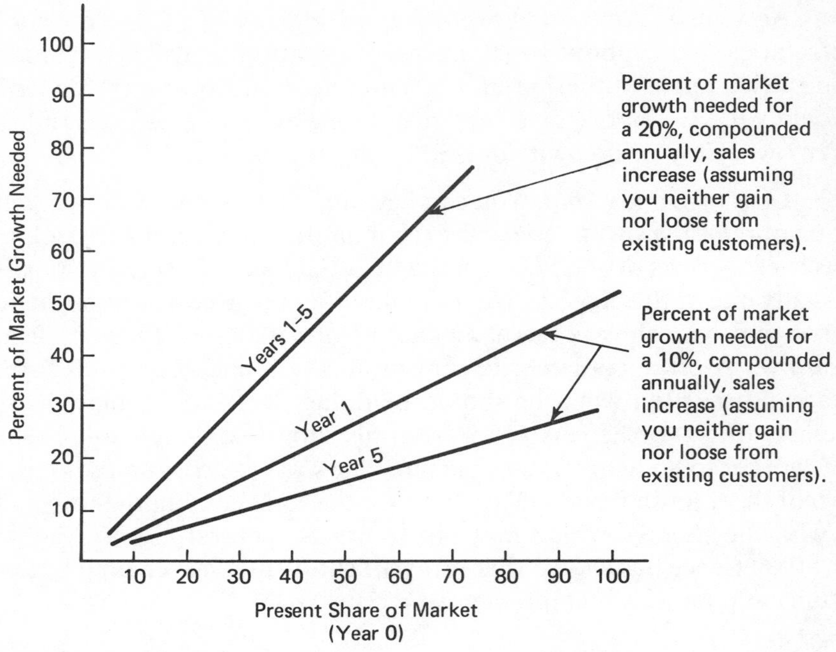

Figure 8-2 Market Growth Rate 20% (compounded annually)

in order to meet your objectives. By Year 5 you only need to pick up 3.5 percent. (Please note: This example was used to show the advantages of being in a growing market. In most cases, a continued loss of market share is disastrous.)

But what happens when the market growth rate is slower than your desired rate? Look at Figure 8-3. If your market share is over 50 percent, right off, in Year 1, you are in an impossible situation—at least in trying to grow by capturing percentage of growth. Your desired growth rate, not only in rate but also in absolute numbers, is greater than that of the total market. If you have a smaller share of the market —say 10 percent—during the first year you'll have to capture 20 percent of the growth. And this rate will have to increase annually because of the difference between the market's growth rate and yours. By the fifth year you'll have to get 28 percent of the new business because now your market share will have increased to 15.4 percent.

You may not have an accurate reading on the size of your market —or its growth rate—but it may be a good idea to make some subjective judgments and then construct a chart appropriate for your situation. Such analysis will help you keep your strategy within bounds

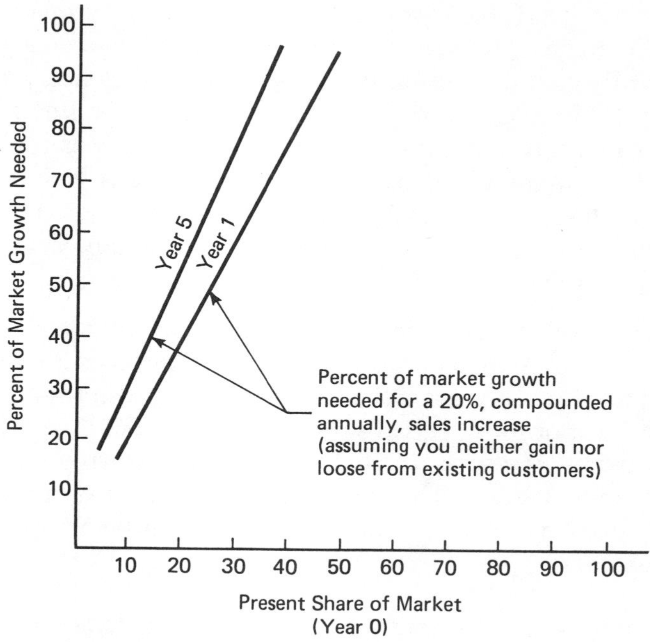

Figure 8-3 Market Growth Rate 10% (compounded annually)

of realism. And it will improve communication among members of the planning team.

A Static Market. Growth is much harder to obtain in a static market. Your competition is also looking for growth, and since they probably have excess capacity (like you), you can expect them to be aggressive. In addition, buyer loyalties are probably well set, and fewer new customers are entering the market. Unless you really have a competitive advantage, or you can make some dramatic internal changes, don't look for much growth.

A Declining Market. If you're operating in a declining market, competitors will be getting out of the business. So you may be able to pick up some business in the short run. But remember that your competitors are leaving for a very good reason. The market is declining. You may find yourself getting more and more of less and less until you end up, finally, with all of nothing.

Of course, the size of the market and the size of your firm determine how attractive the market is to you. Market attractiveness is relative. Many smaller companies have found that what are decidedly declining markets (dogs) for a large firm are actually growth bonanzas (stars) for them. The vice-president of a small chemical company could hardly contain himself pointing out how they had picked up a "real steal" from a major chemical company. "We knew that they had classified this operation as a dog. The market was too small for them. We negotiated keeping in mind *their* point of view—not ours. We got it at a very, very good price." He went on to say that the plant —the whole operation—has worked out exceedingly well, "and extremely profitable."

Price. Raising price may be another way to boost your sales volume. Usually scoffed at as impossible, sometimes it can succeed. In a period of seven years Gary E. MacDougal, who took over Mark Controls Corporation, raised sales from 16.6 to 68.7 million, profit margins from 1.9 percent to 10.7 percent, and return on equity from 5 percent to 27 percent. His competitors believed that at least part of these phenomenal increases were due to getting better pricing terms from customers.[2]

Allow at least two months for developing the strategy. But schedule meetings periodically, and plan them carefully. Set up something to accomplish at each meeting; for example, a review or an analysis of a particular type of expansion. This will help keep the meetings on track.

Avoid criticism at meetings. People like to do the things they are good at, and they dislike being criticized. It's important to avoid criticism in order to encourage participation.

Some other points: If task forces or subcommittees will speed things along, by all means delegate some of the work. But don't worry about the sessions being too long; studies show that people are often most creative when they're tired. A different tactic for stimulating thoughts is to meet some place radically different—at a weekend retreat, for instance.

One rule is crucial: Wherever you hold the meetings, make sure there are no interruptions. It takes only one or two "absolutely necessary" phone calls to drain a meeting of its initiative. Remember that developing strategy deserves the highest priority—it is the firm's most important business.

While you're developing your strategy, you always want to keep asking yourself, "If we follow this course of action, will we be able to meet our short-term objectives as well as the long-term ones?" So, in a sense, while considering strategies you're also doing what we do intuitively: We think of what we should be doing in the long run as well as what we must do in the short run. By the time that you come up with the strategy of the firm, then, you also have a pretty good idea for your operational plan for the following year. As with the strategic plan, the operational plan at this stage does not need to be in great detail, but both the operational and strategic plans should have enough detail to enable construction of very crude P. & L. and balance sheets.

Another point: It's essential that functional area managers consult and work very closely with their subordinates (department heads) while putting together the strategy and the operational plan (even though the operational plan may be pretty much in the rough). The director of marketing, for instance, may not be as familiar as the advertising manager with the immediate constraints—and opportunities—that face an advertising manager. Moreover, if department heads help design the plan, they're more likely to keep their "lights on" to make sure it works. It's the old story of the benefits of involvement.

A FINAL CHECK

Before proceeding, make a final check of your tentative strategy. Review the strategy contingency guidelines. Have you really stuck close to them? It is remarkably easy to inch away, in very small steps, so that we hardly realize how far off base we are. Then, there are some general questions you should ask.

First, is the strategy consistent with the style and philosophy of management? In his book *The Corporate Man,* Antony Jay reports an incident that in various guises we have heard over and over again. A new headmaster of an English boarding school was determined to initiate major changes. Unfortunately (for him), his proposed reforms encountered entrenched resistance from his staff, and he accomplished only a little of what he wanted to do.[3] The situation in a business can be just as touchy—corporate strategy must be in reasonable harmony with the attitudes and philosophy of management.

Second, is there an ample supply of critical resources? According to Murphy's Law, "If things can go wrong, they will go wrong." Not only is that "law" cleverly put, it touches on an unpleasant truth. A gambler once approached this point in a different way. "Don't prepare just for average bad luck,'' he said, ''but for outrageously bad luck.'' If such luck comes your way, will you have an adequate supply of critical resources? Money? Manpower? Physical facilities? Raw materials? Energy?

Third, are the payoffs of the strategy commensurate with the risks? What amount of your company's resources are you committing to this strategy? Is the payoff really worth it? Remember that the more distant the payoff, the more risky the venture. Government has a way of changing regulations. People's tastes change. Technology has a way of advancing in unforeseeable ways.

Finally, does the strategy allow ample time for implementation? The First Law of Aerial Wing-Walking states, ''Never let go of what you are holding until you have a firm grasp on something else.'' When you do, the results are obvious. The same is true with implementing strategies. You must grant sufficient time for your strategy to take hold.

TESTING THE ADAPTABILITY OF THE PROPOSED STRATEGY

Although you've taken into consideration the worst-case future while designing your strategy, pause for a moment and check the flexibility of your strategic plan in your worst-case future. Can the strategy adapt itself to these conditions? Or does its effectiveness depend on the values of the key variables in the most-probable-case future?

This check may encourage you to modify the strategy in order to increase its adaptability. Or you may wish to discard the tentative strategy entirely and redesign a completely new one. Or you may decide the risk is worth taking and that no change is necessary. Or you may decide to develop contingency plans.

DEVELOPING CONTINGENCY PLANS

There is one constant: The future is unpredictable. And Murphy's Law points out which way things are likely to go. (O'Leary's Corollary: ''Murphy was an optimist.'')

Max Gunther, in *The Luck Factor,* analyzed the characteristic of lucky people—not those who win the Irish Sweepstakes, but those who seem to be lucky throughout their lives.[4] One major characteristic lies in what Gunther terms "The Pessimisim Paradox." Lucky people are extremely pessimistic. They are happy—but pessimistic. They always seem to be planning what they will do if things should go wrong. J. Paul Getty, for example, who was one of the richest men on earth, maintained that "When I go into any business deal, my chief thoughts are how I'm going to save myself when things go wrong." Indeed the results of a study of bus drivers revealed that those who have the fewest accidents were those who were always thinking of what they would do if some problem arose. The drivers who were in the most accidents invariably depended upon luck.

Gunther introduces "Mitchell's Law," named after Martha Mitchell. Gunther visited Martha Mitchell in 1975 to try to get her to write her autobiography. He had expected to see a haughty individual. Instead he found a rather meek woman. Here was a person who had risen from a poor background to become a highly paid model, who had married a very successful Wall Street bond lawyer, and who later had become *the* social leader in Washington, D.C. During their conversation she commented on what Gunther later named Mitchell's Law: "Life is slippery like a piece of soap. If you think you have a grip on it, you're wrong."

Murphy's Law says that things are likely to go wrong while Mitchell's Law says that we have very little control over things. Therefore, if you take into consideration these laws, regardless how sound your tentative strategy may seem, it's advisable to develop contingency plans.

Contingency plans are normally developed after you've decided on your strategy, but you should consider contingency planning as an integral part of strategy development. In fact, an examination of possible contingencies may lead you to change your strategy in order to generate a more flexible stance.

If you're developing contingency plans for the first time, and if your planning team is not sophisticated in planning, be sure to keep the process simple. As one executive (of a very large company) cautioned, "Contingencies tend to be downside and people do not like to anticipate negative situations. If people do not like to plan in general, contingency planning becomes an even more difficult task." So accept that the contingency plans will be much less than ideal, but keep in mind that even a very crude plan can have great benefits.

Determining Key Contingency Events

Although there are many possible contingent events, begin with contingency plans for no more than one or two. To help isolate the most important, closely examine the worst-case future you developed. The key variables in this future spell out the events to be considered. However, it may be that your planning team decided that there were no specific contingencies that were deemed as real issues. In that case, don't bother with contingency planning. Your planning team will only view contingency planning as an unnecessary chore.

Although contingent events may be positive as well as negative, in keeping with the policy of simplicity, you may wish to consider only negative events your first time through. As one executive stated: "If we have contingency plans for the 'worst,' that's good enough. Somehow we'll be able to figure out how to handle the 'best'." While that may not be true in every case, simplicity does have a virtue. And it's probably better to have your flank protected.

Specifying Trigger Points

A trigger point indicates when a contingency event has developed sufficient impact that the contingency plan should be implemented. For example, your strategy may be dependent upon a maximum of 7 percent inflation. You may decide that your plan is "triggered" when inflation reaches 8 percent or higher for six months.

Select a trigger point for each key contingent event. It simplifies monitoring if you use commonly reported events, such as GNP, rate of inflation, retail sales, money supply, and company sales.

Developing Contingency Actions

In developing contingency actions, follow these guidelines:

- Keep the plans simple, particularly when developing contingency plans for the first time. Avoiding complex plans will make preparation easier. Limit contingency actions to one page.
- Consider positive as well as negative reactions. To illustrate: In the event of a contingent downturn, a negative reaction would be to discharge personnel. A positive reaction would be to expand to

unaffected markets. Positive actions usually help morale. Furthermore, they're more likely to improve your profits and competitive position.

- Estimate the funding necessary for implementing the contingency action. Make sure funding requirements are realistic and available; recognize that what is "realistic and available" usually varies with psychological perspectives. While business is on the upswing, management is usually optimistic, and funds are approved in this perspective. When profits are threatened, however, management may change its stance and reject what it had previously viewed as reasonable.

Before moving on, recheck your strategy. The contingency plans you've developed may reveal unexpected vulnerabilities in your strategy. You may wish to revise the strategy in order to reduce your exposure to hazards.

MAKING FINANCIAL PROJECTIONS

Through the process of developing the corporate plan, you already have an idea that your proposed strategy and first-year plans are on target with objectives. Now make a rough calculation. The figures you use for this need have only ballpark accuracy—that is, just enough detail to prove that your proposed plans are realistic.

Here's what to do: First, based on your strategy and most-probable-case future, forecast sales for your five- and one-year plans. Then, forecast expenses needed to support projected sales, that is, consider production, inventory, marketing, finance and personnel costs. Forecast capital requirements for plant and equipment, inventories and receivables. Then prepare pro forma balance sheets, P. & L. and cash flow statements. Finally, compare the financial forecasts with objectives. If you're off, one or two actions are in order: Search for more effective strategies or, as a last resort, modify goals downward.

PUTTING THE STRATEGY IN WRITING

To make sure that the strategy you have hammered out is difficult to misinterpret—or forget—formalize it by writing it down. Do so concisely. Two to five pages is adequate for many smaller firms. Just make sure that it is explicit enough to provide guidelines for detailed operational plans. It should include three major parts:

Part 1. *Basic strategies*—types of products and/or services to be offered and target markets and the means by which these markets will be reached.

Part 2. *Contingency plans*—contingency plans for the worst-case future (and when appropriate, for the best-case future).

Part 3. *Timing and financial projections*—a timetable indicating major events such as the introduction of a new product or the entry into a new market area; major capital required for new production and distribution facilities, inventories, and receivables, and the times these funds will be needed; and projected sales, expenses, and profits for Years 1 and 5.

Dividing the written strategy into three parts will aid clarity, as the following example illustrates.

CASE EXAMPLE

The planning team at Acme rated their company strengths and market attractiveness as shown in Figure 8-4. All in all, the company seemed to be in an excellent position (star—invest/grow).

Gap analysis (for the most-probable future) revealed the situation shown in Tables 8-2 and 8-3.

Examining the gaps, the planning team at Acme felt that with careful annual planning they could meet their one-year objectives following their present strategy. However, if they continued their present strategy over the next five years, rough projections exposed short falls. As the most-probable-case future indicated, consumer demand for compact and color coordinated desks would likely increase. At present the company has basically one color and one style. The situation analysis highlighted that while Acme's manufacturing process (electrodeposition painting) has great efficiencies, it is not adaptable to color changes. Furthermore, consideration of the worst-case future pointed out some other disturbing possibilities. If energy and steel shortages should occur, key customer loyalty would probably decrease,

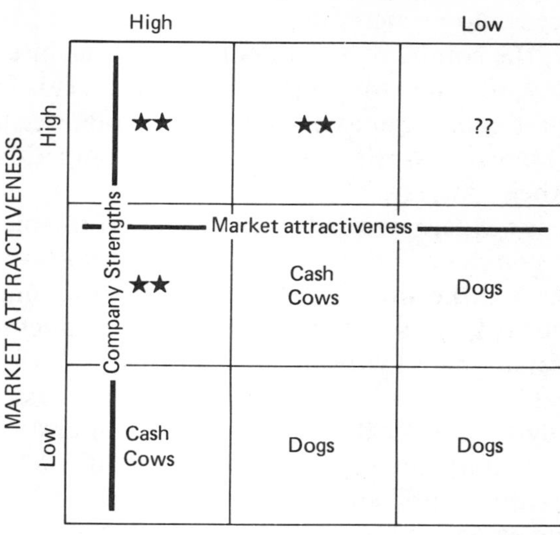

Figure 8-4

Table 8-2

Key Areas	*Five-Year Objectives*	*"Most-Probable" Case Forecasts*	*"Most-Probable" Case Gaps*
R-O-A	12%	11%	1%
Sales	25,000,000	20,000,000	5,000,000
Debt/Equity	50%	50%	—
Earnings	2,500,000	2,000,000	500,000
Dividends	600,000	480,000	120,000

Table 8-3

Key Areas	*One-Year Objectives*	*"Most-Probable" Case Forecasts*	*"Most-Probable" Case Gaps*
R-O-A	9%	9%	—
Sales	14,000,000	13,750,000	250,000
Debt/Equity	1.1 to 1	1.1 to 1	—
Earnings	1,400,000	1,375,000	25,000
Dividends	350,000	350,000	—

and Acme is dependent upon three key customers for 60 percent of its sales. There could be increasing price competition (Acme is selling a commodity; the company has no consumer franchise). Recessions are a possibility, to which the consumer desk market is highly vulnerable. Steel prices could rise faster than the general price level, thereby causing even budget low-price desks to be less competitive with desks made from other materials.

A number of ideas were advanced. (One of the most promising but eventually considered unacceptable, was budget low-price fireproof security boxes for the home. Although there was high marketing synergism, the idea was scrapped because this product required substantially different manufacturing processes).

The final strategy was three pronged. The first, to continue producing budget low-price desks, marketing them through the present channel, and to start investigating how desks might be made more compact and with greater color choice without a great loss of present manufacturing equipment or efficiency.

The second was to expand the sales of desks by tapping the market for budget commercial office equipment. The channel to be used was manufacturer representatives—wholesalers—dealers—commercial users. It was believed that manufacturer representatives could help overcome some of the handicaps of Acme's limited line. Besides expanding the customer base, there was another advantage of moving into the budget commercial office equipment line. Such office equipment would be sold primarily to smaller businesses. Commerical office equipment is less vulnerable to recessions than is home office equipment. There are small businesses that are always starting up and budget office furniture is not much more expensive than used office furniture. Then, too, businesses are less likely than consumers to substitute for office equipment made of less durable materials: Because of heavier use, businesses need rugged desks and cabinets.

The third prong of the strategy was to start the production and marketing of nonsuspension file cabinets. Several of Acme's customers had made inquiries about the possibility of Acme's manufacturing such cabinets. They were seeking backup sources—they still remembered the shortages resulting from the scarcity of steel in 1974 and those shortages that were caused by some plant shutdowns because of energy crises during the severe winters of 1977 and 1978. The production of nonsuspension file cabinets was a good fit for Acme. There was considerable overlap in the production processes for metal file cabinets and metal desks. The drawer fronts, channels, and slides and the drawers for file cabinets would be similar, if not identical, to those for the desks they were already producing. The only manufacturing process that would be different for the nonsuspension file cabinets, besides packing, would be the top panels and body wrap. In general, the same plant equipment and tooling could be used, so production of file cabinets would help to utilize excess plant capacity. Then too, employees were familiar with the general manufacturing process. Unused warehouse space could also be utilized.

Besides being good manufacturing and warehouse fits, Acme could use its present and planned-for channels of distribution for marketing the file cabinets. Then, there was another plus: These file cabinets could be marketed through regional mass merchandisers, thereby opening another new channel and broadening the customer base.

Unfortunately, there were disadvantages to moving into these channels. It would increase Acme's bad debts and extend their accounts receivables (regional mass merchandisers and wholesalers are slower to pay than national mass merchandisers). But Acme was now in a position to extend credit, and willing to do so since there seemed to be market opportunity in the budget line for office equipment. Many of the top-of-the-line producers were moving into the more profitable custom-made modular business (suitable for more automatic word processing systems).

The new strategy seemed to be an improvement over previous ones in that it broadened the product and customer base. Still, the planning team felt that other contingencies should be planned for; namely, the possible shortages of steel and energy.

The planning team therefore decided they would start to buy steel directly from the mill. They had always bought from wholesalers (who offered better terms). But they remembered that in 1974 the wholesalers, who typically bought on "deals," were squeezed by the mills, and since Acme had never bought from the mills, the mills wouldn't talk to Acme. Acme believed it was time that they set up direct relationships with the mills, even though terms were net ten days. They would also increase their stockpile of steel.

As far as energy was concerned, why not have an alternative source, such as LP gas? Several of the members of the planning team noted how a backup system of LP had helped other plants in their area during the winters of 1977 and 1978. Although the plant conservation procedures had been checked, the planning team thought that a more detailed investigation might save money in the long run.

The team's final strategy, when put in writing, was summarized in three parts.

Basic Strategies

1. Continue manufacturing and marketing of budget low-price desks for national mass merchandisers. Start R & D on compact style and multicolor (to give flexibility and still maintain efficiencies of mass production).
2. Start marketing budget low-price desks to commercial users. The marketing channel would be manufacturers' representatives—wholesalers—office supply houses.
3. Start manufacturing budget low-price file cabinets to be marketed to national mass merchandisers (using present channel), regional mass merchandisers (using manufacturers' representatives), and commercial users (same channel as Strategy 2 above).

Contingency Plans

1. Start purchasing steel directly from mills.
2. Increase steel stockpile by 10 percent.
3. Set up alternative energy source and energy conservation procedures.

Timing and Financial Projections

1. Timetable for Basic Strategy 1 (above):
   - February 1, 1980 Start R & D for compact styles and multicolor desks.
2. Timetable for Basic Strategy 2 (above):
   - May 1, 1980 Market research completed.
   - July 1, 1980 Promotion material prepared.
   - Sept. 1, 1980 Manufacturers' representatives network established.

   Significant sales will not be expected until the second year since wholesalers usually order on six-month cycle.

3. Timetable for Basic Strategy 3 (above):
   - May 1, 1980 — Market research completed.
   - June 15, 1980 — Prototypes completed; samples sent to major prospects.
   - Sept. 15, 1980 — Results of prototypes analyzed; establish contracts with major prospects.
     Modify design; if necessary, start manufacturing of permanent dies for automatic machinery.
     Establish contracts with other manufacturers' representatives for regional mass merchandisers and regional wholesalers.
   - March 15, 1981 — Start mass production.

   Sales revenues will not start until October 15, 1981.

4. Timetable for Contingency Plans:
   - Feb. 1, 1980 — Switch over to purchase directly from steel mills.
   - March 1, 1980 — Increase steel stockpile by 10 percent.
   - Nov. 1, 1980 — Complete set-up of alternative energy source and energy conservation procedures.

5. Funds Needed for New Products and Distribution Facilities:
   - R & D on compact style and color $25,000 (Mar. 1, 1980), $25,000 (Sept. 1, 1980).
   - Market research $25,000 (April 1, 1980).
   - Steel rule and permanent dies $50,000 (Jan. 1, 1981).
   - Promotion materials $10,000 (June 1, 1980).

6. Funds needed for Contingency Plans:
   - Increase steel stockpile carrying costs $10,000 (Mar. 1, 1980).
   - Set-up of alternative energy source and conservation procedures $300,000 (Oct. 1, 1980).

Pro forma balance sheets and P. & L. and cash flow statements were prepared for Years 1 and 5. Although these were rough estimates, the planning team felt that they were close enough on target to develop more precise plans for Year 1.

9

Step 4: Developing the Operational Plan

You've decided on broad courses of action for the next five years. And you've got a pretty good handle on your operational plan for next year. The next step is to flesh out the operational plan. You need a better idea of what has to be accomplished during the coming year so you can meet both your short and long-term objectives.

Operational planning means deciding what is to be accomplished, who does what, when it should get done, at what cost, and, in addition, setting up control points and methods of monitoring. It involves developing plans for the corporate level, functional areas, and lower echelons of management.

This chapter describes developing the operational plan at the corporate and functional levels. Planning for implementation and control is covered in Chapter 10.

Perhaps you're reasonably satisfied with your present system of operational planning, and you see how you can blend in the strategic plan. If so, don't make any major changes. Do what you've been doing. It's always a mistake to introduce procedures that aren't really necessary.

If you're not satisfied, the following procedures will help you set up operational planning that will better suit your needs. Of course, the procedure recommended here may be too simple or too advanced for your firm. Then make adaptations. For example, the formal planning in a small job-shop manufacturing company ($2,500,000 in sales) had been carried out by two people—the owners. Other managers received their budgets on almost a "day-to-day" basis. When the owners started formal comprehensive planning, they wanted to involve five others. They formed a planning team, including these five. As a result, the new members were involved in every step of the planning process. Yet the owners felt that asking each of these five managers to develop their own one-year plans—on the first pass—would be asking too much. So they had their planning facilitator—see p. 25—develop the annual plan, working very closely with each of the managers. These managers understood that during the next planning cycle, they would have the responsibilities for developing their own annual plans.

THE OPERATIONAL PLAN

At the corporate and functional levels, operational planning involves three steps: putting together the detailed operational plan; preparing pro forma P. & L. and balance sheets; and making final adjustments.[1]

Putting Together the Detailed Operational Plan

Although you already have a general idea as to the corporate operational plan, you have to develop it in more detail in order to be sure that the pieces will fit together and at the right time.

As far as the operational plans themselves are concerned, naturally, you'll want to keep them as short as possible. But you'll have to itemize major expenses, incomes, and timetables—enough, at least, to show the mesh between functional areas and to be able to construct pro forma P. & L. and balance sheets.

In order to accomplish this, functional areas will have to prepare plans for their areas. To make sure that all of the important areas are covered, have them follow the same format. Standardization will enable members of the planning team to analyze various functional area plans much more quickly. They'll know where to look for certain items.

Here's a recommended format:

THE [MANUFACTURING] PLAN
19xx

Objectives—what the functional area is supposed to accomplish during the year.

Situation analysis—summary statement of the functional area's strengths and weaknesses.

Environmental forecasts—external environment, as relevant to the functional area.

Summary description of the [manufacturing] plan—outline of the functional area's general thrust for the year and statement of relationship of the functional area's annual plan to the general strategy of the firm.

Detailed plan of action.

Contingency plans—key threats and proposed actions to counter them.

Required resources.

As a general rule for smaller companies, the plans for each functional area should not exceed ten to eleven pages. More specifically, objectives should take up one-half to one page; the situation analysis, one page; environmental assumptions, one-half to one page; the summary description of the plan, one page; the detailed plan of action, five pages; required resources, one page; and contingency plans, one page.

As you can see, you have already done part of the work in the previous planning steps—objectives, situation analysis, and environmental assumptions. The functional areas can extract appropriate parts; their major effort will be in developing the plan of action. There's a lot that could be included in this section, so don't get bogged down in detail. But certainly you'll want marketing, for example, to estimate sales volumes from each of the product lines and major customers, as well as the cost of obtaining those sales. To ensure realism, have marketing make a comparison between what they expect in sales from the coming year and what they actually achieved in the year past. The marketing plans should also describe environmental conditions, including the probable activities of major competitors.

Again, there is no point, for instance, in having production struggle to work out the details of factory loading and sequencing, although they will have to do this eventually. What you want now is a general idea of how production intends to produce—at a certain cost—that volume of products that marketing expects to sell. For this, you need cost estimates of energy, raw materials, labor, and equipment. (An overly detailed plan will become useless if the planning team should have to make revisions in the corporate plan.) So you can check for realism have production, also, compare its expectations for the coming year with its achievements during the previous year.

Now is the time for you to consider factoring in next year's inflation (or deflation) rate. Although most firms work with current dollars in determining the next year's operational plan, given the current rate of inflation the use of current dollars may not be the best procedure for you. You may decide it's best to work with projected inflated dollars. Some things, of course, will not be affected, such as long-term debt and multi-year leases on equipment. So on these you don't have a problem. But many other expenditures—and revenues—will be affected by the rate of inflation.

While forecasting the most-probable-case environment for next year, you probably came up with some projection for next year's inflation rate. If you didn't, do so now. (It may be that for your business you'll need to project not only the annual rate of inflation, but also the quarterly rate, or perhaps even the monthly rate.)

Use this inflation rate to adjust your first year's objectives. Quite obviously, if there is an appreciable change in inflation rate, and you don't adjust your growth and earnings accordingly, you'll be getting a distorted picture of your results.

Next, have functional areas use the same inflation rate in developing their plans. Remember that this will take considerable translation on their parts. For example, production will have to estimate how the inflation rate will affect, among other things, the costs of materials, transportation, and utilities; personnel will have to judge the increase in wage rates and salaries; marketing will have to estimate sales costs and possible changes in product pricing to reflect the new inflation rate; and finance, how the projected interest rate will affect the cost and availability of money.

There must be close cooperation between the various functional areas while they prepare their plans. For example, manufacturing cannot make production schedules until it has sales estimates. Similarly, marketing may have to change its plan in order to achieve manufacturing cost efficiencies. Manufacturing must likewise consult with personnel about labor costs; and so on. This interchange, besides being necessary, can have additional benefits. While working out detailed plans, unexpected opportunities as well as problems are exposed. Close coordination among the functional area managers makes it easier to take advantage of the former and better deal with the latter. Besides, it helps functional area managers to understand better the problems of other areas and to think more of the firm as a system. Be sure to let them know they've got to work together. And that it's their responsibility to do so, and to make it work.

Of equal importance, at this time there should be a general agreement, within each of the functional areas, as to department heads' plans and budgets for the coming year. For example, the director of marketing should consult and work very closely with the sales and advertising managers. In fact, the director of marketing should have them develop tentative plans for their departments. This is necessary so that later on, when department heads submit formal plans and budgets, these will be in line with the overall functional plan. But there's no need to have department heads prepare formal plans and budgets now. All you want is a general agreement. There's usually some last-moment negotiations involving "final" functional area plans and budgets, and these will almost certainly require changes in department heads' plans and budgets. Department heads should be conscious, however, of the importance of their estimates—and that later on they'll be expected to live up to their commitments.

You may find it necessary to get the planning team together once or twice while functional area plans are being developed. These meetings will help ensure that functional area managers are working on their plans and are on schedule and on the right track and, perhaps of most importance, give everyone a chance to be exposed to tentative plans and problems of other functional areas. That will tend to ensure that the pieces will fit together.

Set a date when functional area plans are to be completed. Have each functional area manager distribute his or her completed plan to members of the planning team. Then, about two weeks later, have each functional area manager give an oral report of the completed plan. But make sure members of the planning team have copies at least two weeks before the oral reports are given. If they have time to think the plans through, they'll be more likely to be able to spot potential flaws. Furthermore, early study of the plan makes it less likely that a smooth presentation will obscure the rough spots.

Have the most critical functional area give its oral report first. If there are any serious "bugs" there, you might as well find out about them as soon as possible. Usually, the marketing plan is most critical.

But not always. A firm having difficulty producing enough to meet demand, for instance, would probably begin with the production plan first.

While examining each plan, make sure it is geared toward achieving the basic strategy. For example, does the proposed action follow the strategic direction indicated by the market opportunity/company strengths matrix? If the product falls into the earn/protect category, for example, is promotion highly selective? Are pricing policies likely to stabilize prices for maximum earnings?

Closely examine the reasonability—the logic—of each plan. Do production schedules seem realistic? What about materials availability? Warehousing for raw materials and finished goods? Do sales forecasts seem reasonable given projected economic conditions and the past history of key customers' purchases? Be particularly on the lookout for "hockey stick" projections: plans that show a quantum leap to being "there" tomorrow without specifying how to get there. If production projects a 10 percent reduction in manufacturing costs per unit, just how will it achieve that? Through lower costs for raw materials? Or more efficient use of raw materials? When, precisely, will the reduction occur? Do recent trends support these projections? If sales are to increase by 20 percent within the next year, just how will this be done? What was the increase last year? If it was only 5 percent, what in marketing's program will create such a surge? Who is to make these additional purchases? Are they to come from new customers or from existing ones? If from existing customers, what will marketing be doing to encourage them to buy more? If from new customers, how is marketing planning to entice them from your competitors? And how will these competitors react to your intrusion into their markets?

Besides checking each plan, of course you'll have to analyze carefully the fit of the functional areas' plans. Do the production and inventory schedules meet the demands of sales? Given the factory employee labor situation, are production schedules realistic? Is the available labor pool large enough? Is there a good possibility of a strike during the year? If marketing has plans to open new territories, does it have the trained personnel to do so? Is there adequate cash available (through cash on hand, lines of credit, factoring of accounts receivable, and/or cash flow) to finance increased production and sales costs and accounts receivables?

What happens if a functional area plan should not conform to the firm's strategy, fail the test of logic, and/or give a poor fit? Straighten it out now. If it's something the functional area manager can do, have him do it. But if he can't do it, and the problem area is critical to the success of the corporate plan, it will require the work of a subcommittee or the whole planning team. Hopefully it won't require radical changes in the corporate plan. But face the fact that it may.

Preparing Pro Forma P. & L. and Balance Sheets

Once the functional area plans are in order, prepare pro forma P. & L. and balance sheets to see how close you are to your one-year objectives.

Finalizing the Operational Plan and Making Final Adjustments

If you're lucky, you're right on target. If you're very, very lucky, you may have surpluses of profits and cash flow. In such a case, why not make "insurance" investments to strengthen your future position for the second, third, fourth, and fifth years? Such investments might include improving production facilities, increasing expenditures in R & D, opening of new territories, and/or manpower development. And your job's done.

But probably there's going to be a gap between what you'd like to achieve and what the P. & L. and balance sheets show. If you've been working carefully through the planning steps, the shortfalls will likely be minor. You'll probably be able to make necessary adjustments by cutting costs, or increasing income, through a change in one or more of the functional area plans. Probably the gap will be in one of three areas: sales, earnings, or return on investment. If it's in sales, then check Sector 1 of the opportunity chart (Chap. 7). You might be able to increase sales by opening new geographic areas, increasing present customers' usage, and so forth. If the gap is in earnings and/or return on assets, again the du Pont Chart may provide ideas as to where you can "plug these holes" (see Fig. 8-1). Recall that besides increasing sales, you can increase earnings by cutting costs. For example, you can buy cheaper; lower manufacturing costs; cut back on product quality or services; reduce selling expenses; lower the inventory levels; or cut back on administrative expense.

If your sales and earnings are pretty closely on target, but your R-O-I is low, then you've got to bring R-O-I in line. Increasing earnings will of course help to boost R-O-I. But there's another way to raise

R-O-I: reducing your asset requirements. The first place to look is in fixed investments. Are you making any new capital expenditures that can be postponed without affecting your short- and long-term objectives?

After you've taken a hard look at capital investments, check other ways to reduce cash requirements. Can marketing open up new territories by using manufacturers' representatives instead of a direct sales force? Can you reduce inventory? How about cash management —is your checking account's balance too large? What about your credit policy—could terms be tightened? Are you maximizing potential cash flow from accounts payable?

But in bringing your short-range plans in line with objectives, don't make cuts recklessly. Make sure that you're not sacrificing long-term opportunities, thereby putting your strategic plan in jeopardy. Consider the following cautionary example. In 1971, when price controls came into effect, Simmons Company switched to cheaper mattress materials in order to maintain profits (controls were on finished goods, not on raw materials). The company also cut inventories and despite soaring media costs held its advertising budget constant. This strategy fared poorly. Customers noticed the differences in the finished mattresses, and the inventory changes upset delivery schedules. Then, too, the number of impressions declined because of "watered down" advertising dollars. As a result, Beautyrest's image declined in the minds of both customers and dealers, and sales suffered.[2]

Probably you're not going to be fortunate enough to uncover profit-generating and/or cost-cutting opportunities that are going to be agreeable to all members of the planning team. Manufacturing may wish to lower inventory in order to keep costs in line, but too low an inventory level will alarm marketing. Then too, marketing usually prefers as wide a product line as possible, but probably has to arrive at a compromise with manufacturing, whose instinct is to have a few products in long production runs, thereby cutting its own costs. There will have to be a number of negotiations.

You can, of course, impose your will on your subordinates, but you should do so as little as possible. When you do, you're forcing them to accept numbers they believe not to be realistic. They may go along with you—while hoping for miracles (and perhaps while circulating their resumes). But at the end of the year you'll just have another bunch of missed projections. If you don't have confidence in the people reporting to you, perhaps you'd better start thinking of replacements.

Have your subordinates make their own plans—and numbers. Certainly you will review their plans and make final approvals, but it's much better to have your managers design their own plans, thereby committing themselves. It's comparatively easy to fail tasks that are imposed upon us. Failing our own plans involves a much more painful and personal defeat.

With luck, negotiations will keep the operational plans close to the corporate objectives. If not, and if you have time, perhaps the planning team can make some basic changes in the operational plan (and perhaps modify the strategy). Otherwise, shore up the plan the best you can. More demanding objectives will have to wait until later. In any case, the company is better off knowing what the gaps and potential problems are going to be. You will be in better shape to solve them next year, if not before then.

After you've arrived at a final agreement as to the operational plan, put together one for the company as a whole, and have each functional area manager make necessary adjustments on their plans. Chapter 12 suggests a format for the corporate plan.

FUNCTIONAL LEVEL CONTINGENCY PLANS

Functional area managers (and other managers throughout your company) should be aware that plan approval does not release them from responsibility should the plan fail. They should expect to be judged according to results—not on how well the plan was implemented. Plans carried out are worth nothing unless objectives are reached. Of course, things may happen in the environment that were unplanned for. To compensate for these, managers should have contingency plans.

There are two basic ways functional area managers can develop contingency plans. The first is by handling contingencies in the same manner as recommended in Chapter 8 for strategic planning: Determine contingent events, specify trigger points, and develop contingency actions. Experience has shown, however, that this method is advisable only when specific contingencies are deemed as a very real issue. For example, you may have to negotiate a new contract with labor during the next year and a strike is likely. The contingency plan, in the event of a strike, then, should spell out what actions should be taken. The plan of action does not have to be highly detailed, but you need to make sure that the general plan makes sense to other members of the planning team.

The second method by which functional area managers can prepare for contingencies is through variable budgeting. Detailed aspects of budgeting are beyond the scope of this book, but the references at the end of this chapter list some excellent sources. Several points on budgeting, however, should be stressed. Operational plans create the framework for budgets. Following this procedure adheres to the basic tenet of zero-based budgeting: *Programs determine budgets.* In other words, budgets are not automatically adjusted for inflation and then approved. Instead, managers must first justify the needs for funds; programs must contribute to the strategic and annual plans of the company. This procedure, however, is less sophisticated than formal zero-based budgeting in that managers are not required to put together decision packages. Even so, you judge effectiveness through careful review of plans.

Since plans do determine budgets, and managers develop the plans, you're adhering to two basic principles of effective budgeting: That budgets follow organizational lines and that those who must live with the budgets are involved in setting them. And your budgeting system should be simple since you're keeping planning on a shirt-sleeve basis. Highly detailed budgets cause exasperation and finally spur efforts to beat the system.

Of course, managers should never feel (or be) chained permanently to the requirements of their plans. In the event of unpredicted changes in environmental or other conditions, they must feel that a request for additional funds will receive a fair hearing. If they don't, they will try to deal with the unexpected ahead of time by padding their requests. Such attempts lead to two major types of wastes. First, the waste caused by managers submitting requests for more than they really need: "cushionitis." If the practice is followed throughout the company, it can lead to a considerable sum in "locked-up" nonproductive accounts. Then, wastes often occur because managers believe that they have to spend all of their budgets. If they don't, next year their budgets will be cut. We've all watched mad spending flurries near the end of fiscal years and have shuddered at the resulting losses. The exposure created by formal planning (where everyone on the planning team takes a close look at each of the functional areas) does much to help prevent "cushionitis."

"End-of-the-year spenditis" will be prevented, in the large, by following the procedure recommended in this book: Planning precedes budgeting. Managers will be less likely to dump their reserves at the end of the year, because they know that the next year their budgets will not be determined mainly by how much they spent last year. Their budgets will depend on their plans.

But even with this increased exposure, it's essential that managers believe that if emergencies—or opportunities—should arise, reasonable requests for funds will be approved. Starting with the president and permeating throughout the firm, management must be willing to examine what has happened (and what is happening) in light not so much of what was budgeted but of what has really happened (or is happening). And they must adjust budgets accordingly.

Two ways of implementing flexible budgeting are through supplemental and variable budgets. Supplemental budgeting simply means that the company keeps reserves so that, in the event of an emergency or an opportunity, a functional area can make requests for additional funding.

Variable budgeting, however, means that functional area managers plan for contingencies of increases and/or decreases resulting from nonspecific causes (in addition to planning for those specific contingencies deemed very real issues, such as a strike or an energy cut-off).

Fundamental to variable budgeting (on the downside) is that some expenses will vary with different levels of output and that some fixed expenses are really discretionary; that is, some fixed expenditures can be cut back—or postponed—without having an immediate impact on sales. For example, recruiting and training might be curtailed, marketing research postponed, expense accounts reduced, and secretarial support trimmed back.

A procedure for implementing variable budgeting is described below.[3] Although the example given below is at the company level, the same general process can be used by any echelon within the company. If you would like additional methods of variable budgeting, check the references in Appendix 9A.

Determine Expense Structure. Have each functional area divide costs into variable, fixed (bedrock), and fixed (discretionary). For example, for marketing:

- *Variable costs* are those that vary directly with sales, such as commissions and bonuses or co-op advertising.

- *Fixed (bedrock) costs* are those that are essentially unchangeable during the planning period, such as salaries for key people or a lease on branch offices.
- *Fixed (discretionary) costs* are those that can be cut back within the planning period without having an immediate impact on sales, such as recruiting, training, advertising, the use of outside agencies (market research, consultants), the use of employment agencies, expense accounts, or staff reductions.

Consolidate Costs. Arrive at total costs of the firm according to variable, fixed (bedrock), and fixed (discretionary) costs.

Prepare Pro Forma P. & L. Statements of Various Levels of Sales. If you only produce one product, this will be pretty easy to do. But you probably have a number of products, each having different cost structures. So if you really wanted to do it right, you'd have to calculate profits for different levels of sales for all of your products.

That will be pretty difficult unless your planning system is highly computerized, which it probably isn't. So why not do the next best thing: Figure your profitability for an across-the-board sales decrease. (You could also make such calculations for a sales increase, but for simplicity only contingencies for sales decrease will be explained). Doing this would simply involve decreasing variable costs in proportion to a sales drop.

Determine Actions to Be Taken in the Event of a Sales Slowdown. Suppose that sales would be 10 percent lower than forecasted. Further, assume the slump would call for a reduction—or postponement—of $100,000 in fixed-discretionary expenses in order to meet profit projections.

In determining the expense structure, you singled out these discretionary expenses. Although these expenses may be postponed without having serious short-term effects, the long-range effects may range from minor inconveniences to those of disastrous proportions. Since long-range effects vary, those fixed-discretionary expenses "selected" should be ones whose effects, as much as possible, would involve only minor inconveniences.

The basic idea is similar to Emerson Electric Company's ABC system of budgeting. Budget A is the base plan, Budget B is for a 10 percent drop in sales, and Budget C is for a 20 percent decline. Managers are serious about the development of the plan since up to 40 percent of their salaries is based on meeting their commitments.[4]

To get cooperation from your managers, however, you must let them know that they will not be penalized for developing pessimistic plans. And be scrupulously fair. Otherwise, managers might take variable budgeting—and contingency planning—as an invitation to budget cuts.

DEPARTMENTAL PLANS

Although you've developed basic plans for the functional areas, plans still need to be drawn up for the various departments. For example, although the general marketing plan may already be approved, the advertising manager and the sales manager still need to work up formal plans for the coming year.

The functional area managers have been working with their department heads while preparing the functional area operational plans. Furthermore, their department heads have already committed themselves to tentative plans and budgets that mesh with those of the functional areas. Now is the time to formalize these department plans and budgets.

For example, let's assume the director of marketing calls a meeting of the people reporting to him/her (for simplicity, let's assume she runs two departments, advertising and sales). She supplies each with a detailed description of the marketing plan (to which, she ought to point out, they have already committed themselves), and asks them to prepare their formal plans and budgets. She allows them about two weeks (two weeks is probably adequate since they have, in general, already developed plans). After giving everyone a chance to review his/her formalized plans, the three get together to critique them.

Particular attention should be paid to departmental "outputs" and expenses. Make sure they mesh with the functional area plan—in this case, marketing's. For example, the sales manager's forecast should match the sales forecast of the marketing plan. If it doesn't, negotiations can probably iron out minor differences. A major discrepancy, however, is likely to necessitate a change in the corporate plan. If such a discrepancy occurs, let the corporate planning team know about it as soon as possible. Hopefully, the "slack" can be made up somewhere else. If not, it's going to call for making major adjustments in the corporate plan.

If you do have to make a change in the corporate plan now, it will probably create havoc in the planning cycle. But better that than to ignore the discrepancy. Console yourself that you took every precaution to make sure that it wouldn't happen. Then, since you're gaining experience in planning, it probably won't happen again.

It is obvious that while the planning process should cascade downward throughout the organization, much of the work goes on simultaneously at all levels. For example, as the director of marketing assembles the marketing plan, she checks with the sales manager about the levels of projected sales. And to put together a dependable sales estimate, the sales manager depends at least in part on the knowledge and information he receives from his salesmen.

The planning process, then, is neither "top-down" nor "bottom-up," but both. While top management always retains control of the overall process, it makes its final decisions only after close consultation with the lower managerial echelons.

Figure 9-1 illustrates the involvement you should having during the various steps in the planning process. Setting objectives, mission, and policies is top-level management's job. There's no sense in getting others involved in this one. When it comes to the situation analysis, the planning team sets the guidelines—deciding what should be gathered, how thoroughly, and so forth. But then there can be—and should be —a great deal of delegation in gathering information.

Functional area managers should consult with people reporting directly to them concerning the feasibility of proposed strategies. But because of the abstract level of strategies, lower echelons usually need not be consulted.

When it comes to developing operational plans (at the corporate and functional areas), here's where lower echelons should become involved. Functional area managers should get commitment from their department managers. Department managers, too, will probably want to consult with people reporting to them to check feasibility and, in addition, to get their commitment, and so down the line.

Objectives for the department plans will be set by the functional area manager (these objectives, after all, are the plans of the functional area plans). Developing department plans calls for involvement of lower echelons. There's not likely to be many conflicts, however, since these lower echelons have previously committed themselves.

And so on, until you've reached the lowest level of management.

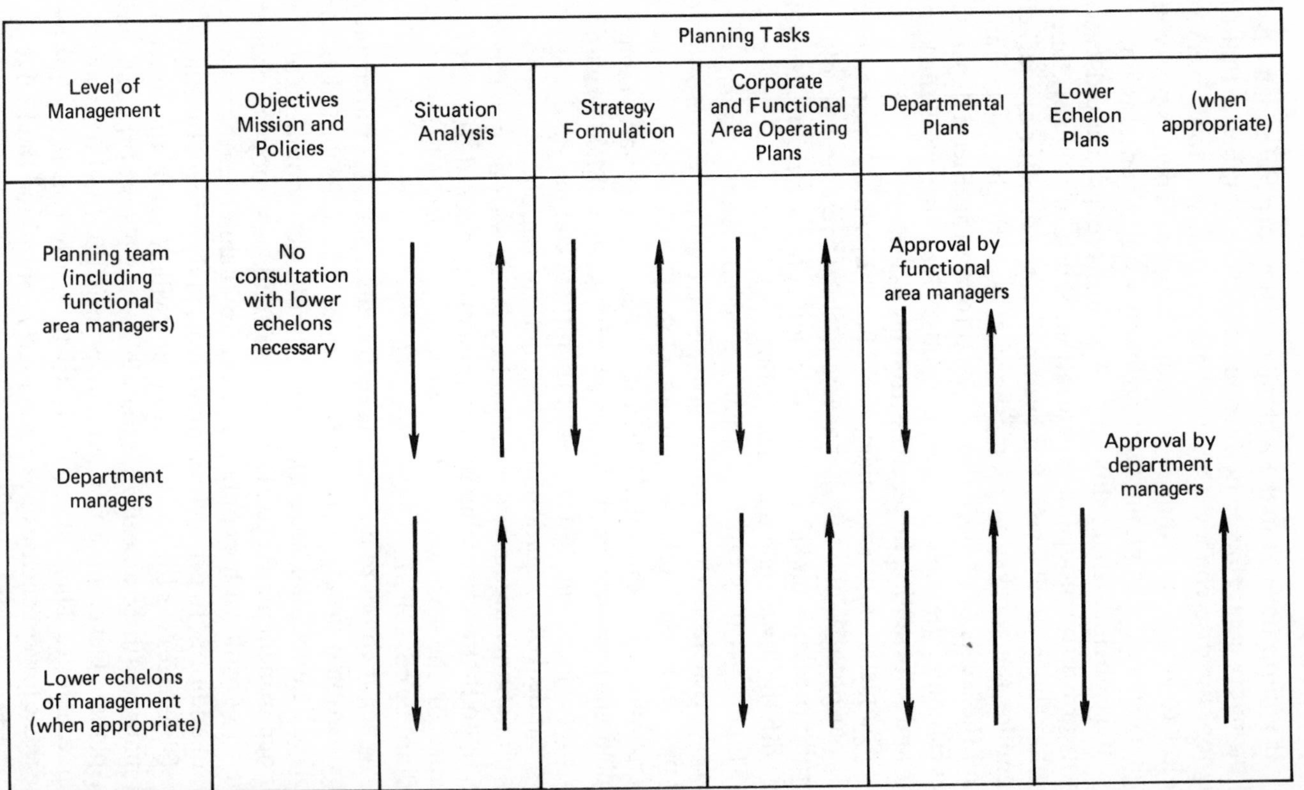

Figure 9-1. Involvement of Personnel in the Planning Tasks

APPENDIX 9—A Supplemental Readings

ALLEN SWEENY and JOHN N. WISNER, JR., *Budgeting Fundamentals for Nonfinancial Executives.* New York: AMACOM, 1975, 137 pages. An easy-to-read primer on budgeting. Explains what budgets are, how they work, and how to prepare and present them.

REGINALD L. JONES and H. GEORGE TRENTIN, *Budgeting: Key to Planning and Control.* New York: AMACOM, 1971, 320 pages. A more detailed explanation of the fundamentals. Includes step and variable budgeting. Deviation analysis. Examples, tables, evaluations and forms.

M. EDGAR BARRETT and LE ROY B. FRASER, III, "Conflicting Roles in Budgeting for Operations," *Harvard Business Review,* 55, No. 4 (July-August 1977), 137–46. Presents five functions of operational budgets and their potential "people" conflicts. Gives suggestions as to how these stress points might be minimized.

RONALD R. FEINER, *Operational Financial Analysis: A Practical Handbook with Forms.* Englewood Cliffs, N.J.: Prentice-Hall, Inc., 1977, Chap. 11, pp. 200–215. Gives practical how-to-do-it steps on how to use and benefit from flexible budgeting.

10

Step 5: Planning for Implementation and Control

The final step in the planning process is to plan for implementation and control. You need to know if and when individual projects have been started and what your progress has been toward your objectives. Planning for implementation and control, then, provides you with yardsticks to measure action and results against the plan on a periodic basis.

Most of the work of planning for implementation has already been done. Your operational planning has given you a pretty good idea as to who is to do what and when. For example, in working out the details of a plan for plant modernization, you've already decided who needs to accomplish various tasks and the time sequences. But that's not enough. Left to their own devices, managers (like everyone else) tend to become more engrossed in the daily crises, which are immediate and very concrete. New projects necessary to the requirements of the overall plan—whose payoffs are less immediate—tend to get put aside. Consequently, you need check points along the way so that you can easily monitor activities to make sure things get done according to the corporate plan. Although in many ways this is the easiest part of the planning process, it's time consuming. And since everybody already has a pretty good idea as to who is to do what and when, it's the part of the planning process that's usually skipped or brushed over. As a result, programs often don't get implemented when they should. The consequence is that corporate plans never really come off.[1]

But even if properly implemented, things don't always go according to plan. The unpredictable may happen. Perhaps there'll be a wildcat strike or a recession instead of the steady growth everyone expected. Or another firm acquires one of your key customers, who now buys from one of its new parent's subsidiaries. Or all three of these happen at once, plus a few extra. Consider the implications of the "Butter-Side-Down Law": "An object will fall so as to do the most damage." The corollary to this law serves as a painful emphasis: "You cannot successfully determine which side of the bread to butter."

This unpredictability means that you must continually check the validity of your assumptions and make-or-break variables (labor stability, GNP, what your competition is up to, inflation, etc.), the logic of your strategies (is the strategy still applicable given the new situation?), and the effectiveness of programs and budgets (are they doing what they're supposed to? are you receiving the "profits" within the planned-for constraints?). Take for granted you'll have to act to keep results on track—and you'll find this considerably easier to do if you've planned for control *before* the plan is implemented.

Control does not mean a larger stack of reports and data. It is far more practical. It tells you *when* you should take action to adjust for changing conditions and/or improve substandard performance. By establishing standards, you know what to monitor, and the triggers you set up let you know when it's time to make changes.

This chapter gives pointers on how to plan for implementation and control. Use a time frame of one year. You're going to replan at the end of this year, so you'll be making changes in the corporate plan. There's little point in trying to detail responsibility five years from now. So make it easier on yourself and only concern yourself with one year.

THE PROCESS OF PLANNING FOR IMPLEMENTATION AND CONTROL

There are three major steps to planning for implementation and control: documenting responsibilities; setting up responsibility charts; and setting up activity schedules. The end results of the process will provide the president and each manager with sets of objectives (standards), responsibilities, and activity schedules. The procedure is the same at every managerial level; only the substance is different. So it's really not complicated. Once you understand the forms, you've got it.

Figure 10-1 demonstrates responsibility charts and activity schedules and their "overlap" for three echelons of management.

While you plan for implementation and control, keep in mind you must assign responsibilities to specific individuals (not departments); make sure that planning for implementation and control is carried out at every echelon of management; and make sure that plans for implementation and control "dovetail" from one echelon to the next.

Documenting Responsibilities

Let's start at the top. The president is ultimately responsible for corporate goals. Let's assume, for simplicity, that these are specified levels of sales, rates of profits, and debt/equity ratios. These annual objectives should be divided into monthly subobjectives to show if the firm is on target.

Obviously the president has to delegate responsibilities. But with these objectives, right off there's a problem. Everyone has a hand in them, so none of them can be assigned to any one person. Fortunately, this issue has been addressed by the planning team while putting together the corporate plan. Their judgment has told them that if a certain level of sales volume is attained, if manufacturing costs are at a specified level, and so on, then the corporate objectives will be reached. So, objectives for each of the functional areas can be gotten from the corporate plan. And, if the corporate plan goes according to schedule, these objectives (sales, profits, debt/equity) will be met. But, of course, the president still wants to monitor sales, profits, and debt/equity.

In documenting responsibilities for each of the functional areas, examine the corporate plan closely. What, in essence, is each of the functional areas' key objectives? Split these out. The president can then monitor the progress of each of the functional areas toward these objectives. If all goes well, and all of the functional areas meet their objectives, the corporate objectives should also be met.

This completes the president's documentation of his responsibilities and those of the functional area managers reporting to him.

Let's now take a look at the functional area managers. Their key responsibilities have been assigned. Now they must decide on the

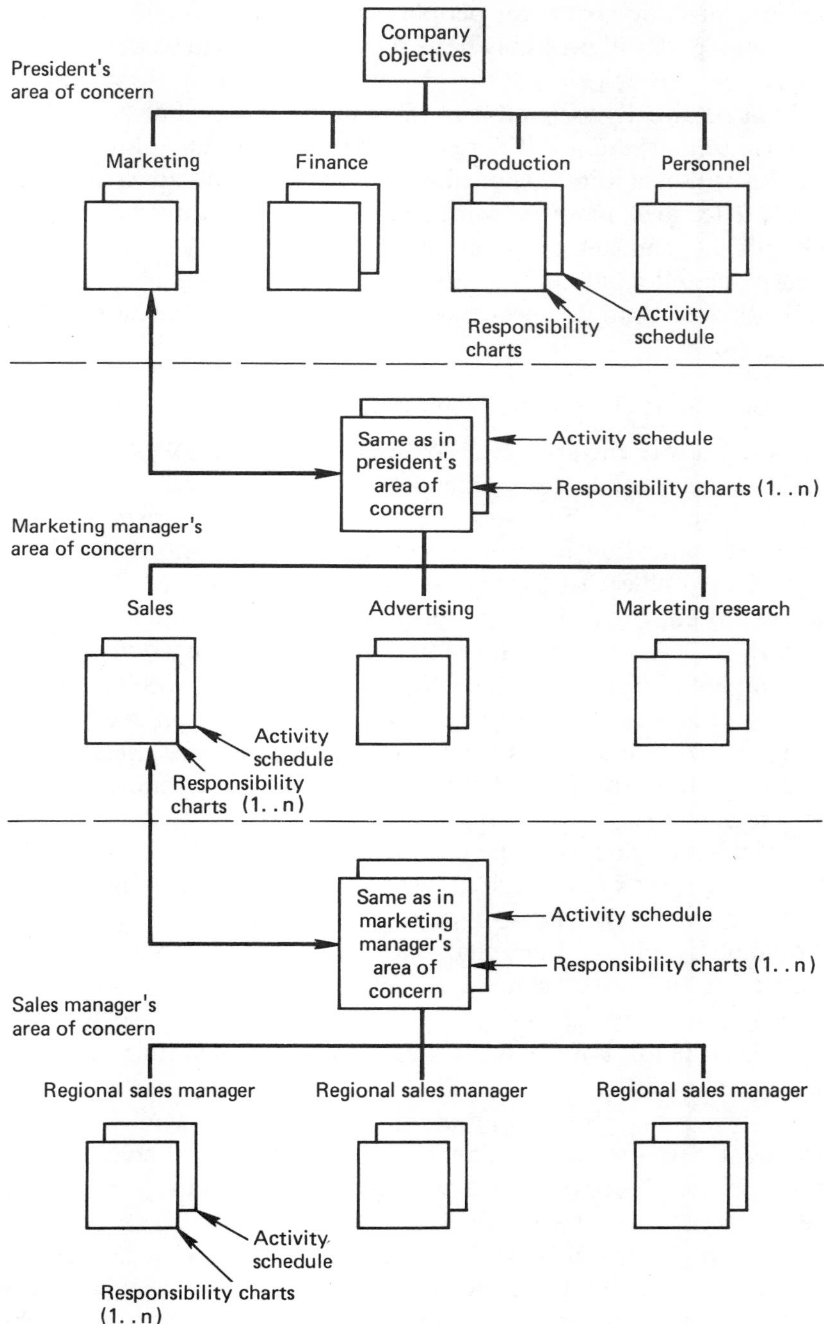
Company objectives
President's area of concern
Marketing
Finance
Production
Personnel
Responsibility charts
Activity schedule
Same as in president's area of concern
Activity schedule
Responsibility charts (1. . n)
Marketing manager's area of concern
Sales
Advertising
Marketing research
Activity schedule
Responsibility charts (1. . n)
Same as in marketing manager's area of concern
Activity schedule
Responsibility charts (1. . n)
Sales manager's area of concern
Regional sales manager
Regional sales manager
Regional sales manager
Activity schedule
Responsibility charts (1. . n)

Figure 10-1

key responsibilities of those people reporting to them. The functional area managers will probably have the same problem as the president. Many—or perhaps all—of the objectives assigned to these managers will not be directly assignable to their subordinates. For example, the director of marketing will be responsible for a certain volume of sales, but this will be a joint responsibility of the sales and advertising managers. The sales manager will be responsible for direct contact, the advertising manager for creating brand awareness. The functional area plans tell what specific objectives should be assigned to which subordinates. And this process spirals down to the lowest echelon of management.

Setting up Responsibility Charts

Let's go back to the president. We assumed, for simplicity, that he or she was responsible for achieving three objectives: sales volume, certain rates of profits, and debt/equity ratios. A form should be prepared indicating how the company is progressing toward these objectives. Table 10-1 shows the form used by Acme. The monthly basis is of course arbitrary, and may not suit your company. (More on how to determine the right interval will be discussed at the end of the chapter.) The point is that proper control points will let you know how you're doing. If things begin to go wrong, you can begin to make changes before it's too late for anything but regrets. The end of the year is no time to discover that you're hopelessly behind what you need to achieve.

Let's examine what the president's responsibility chart for marketing might look like. Each major objective for marketing should be placed on its own chart—if there are five major objectives, there should be five charts. Each chart should be divided into four elements: the major objective, general program, subobjectives, and critical assumptions. (See Fig. 10-2.)

Since all this information is in the corporate plan, this step doesn't require uncovering new ground. When to measure the objectives of major programs—by week, month, or quarter—depends on what the president needs to know. There should be a general statement that indicates the objective to be achieved. There should also be a general statement as to how this objective is to be achieved (program). A sentence or two is all that's necessary. And, when necessary, each major objective should be broken down into a series of subobjectives that show how the major objective will be achieved. Finally, there should be a list of critical assumptions for each objective—that is, a

Table 10-1 Corporate Objectives for Acme Metalworking Company

Sales (in $000)	*Jan.*	*Feb.*	*Mar.*	*Apr.*	*May*	*June*	*July*	*Aug.*	*Sept.*	*Oct.*	*Nov.*	*Dec.*	*End of Year*
Objective	900	1100	1200	1200	1200	1000	1000	1000	1400	1600	1500	900	14,000
Actual													
Variance													
Profits (in $000)	*Jan.*	*Feb.*	*Mar.*	*Apr.*	*May*	*June*	*July*	*Aug.*	*Sept.*	*Oct.*	*Nov.*	*Dec.*	*End of Year*
Objective	90	110	108	106	108	88	89	90	160	185	176	90	1,400
Actual													
Variance													
Debt/ Equity	*Jan.*	*Feb.*	*Mar.*	*Apr.*	*May*	*June*	*July*	*Aug.*	*Sept.*	*Oct.*	*Nov.*	*Dec.*	*End of Year*
Objective	Maintain a 1.1:1 ratio throughout year												
Actual													
Variance													

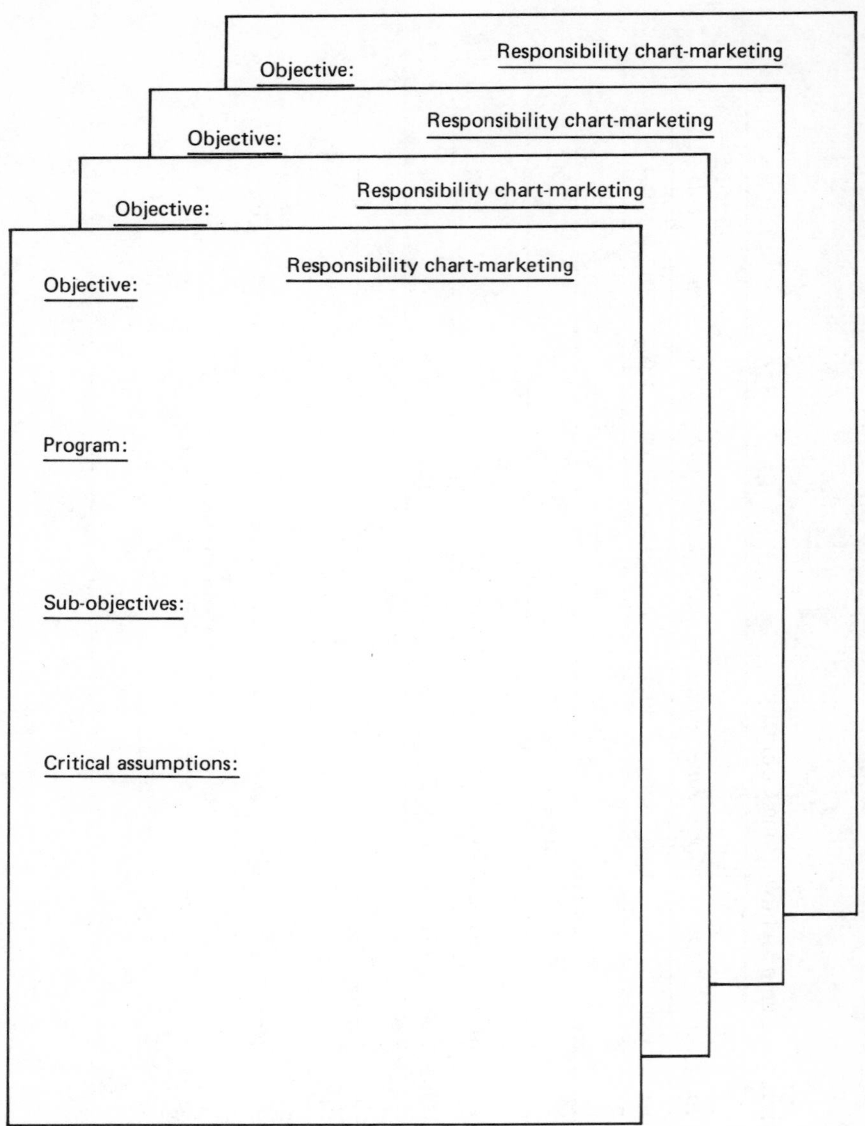

Figure 10-2

Source: Adapted, by permission of the publisher, from *Long-Range Planning for Your Business: An Operating Manual,* Merritt Kastens, © 1976 by AMACOM, a division of American Management Associations, p. 137. All rights reserved.

list of events and conditions that the program depends on for success.

A form of this sort serves as a constant reminder to the managers responsible for carrying out the corporate plan. It helps ensure that the plan becomes a working tool in their minds, not some "theoretical stuff" isolated from the guts of the business.

The president will have responsibility charts for each functional area reporting to him. Normally each functional area head works closely with the president in preparing these charts, although the president may simply have the functional area head present them for approval. After the responsibility charts are agreed upon and prepared, each functional area manager, as well as the president, should have a copy. For example, the production manager would have a copy, the same as the president's, of the responsibility charts for production.

Setting up Activity Schedules

The responsibility charts indicate when the various objectives need to be achieved. These are the "final results." To make sure, however, that there is proper implementation, you want to make sure that certain activities get started when they should and that they are completed on time.

Every executive should have an activity schedule in addition to responsibility charts. This calendar divides each activity into start-up and completion dates. The schedules would normally be prepared by the area managers and presented to the president for approval.

Let's assume that the president has four major functional area managers reporting to him. He would have an activity schedule for each. (Figure 10-3 offers an example.) With only a glance, the president can tell if his director of personnel, for example, is more or less where he or she should be. And the director of personnel uses the same method to check the progress of his or her own immediate subordinates. In this way the use of activity schedules cascades down through all echelons of management.

Action, Activity or Task	Start Date		Completion Date	
	Planned	Actual	Planned	Actual

Figure 10-3 Activity Schedule, Director of Personnel

GUIDELINES FOR ESTABLISHING CONTROLS

Deciding What Should Be Monitored

You can't monitor everything even if you wanted to. And while it's vital to know that your subordinates are keeping pace, it's also important to minimize paperwork. Too much paperwork has at least two devastating effects: It obscures the really important facts and creates so much "shuffling" that it's hard to get productive work done. The trick is to monitor only what you "must" know. Forget about those things that would be nice to know. You must select key objectives and programs to check, and check them selectively.

How many objectives can a competent executive monitor? As Kastens points out, experience suggests five, assuming that each key objective has five subobjectives. The logic behind this number is as follows: Let's assume you have five people reporting to you; each has five key objectives, and each key objective has five subobjectives. That gives you 150 points to monitor, not to speak of your own control calendar. The importance of being selective should be obvious. But since you aren't watching everything, there are going to be some surprises. Some things you thought minor will turn out to be critical. But what's the alternative? You could monitor everything—but you don't have time to do this and still do productive work of your own.

You must decide which objectives require your attention the most. Choosing among them is largely a matter of common sense. Here are a few suggestions you might find helpful. First, consider relative stability. Generally, it's wise to keep an eye on new activities —and personnel—whose behavior you don't know much about. Similarly, it's a good idea to monitor any activity—or person—whose performance has been inconsistent or not wholly dependable, and decrease the frequency of monitoring those you really can count on. Finally, consider the cost, in money and manpower, of gathering the information for these standards.

Accept the fact that even in the best of situations you can't monitor everything. So try to choose objectives (standards) that give you a sense of the overall operation. That way you'll be aware when something starts to go wrong, even if you're not sure at first where it is.

Let's see how the president might select objectives to monitor, using the Acme Metalworking Company as an example. When the president turns his attention to the director of marketing, for instance, he must select what to monitor among a welter of activities. The director of marketing is responsible for, among other factors: sales; market forecasting; market research; developing new customers; advertising; public relations; advertising, research and selling activities that are legal.

The president might decide that although he would like to know how the director of marketing is doing on all of these factors, he will monitor only sales, development of new customers, and results of market research. These are the key marketing objectives essential to the successful attainment of the annual plan. The rest of the items can be covered in informal discussions or, if worse comes to worse, on a crisis basis. In addition to monitoring objectives (accomplishments), the president must also be sure that start-up activities have been implemented on time. Again, it would be nice to know everything but for practical reasons the president should restrict monitoring only to those activities that have a make-or-break potential on the firm's plan. These would be: the start up and completion of the market research for budget low-price desks and file cabinets; the start up and completion for contacting national wholesalers; setting up manufacturers' representatives network for budget low-price desks; and the start up and completion dates for establishing contacts with other manufacturers' representatives for budget low-price file cabinets.

A word of caution. Your people will inevitably direct their energies toward the key areas. You've set objectives (standards) for them. So make sure those areas really are key. Some important objectives are hard to quantify, but don't pass over them simply because they're hard to measure. And it's just as bad to force a quantitative measurement on a situation where it doesn't belong—or where the quantitative measures leave loopholes.

We're all familiar with the sick results these kinds of situations can produce. Here's a minor, but typical, example: A number of years ago certain bomber squadrons had to meet gunnery standards periodically so that in the event of war they would be prepared. The measurable standard was to be able to fire, at 40,000 feet, 80 percent of their 20 mm. cannon load into the ocean below—not exactly comparable with firing at jet fighters approaching at Mach 2. To make matters worse, unfortunately, their guns often froze at this altitude. On at least several occasions, enterprising aircraft commanders dropped down to 2,000 feet, let their guns thaw out, and climbed back to 40,000 feet, where they resumed firing.

Determining Benchmarks for Acceptable Performance

Establish minimum and/or maximum acceptable standards. Recognize that seldom will a single point be practical; usually you're going to have to allow for upper and/or lower limits. For example, past experience may have shown that, for a given month, sales may vary ± 10 percent. In such a case, any volume within these boundaries should be considered normal. Only if the sales volume falls above or below these limits should action be taken.

Establishing Early Warning

Control is the means of keeping progress and results within tolerable limits. But this is sometimes hard to do since the results which you are concerned with are often the effects of a chain reaction. Take company sales and profits (as depicted in Fig. 10-4). This "domino" set-up suggests lags in the system, which Figure 10-5 demonstrates more clearly.

As a case example, suppose there is a decline in Acme's sales. There is a certain time lag before the president receives this information

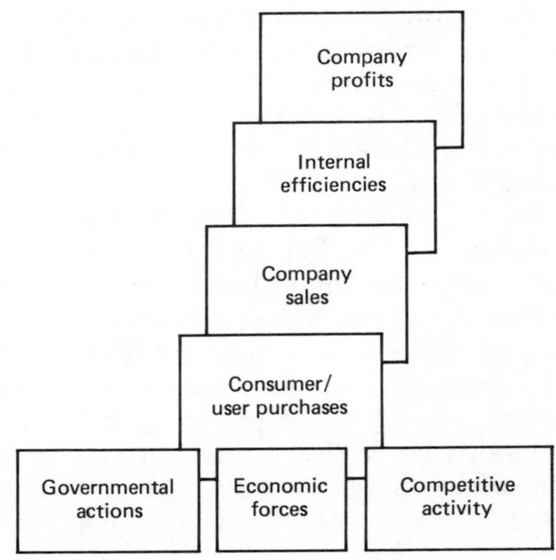

Figure 10-4

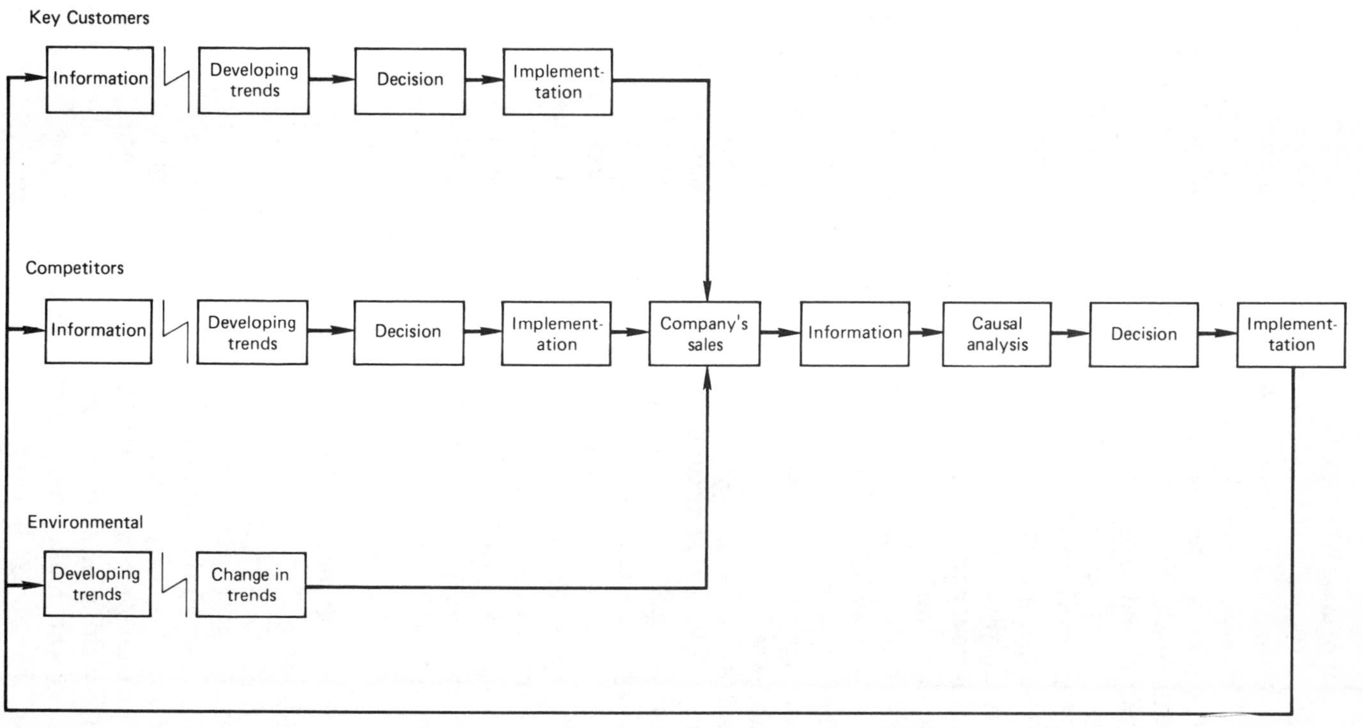
Key Customers
Information
Developing trends
Decision
Implement-tation
Competitors
Information
Developing trends
Decision
Implement-ation
Company's sales
Information
Causal analysis
Decision
Implement-tation
Environmental
Developing trends
Change in trends

Figure 10-5

(the amount of time will depend upon the efficiency of the company's information system). Then, he has to determine the cause of the drop in sales. Sometimes this will be obvious; in other instances, not so obvious. Then, a decision has to be made. Again, the time length will vary. Then, even after the decision has been reached, there's a lag before it's implemented. Suppose the decision was to make certain modifications on the file cabinet drawers. Before this can be done, however, the present production run of desk drawers must be completed. And even after this run, there will have to be a major retooling, with a loss of production time, and then the file cabinets have to be gotten to the point of distribution. And there are similar types of lag on the customer end.

Perhaps this illustration is extreme. But the point is that if you always wait for a decline in company sales before you take countermeasures, it may be too late to keep results within a tolerable band.

These examples underline the importance of early warning systems. Managers simply must be alerted to the "quiet" symptoms that can lead to serious deviations from the plan. And it is at this point that the critical assumptions on the responsibility charts play such an important role. These assumptions should not only be noted, but periodically checked. For example, assume the rate of housing starts is a leading indicator (six months) of industry sales of budget low-price desks. In such a case, a manufacturer of budget low-price desks (Acme) should check this statistic every month (and record it as well). If the actual number of housing starts drops below the forecast, the manufacturer will have time to act before more dominos start to fall. Success is never a certainty, but advance warning to adverse consequences—and timely countermeasures—make it more likely.

Deciding How Often a Standard Should Be Monitored

Deciding on how often to monitor a standard is a tough one. The general answer to this problem is easy enough: You monitor as often as necessary—that is, enough to ensure that the plan is progressing and to pick up symptoms of serious deviations. But what's "enough" varies from situation to situation. A company with a large number of customers who make frequent purchases might find it sensible to monitor sales daily. But it would be practical for a company with several key accounts to check sales levels less often—perhaps every month. Daily reports would serve little purpose. Probably they would just get people upset over "random walks."

Simplicity is vital. Whenever possible avoid clutter which can obscure data that really is important. So be selective. Don't check the performance of all your personnel indiscriminately, for instance. Your really dependable people don't need frequent checks, and they will appreciate the confidence you show in them. (Don't overdo your confidence, of course.)

Planning for implementation and control will be a much simpler task if everyone is aware of the process as they work through strategic and operational planning. Then when it becomes time to create (and then fill out) these forms, your people will understand what's involved. And the next time through the planning cycle, you'll find that your people are developing the process of control even as they work out the strategic and operational plans.

It's something to look forward to. Not only will everyone do it faster each time, but better.

11

Scheduling the Planning Process

Although previous chapters discuss times and stages for each of the planning steps, these recommendations are scattered throughout the text. As a result, the entire process may be hard to visualize. Anyone using this book as a general guide for introducing planning to his or her firm needs something easier to work with.

This chapter offers comprehensive schedules for five separate situations. The first, which is covered in most detail, is the "normal" planning cycle the first time around. However, because sometimes there isn't enough time for the "normal" cycle, the next three situations offer increasingly "compressed" versions. The fifth situation offers suggestions what to do the second time around.

Since this is probably your first introduction to formal comprehensive planning, it's best to stick closely to the recommended schedule (it works!). After you've been through the process once, you'll be in a better position to adapt to the special needs of your own firm. Please note: The chapter does not cover *all* possible meetings of the entire process, but only the essential ones which, if mismanaged, are likely to cause problems.

SITUATION 1: SCHEDULING FOR THE "NORMAL" PLANNING CYCLE

Figure 11-1 offers an overview of the timing for the "normal" planning cycle. The schedule is set according to the calendar year, so you may have to revise it if your company operates according to some other fiscal year.

The first thing to note is that planning stretches throughout the year. There are at least two good reasons for this. First, because operating managers are extremely busy, a few hours here and there are much easier than two or three solid weeks. The second reason for planning throughout the year is because some of the steps can't be rushed. It takes time to gather information, conduct vital surveys, and so forth. Then managers need time to absorb the information they gather; they need time to think.

	Jan	Feb	Mar	Apr	May	June	July	Aug	Sep	Oct	Nov	Dec
Objectives												
Mission												
Policy												
Situation analysis												
Environmental analysis												
Strategy development												
Operational plan												
Pro-forma P & L and balance sheet												
Final adjustments												
Departmental plans & budgets												

Figure 11-1

Background

After you decide on the members of the planning team—you should do so by mid-December—hold an introductory meeting. An hour and a half will be long enough. The president should explain the importance of the planning team and what it should accomplish. Then distribute copies of this book which will supply planning team members with a common background. They should read the book before the next meeting, and be particularly familiar with Chapter 4—because at the next meeting you'll start working on objectives, mission, and policies.

Objectives, Mission, and Policies

In two meetings you should set your objectives, mission, and policies. Schedule the first for about three hours in mid-January. At the meeting have the planning team determine key areas for which the firm should have objectives. You'll probably want to use some measures for the key areas of growth, earnings, and stability. Take no more than one hour to decide what these should be.

The next step is to analyze your company's track record in these areas. Since you probably won't have all the information at hand that you need, assign someone to put it together for the next meeting. Then move on to formulate the firm's mission.

First have the planning members arrive at a consensus on the nature of the firm. Do they see it as single industry, diversified, or conglomerate? Allow an hour or two, but no more, for this job. As you go through the process you'll gain insights that will help you to define better your company's mission. Of course you might arrive at an impasse. If you do, set up a task force to come up with a tentative statement of mission that it will present to the planning team at the next meeting.

Briefly discuss policies before disbanding. Set up a second task force, or use the same one, to prepare tentative policies for discussion at the next meeting.

Schedule the second meeting for about three hours during the third week of January. Analyze the firm's track record in the key objective areas. This will help "bracket in" acceptability and reasonability. Then determine amounts for each area. After this, finish up any work you have left to do on the mission, and turn your attention to policies. If there are still some areas of disagreement or uncertainty, assign the task force to refine further the policies and report back to the team as part of the agenda of a later meeting.

But don't let minor obstacles of this kind prevent you from moving on to the situation analysis.

Situation Analysis

Sometime in the first week of February hold a meeting to embark on the situation analysis. Make sure that the planning team members are already familiar with the material in Chapter 5. Set up timetables at this meeting. Consider using the following one (of course, as discussed in Chapter 5, you may wish to use a more simplified procedure):

February 1:	The initial meeting. Allow about two hours; meet on the premises.
1–7:	The functional areas devise forms for their areas and circulate them to the members of the planning team at least a week before the next meeting.
14:	A three-hour meeting on the premises. Discuss the forms; make any necessary revisions.
March 21:	The functional areas conclude their self-analyses and circulate the completed forms to members of the planning committee.
31:	A one-day conference, preferably off the premises. Discuss the completed forms thoroughly and reach agreement on the firm's major strengths and weaknesses.

Environmental Analysis

After you finish the situation analysis, start on the environmental analysis. Get away for an entire day somewhere around the first of April. Try to schedule the meeting, if possible, at a country club or resort area—someplace special. Have the planning team reread Chapter 6 before the meeting.

This one-day affair requires some advance preparation because you'll want some members to report on past trends. You may even wish to bring in an outsider for this part of your meeting. Spend a lot of time talking about what the future might bring for your company. Decide, on a preliminary basis, on your assumptions and make-or-break variables. Assign a task force to check into these assumptions and forecast plausible ranges for the key variables. Remember: This is almost identical to conventional forecasting, except that now you're projecting ranges as well as the most probable case. Because of the similarity, you may wish to use the forecasting techniques you are already familiar with. Also charge the task force with developing a tentative industry forecast for the coming year.

Give the task force about six weeks to come up with their findings, or about the same amount of time you allow for conventional forecasting. After all, the task force may have to write to associations and other groups for information, conduct surveys, analyze results, and the like. But by May 15 the task force should be circulating their findings to the planning team. Have the members study the findings and be ready to discuss them at a meeting during the first of June.

Once again, get away for a day (if you can, try someplace different). After the task force formally reports their findings, invite discussion. After you reach a concensus, which may not be easy, hammer out two or three plausible descriptions of what the future for your company might be like. Be sure to include the most-probable- and worst-case futures.

Before you adjourn this meeting, spend some time discussing the tentative industry forecast for the coming year and general ideas about strategy formulation.

Strategy Formulation

At your last meeting on environmental analysis discuss your approach for strategy formulation. At this time appoint a task force. Have them use projections from the most-probable-case future to estimate your position on the market attractiveness/company strengths matrix, and perform gap analysis.

Give them two weeks to do the job and then have them circulate their findings to members of the planning team. Schedule your next meeting about one week later (approximately June 21). Before the meeting assign someone (the planning coordinator, if you have one) to prepare several "rough" charts. These should be about the size of a flip chart pad—the 27-by-34-inch size is fine—and posted on a wall so that all the participants can see them clearly. Use a broad-tip felt marker.

You should have one chart for each of the following:

- Objectives
- Mission

- Policies (summarized)
- Strengths and weaknesses of the firm
- Most-probable-case future
- Position on market attractiveness/company strengths matrix
- Gap analysis

One hour to draw up the charts is plenty. After all, the information has already been gathered, and rough charts are all you want at this point.

The planning team members should be completely familiar with the material in Chapters 7 and 8 before this "June 21" meeting (schedule it for one-half day on the premises). With the charts as reference, the president should review the company's objectives, mission, policies, situation analysis, and most-probable-case future. Then he or she should invite the members to discuss the firm's position on the market attractiveness/company strengths matrix. This may turn out to be a heated issue, but you might as well resolve it now. If the team members end up hopelessly deadlocked, consider stopping to gather additional information. But if you can't get the information in two weeks, you'll have to wait until the next time for definitive answers and do the best with what you have. Certainly it's to your advantage to arrive at a compromise decision now.

Move on to the last chart: gap analysis. After you reach agreement on this one, you'll have a pretty good idea how much you can accomplish by pursuing strategies within Sector 1. Remember that you should move into Sectors 2, 3, and 4 in order, and only after you have thoroughly explored the opportunities in Sector 1.

How and when you schedule meetings after this point depends on what you need to get done, vacation schedules, and the like. (Incidentally, you should post the rough charts at every meeting.) But follow the guidelines suggested in Chapter 8, and by all means consider using task forces.

In any case, you should arrive at your tentative strategy by July 31. This gives you a month to (1) make financial projections, (2) develop contingency plans, and (3) make any revisions that become necessary because of the results from (1) and (2).

At the end of the month put the strategy in writing. This should take only a few hours. At the last meeting on strategy, when you approve it in its final form, assign the functional areas to begin developing their operational plans.

Putting Together the Operational Plan

If your present system has operational planning pretty well under control, you may wish to follow your present procedure. It's to your advantage to change as little as possible. However, you may wish to use the procedure recommended in this book, particularly if you're not all that happy with what you're doing.

Post the flip charts on the wall during each meeting on operational planning. This will help to keep the tactics you develop "on strategy." If you're adhering to the schedule, have the functional area managers circulate their respective operational plans to each member of the planning team by September 15. A week later get away from the plant for an entire day to discuss, very closely, each of these plans. Allow a week for any necessary changes.

Preparing Pro Forma P. & L. and Balance Sheets

Run pro forma P. & L. and balance sheets. These shouldn't take your finance officer any longer than several days to develop. Of course, he (or she) could do it in several hours if he had all the data. But probably he's going to have to get some additional information from other functional area managers.

Making Final Adjustments

About the second week in October get the planning team together for another one-day meeting. Have the finance officer go over the P. & L. and balance sheets (make sure these were distributed at least several days before the meeting). Make up your mind that during this meeting you're going to have to make some final adjustments and negotiations. You may find that you'll need a number of meetings during the next three weeks to get these jobs done.

Since the next step is to set detailed programs and budgets within each functional area, the planning team need not concern itself with further steps. In fact, the planning team has accomplished everything the president hoped for back in December, at least for the time being.

SITUATION 2: YOU'VE GOT NINE MONTHS INSTEAD OF TWELVE

It's already April.

You might say, "O.K. We've lost three months. Let's wait until next year."

Don't. The benefits of long-range planning will still be great, and the greatest benefit of all is what you learn from working through the process. The schedule you should follow is charted in Figure 11-2.

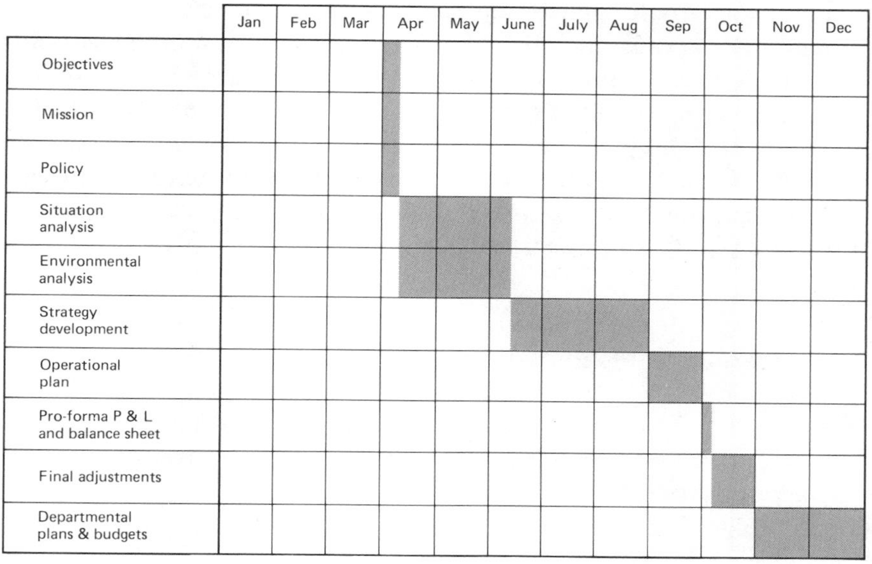

	Jan	Feb	Mar	Apr	May	June	July	Aug	Sep	Oct	Nov	Dec
Objectives												
Mission												
Policy												
Situation analysis												
Environmental analysis												
Strategy development												
Operational plan												
Pro-forma P & L and balance sheet												
Final adjustments												
Departmental plans & budgets												

Figure 11-2

Objectives, Mission, and Policies

Follow the schedule for the normal planning cycle in setting objectives, mission, and policies.

Situation Analysis

With less time available you eliminate one major step in the situation analysis. Instead of deliberating on the proper forms, simply ask each functional area to give their reports. Then hash out the strengths and weaknesses of the firm.

Environmental Analysis

The environmental analysis should coincide with the situation analysis. Clearly there will be less time, so compress it where you have to.

Strategy Development

Prior to strategy development, as in the normal planning cycle, the task force will determine your position on the market attractiveness/company strengths matrix and perform gap analysis. But the task force will have only one week to compile the results, and the planning team only two to three days to study them. There will also be less time to cogitate over the proper strategy, which means you'll be less likely to make major changes (naturally you don't want to make such modifications unless you have more complete information). And you will have to shorten the time you allow for developing (1) financial projections, (2) contingency plans, and (3) any revisions in the base plan.

Operational Planning

Don't compress the time you allow for operational planning. But if you're accustomed to doing it in one month, fine. You can use the extra month for strategy development.

SITUATION 3: YOU'RE STARTING VERY LATE—IN ONE MONTH YOU MUST GET TO WORK ON OPERATIONAL PLANS

Objectives, Mission, and Policies

In determining objectives, mission, and policies, stick to the recommended time span in Situation 1.

Situation Analysis

Schedule a one-half day meeting for situation analysis and come up with a list of strengths and weaknesses.

Environmental Analysis

Hash out your analysis of environmental factors in half a day. You'll just have to go with best estimates.

Strategy Formulation

Spend one day and come up with a basic strategy. Try to follow, in abbreviated fashion, the guidelines for Situation 1. Clearly it would be better not to make major changes this time around.

You might consider a weekend "retreat" where you can do both the environmental analysis and strategy formulation.

Operational Planning

Once again, don't change your operational planning procedures unless you think it's essential to do so. If you have some extra time to devote to strategic planning, that's great. But don't create some at the expense of operational planning.

SITUATION 4: YOU'RE STARTING VERY, VERY LATE. IN FACT, YOU'RE ALREADY INVOLVED IN OPERATIONAL PLANNING

Forget comprehensive planning this year. If you stop and go back to establish objectives and so forth, you're liable to foul everybody up. Compression of long-range planning is valuable up to a point—which you are now past. Wait until next year. And then do a good job of it.

SITUATION 5: THE SECOND TIME AROUND

Congratulations! You're already through the hardest part. You now know more about which planning processes will work in your company than the author of this book does.

Make whatever changes you know are necessary. You'll be pleased at how much easier it is the second time—and more fun, too. And even more so the third time around.

12

The Finished Plan

Commit the plan to writing. But don't try to make it a masterpiece of prose. In fact, make it as short as possible—a summary, in effect, of the objectives, mission, policies, situation analysis, and so forth.

Call the plan the "Corporate Plan." There is no need to separate the long-range and the short-range plans. Since this is comprehensive planning they should be kept together.

SECTIONS OF THE PLAN

The suggested page lengths are for the smaller, single industry firm. If your company should have several product lines that are affected by different environmental forces and require separate basic forecasts and strategies, then, of course, certain sections of the plan will have to be longer.

Objectives (one-half to one page). Here's how *NOT* to start: "After careful deliberation the Corporate Planning Team decided that objectives should be energizing as well as. . . ." Avoid this sort of nonsense in all the sections. Just state the objectives for Years 1 and 5. You won't need any prose on this page.

Mission and Policies (one to two pages). Copy down the mission and policies you've already agreed upon. Have one subsection for mission, another for policies.

Situation Analysis (one page). Insert the summary sheet of the corporation's strengths and weaknesses.

Environmental Forecasts (one to two pages). List your long-range assumptions and make-or-break variables. In one or two paragraphs describe the most-probable-case future.

Basic Strategies (one page). Part 1 of the strategy (see page 218). This should consist of two sections:

Types of products and/or services.
Target markets and how they will be reached.

Short-Range Environmental Forecast (one page). List short-range assumptions, the predicted values of the make-or-break variables, and the resulting forecast.

The Annual Plan—Summary (one page). Summarize the major activities your corporation wishes to undertake and/or complete during this next year.

Functional Area Plans (one page for each functional area). Summarize the major plans for each area.

Statement Describing How the Annual Plan Contributes to the Corporate Strategy (one page). This section helps assure that the short-range plan is geared to the firm's overall strategy.

Schedule of Implementation, Required Resources, Revenues, and Profits (two to three pages). Divide this section into two parts:

Operational: one to two pages
Strategic: Part 3 of the strategy (see page 218)

Risks/Alternative Future Operating Environments and Contingency Plans (four pages). Divide this section into two parts also:

Operational: two pages
Strategic: Part 2 of the strategy (see page 218)

The members of the planning team and the functional area managers should receive a copy of the Corporate Plan. In addition, each functional area manager should keep a detailed copy of his or her functional area plans and budgets immediately following a copy of the corporate plan.

The final section, for all members of the planning team, should contain their individual responsibility charts and activity schedules.

If you've proceeded carefully, step by step, you'll find that you've actually written the Corporate Plan by the time you finish operational planning. All you need to do is put it together.

Perhaps you've been wondering, "Should our company have a planning manual?" The answer is, "No." You bought this book to get you off on a start. By now it should have done that. In the future, as you work together, you'll develop your own model—and it will be one that really suits you. Prepare a planning timetable (see Fig. 11-1). But don't write out what you're going to do at each step. Spend the time developing workable strategies and plans.

13

Delegating Authority

For comprehensive planning to work, as has been pointed out throughout the book, you'll have to have a high degree of involvement. And since now your company will be more participative, you'll have to have more delegation—at all levels within the organization. In fact, the success of the planning process may hinge on the diffusion of effective delegation. Often, of course, delegation is not necessary. But if you've accumulated people under you—whether in your department, division, or business—you've presumably hired them because the volume and nature of the business demand it. There is work for them to do; they have a job and you must define what it is and permit them to go about doing it. As one moves to higher echelons of management, the need for delegation becomes more and more apparent. As one president commented:

> When our audit was complete, we discovered we had lost money. I had been president for a number of years and we had never experienced a loss before. It really shook me up. I called my group together. From

This chapter is a modification of the author's monograph *Delegation at the Chief Executive Level,* © 1972 by the President's Association Inc., American Management Associations, 135 West 50th Street, New York, N.Y. 10020. Adapted with permission of the publisher.

> their comments I realized that a major cause of the company's problems was that I had been running a one-man show. I decided that my style wasn't right, so I set out trying to delegate. But I would not want to give the impression that I became an effective delegator overnight.

To be willing to delegate does not come easily. It can be particularly hard for people who are not used to doing it. Many executives, when they first become managers, want to do nearly everything themselves. As time goes on, they find that if they want to get things done, they have to delegate. Sometimes this realization does not come early or without pain.

Although developing delegation skills often requires tough self-discipline, payoff potentials are high. The way to good management is to let people make their own decisions. The president of a large food store chain emphasized this:

> Most people have a lot more potential than they are given credit for. Usually they are not given an opportunity to use their natural skills. But if you throw them in, they will swim.
>
> A good manager doesn't expect his executives to operate at 100 percent efficiency and don't expect their judgments to be like yours all the time. If you limit judgment making in your organization to your capabilities, you limit the amount your company can accomplish.

By having people who can—and are willing to—make decisions, you can capitalize on opportunities that might otherwise be lost. If you involve people and they believe that their help and confidence are necessary, you create an atmosphere that is beneficial to all.

Are there short-term losses? Perhaps. Certainly there are instances when you could do the task better than the person to whom it has been delegated. Often, however, a person who has been devoting his or her full time to managing an area may be able to do a better job.

Sometimes, too, subordinates have more capabilities than you imagine. Here's an example given by the president of one company:

> Over a period of several years we had union elections. In my mind, whether we had a union in the company was an important issue. I considered management representation to be my responsibility.

Then, in another year or so, we were again faced with a union election. I said to myself that if I'm going to practice what I preach—because I started practicing differently after I had become aware that I had been making a lot of operational decisions—the vice-president of manufacturing should represent management. So I turned the responsibility over to him.

For the three or four weeks before the election, I deliberately got away from the office as much as I could so I wouldn't interfere. The result of the election? Well, he did a lot better job of representing management than I previously had.

Because of the importance of delegation—and the difficulty of effective implementation—this chapter offers some practical pointers on how to delegate effectively.

IDENTIFYING WHAT SHOULD BE DELEGATED

Hard and fast rules are not very helpful in determining what you should delegate. However, certain general guidelines can be followed.

Is there any doubt whether the task should be delegated? If there is, delegate. Most people underdelegate.

Are there capable people to whom you can delegate the task? If so, delegate. But, as an executive cautioned:

> There is one most important thing about delegation: You have to have capable people. If I were to bring an eighteen-year-old in and make him vice-president of manufacturing it would be a mistake to delegate almost anything to him because he would not possess the capability.

How important is the task to your company's functional areas, departments, or the company's future? If the task is not important (relatively), delegate.

Is the organization in crisis? Regardless of the merits of delegation in the normal operating situation, you may have to plunge in yourself in a crisis situation. For example, a man who took over a company with a net worth of $30 million that was losing $1 million a month made substantially all major management decisions himself until the crisis had passed.

SPECIAL CONSIDERATIONS AFFECTING EXECUTIVE DELEGATION

As a practical matter, you have to vary your manner of delegation. The extent of delegation depends, in part, on competency. New people should report to you often. When you're sure they understand their responsibilities, the frequency of these meetings should be progressively reduced. On the whole, capable people need fewer and less detailed directions. Not only can you depend on them to do the job, they'll also report back on how they're coming along. Others, unfortunately, need to be prodded every step of the way. Moreover, an individual can be extremely capable in several areas but inexperienced in some essential part of a new job. Under these conditions carefully weigh assignments of responsibility and set up tighter controls in the areas of lesser experience.

The approach to delegation should be adapted to meet the needs of each executive. Few people can be treated in exactly the same way; personality and temperament have an enormous effect on working relationships. When executives tend to cut across established lines of responsibility, delegate authority to them very explicitly, in writing. For others, more informal instructions may be adequate. Some people need suggestions to spur their imaginations on. For others, it is inadvisable to recommend that a task should be accomplished in a certain way. Even a casual suggestion may make them reluctant to consider alternative approaches.

The same applies to the style of delegation. As one president noted, "With some people you can lay it right on the line. Others are sensitive; you have to lead a bit. If you lay it on the line with these people, a wall comes up and then you have to knock down the wall."

How specific you are in giving your instructions should also vary. Be more specific in critical areas. Another president advised, "It's sort of a rationing of time. It takes more effort to be specific, so you tend to do it only when it is important."

Vary the pattern of delegation with your own experience. You can be more specific in areas where you have your greatest competence.

Where you are less knowledgeable, you can still have specific objectives, but you have to rely more on your people to help establish specific objectives.

DESIGNING THE ORGANIZATIONAL STRUCTURE

What you delegate, and who you delegate it to, are inseparable from your organizational structures. In theory, organizational structure should be simply and logically oriented—for example, according to division, function, process, product, territory, or customer groupings. As a practical matter, however, the specific strengths of available personnel often influence the structuring. Usually a person does not have all of the necessary capabilities for the job; and one of the major delegation pitfalls is assigning tasks to individuals who are not fully equipped to handle them. Consequently, in some organizations there is no attempt to reflect a rigid departmentalization of responsibilities. Naturally there are titles. But in those companies you will see people handling jobs that you would not expect them to handle in terms of their job titles.

Consider modifying the structure when necessary to meet the qualifications of personnel. As a chief executive officer emphasized:

> An organization structure must be fluid and suit the capabilities of the best men you have available for the jobs. If a man doesn't have the experience, background and/or talent for a certain function that his predecessor had, then you assign that particular function to somebody else. This may be at variance with authorities who say that if a certain job requires ten qualities, find a man who has these ten qualities but don't change the job requirements. However, if you find a man with these ten qualities, you are going to find a guy with ten mediocre qualities, and you will get a mediocre cluck. I'd rather get a person with six strong qualities and then give those other four functions to a person who is strong in those areas. That way you will have two superstars.

For example, perhaps your manager of manufacturing is an excellent production man but not suited for labor negotiations work. Consider shifting the responsibility for labor negotiations to another executive.

Tailoring the job to the individual, of course, can result in difficulties when that position becomes vacant. For example, suppose a vice-president of administration fills an unusual combination of roles: director of materials procurement, director of engineering, and chief of the management information system. If he or she should leave suddenly, it might be impossible to find someone with all those talents.

But contingency planning may help minimize this inherent danger. In one company the president has developed five different organizational charts for the next six years, taking into account retirements and potential vacancies that might result from the death or withdrawal of key executives.

DELEGATING RECURRING TASKS

Most delegation involves recurring tasks. Use job descriptions and performance standards in delegating such responsibilities.

The main purpose of job descriptions is to outline general areas of responsibilities, so everybody knows who is to do what. Job descriptions are usually couched in general, qualitative terms, and there are several ways to prepare them. They can be prepared jointly by the executive, the subordinate, and the personnel department. Perhaps the best way is to let the person with that job describe it himself (preferably in his own handwriting—otherwise you're likely to get his secretary's version of what he does). His involvement will help make the description more than just another piece of paper. In any case, the draft should be reviewed by the manager and circulated to other executives whose responsibilities may overlap or conflict with that position.

Job descriptions should be considered flexible. Since circumstances may change or problems arise, they should be reviewed periodically. Moreover, since jobs have a way of forming themselves around their present incumbent, it's usually wise to reexamine them whenever there is a change in personnel.

But you need more than job description for effective control. Because job descriptions are generally written in qualitative terms, it can be difficult to measure performance against them. And, the more you delegate, the greater your need to know if your subordinates are performing adequately. Defining responsibility and authority has to be followed by quantified performance standards. So a monitoring system is crucial. You should have few problems installing one if you have gone about corporate planning in a systematic fashion. In fact the responsibility charts and activity schedules (Chap. 10) derived from the corporate plan serve such a purpose.

DELEGATING NONRECURRING TASKS

Job descriptions and performance standards will not cover everything. Even without emergencies there will be occasional tasks that lie outside of everyone's normal work. Too often the delegation of nonrecurring tasks is handled casually. The order is given in an offhand manner. Or it's given in the plant—and before the manager gets back to his office, something comes up and, as a result, he doesn't get the job done.

To effectively delegate nonrecurring responsibilities, make sure that the person knows what he (or she) is expected to do, when he is expected to do it, and that he is responsible for his performance. In some companies, where the order is issued orally and not completed, the delegator is responsible. If you wish to delegate nonrecurring responsibilities in writing, consider using duplicating, autographic forms. Give the original to the person who had been assigned the responsibility and keep the carbon. The file copy should be checked periodically until the task is completed.

NONINTERFERENCE

Often the hardest part of delegating is keeping out of your subordinates' way so that they can do their jobs. If you become involved in their day-to-day operations, you undermine them. And, when you become involved, there's a tendency for the person who is running a program to turn it over to you.

But avoiding involvement is not easy. It's also difficult showing interest without unduly influencing subordinates. As one president stated:

> It doesn't matter what you say, you are the guy whose picture is on the annual report. Your subordinate knows who you are. He is going to hang on to everything you say. Even a casual opinion will be accepted

in a much stronger way than you intend it. Consequently you can't get involved and at the same time expect others to take the major responsibility.

Unless you want the responsibility yourself (and why, then, did you delegate it in the first place?), you'll have to minimize your involvement. There are a number of ways to do this.

Keep Your Hands off Delegated Tasks. You can take the approach that, although you're ultimately accountable, most crises that happen in your company/functional area/department are not yours. The resolution of a crisis really belongs to the person to whom the responsibility has been delegated.

Counsel Subordinates but Don't Make Their Decisions. Except in extreme cases, don't help your subordinates. If you have an executive who constantly hesitates to make decisions about hard problems, he's probably the wrong man for the job. Let them know that you expect them to solve their own problems. Able people like it that way. On the other hand, keep your door open. Subordinates should feel free to talk with you when they have problems. There's a subtle technique of giving counsel, but avoiding decision making. Ask your executives questions until they have formulated their own plans.

Avoid Committee Meetings of Subordinates When It's Not Essential You Attend. Your presence tends to inhibit discussion; your executives just sit. Your absence will usually provide a permissive atmosphere that allows upcoming executives to express their own opinions, fight their own battles, and ultimately become more effective managers.

Be Aware of Exerting Unintentional Influence. Your very presence influences subordinates; they will not act freely when you are around them, even if you attend a meeting at which you say nothing at all. They know your ideas, your attitudes, how you've dealt with problems in the past—and this will inevitably influence how they act now. It is vital, by the way, that they really believe you want them to handle the delegated responsibility in their own way.

Exercise Care in Dealing with Lower-Level Managers. Be particularly careful in dealing with personnel below the level reporting directly to you. You may find that you're unintentionally undercutting the authority of those who report to you. Even "friendly chats" can be dangerous. One president remarked:

> A president can't go out into the plant and be the same guy he was before he was president. For example, an old buddy who was and still is a foreman comes up and says, "Hey boss, do you know what the hell is happening now? The whole place is coming apart since you no longer are plant manager." So the president goes into the new manager's office and says, "What the hell is going on out there?"... Some guys are smart enough to try to use a higher-level manager as a tool.

A casual question may cause you to become more involved than you had intended. Never ask an employee, who does not report directly to you, "How are things going?" Of course you should talk to people, but you just don't leave that kind of door open.

Stay out of the Way. When you feel the temptation to involve yourself with work you've delegated, resist it. If that's too difficult, try to get out of the office. Make an inspection trip. Visit customers. Attend a conference. While you're gone, your subordinates will have to make their own decisions, which is what you want them to do. If you're around, they're likely to drop by and ask your advice, thereby taking the pressure of decision off their backs. Let them know that you expect them to take over.

LIVING WITH DELEGATION

Perhaps the hardest part of delegation is to keep from personally taking corrective action. A number of psychological factors make it difficult. You're self-confident, and you feel you can do the job better than anyone else. You've achieved your position by reaching for responsibility; it's painful to watch others. It's often easier, quicker, and more efficient to do things yourself. You're action-oriented and want to get things done immediately. Nonetheless, there are some techniques for learning to live with delegation.

Living with Minor Differences in Procedures

Subordinates will usually use methods different from the ones you advocate. But you should recognize that to develop strong people you have to be guided by results rather than by methods. After all, as long as their actions attain results, are legal and ethical, and don't cause problems in other divisions of the company, that's all you're interested in. Refrain from nagging subordinates and making them overly dependent.

In addition, remember that your people are bound to make some mistakes, that it's impossible to be aggressive without making errors. Too much criticism will undermine that aggressiveness, and in a very short period of time.

Here are techniques some executives have found useful in living with minor differences.

> I bite my tongue and walk away.
>
> I think of my past mistakes to remind myself that I am not so smart after all.
>
> I keep my own mouth shut and only open it when my advice is requested.
>
> Having established specific performance criteria, I adopt an attitude that if a subordinate meets these criteria then he has done a satisfactory job. If I'm unhappy with the methodology, then I haven't established tight enough performance standards.

But times will come when a subordinate does something that you don't intend to reverse but that you strongly disagree with. When this happens, nothing is better than an old-fashioned person-to-person talk. You may be surprised when you hear your subordinate's point of view. Of course if you think there's a much better way of doing this particular piece of business, you can make that clear. But don't make the decision for him, and do support him even if you disagree with the decision he finally arrives at.

Handling Major Differences in Decision Making

Reverse your subordinates' decisions only as a last resort. Even though it may be absolutely necessary, your action serves to undermine the whole system of delegation. Everytime you reverse anyone's decision, it tends to undermine the credibility of delegation. As one president stated:

> Besides, it [a reversal] bruises a man's ego. If you can live with the decision, it's much better than to destroy the guy. Your job is to build self-confidence in people, and to improve their self-reliance to the point where they will accept the delegated responsibilities and carry

> them out as their own. If you are constantly reversing them, you are going to have trouble getting these people to accept the responsibility. So you're better off suffering a loss.

Another executive claimed:

> If you are careful you can, perhaps, veto once—maybe twice—but if you have to do it more than that, you had better get yourself a new executive, because you've spoiled the one you've got. When it happens the second time the executive is apt to ask himself, "Who is supposed to be running the show?"

On the whole, you may often be better off taking a loss, if it's one you can afford, than making a reversal.

One way of avoiding reversals is to avoid assigning responsibility in areas that might lead to reversals. Instead, have your subordinates make recommendations in place of decisions. Another, as we mentioned earlier, is to have someone who has just taken on new responsibilities report to you more often.

Backing up and Turning Around

In the longer view, if you're unhappy with the results of delegation to certain people, you're going to have to make changes. The way you do so is important. Your action will affect not only individuals, but (indirectly) the delegation process itself. Changes that are not manifestly fair, or warranted by the facts, or reasonably considerate of the individuals involved, will discourage other executives from accepting the risks and opportunities inherent in all delegation.

If you and a subordinate are unable to work together effectively, the options are essentially to transfer the executive to lesser or other responsibilities, retrain him, or let him go. The normal result of demotion is that the down-graded executive leaves the company. Transfers that are tantamount to demotion have much the same effect.

Usually retraining doesn't work at the executive level. Many difficulties stem from a lack of common sense on the part of some executives. Some stem from personal troubles. And possibly most important, some stem from the lack of skills in handling conflict situations. Often these problems are fundamental and too difficult to correct, at least in the short run. Usually effective performance of delegated responsibilities is so important to the success of the company that long-term development of the subordinate is not a feasible alternative.

When the subordinate is relatively new to the organization, or it's impossible to use him in another position, termination may be the only answer. Such dismissals are painful for everyone.

Timely evaluations of performance will reduce the need for this final step. Be frank, even brutal. After such appraisals most executives manage to get the job done, or begin to look for new jobs. Another useful tactic: During staff meetings have each executive respond to four basic questions: What was the plan? Where are you in relation to the plan? Why are you behind? What are you going to do about it? Few people can bear to stand up day after day and tell their peers that they are failing. Either they manage to get the job done, or they leave.

MOTIVATING SUBORDINATES TO DELEGATE

If you accept the philosophy that the potential rewards of delegation exceed risks, then you also recognize that the process should be extended throughout your organization. To make sure this happens, create an atmosphere in which this delegation cascade can function. You must also take the steps essential to ensure its operation at all company levels.

Creating the Atmosphere

If you expect subordinates to delegate, you must delegate. When you do, you create an aura that spreads. If, for one reason or another, you don't delegate, everyone else will readily find excuses for not doing so either.

At periodic meetings stress the importance of effective delegation. Subordinates must know that they are expected to delegate, and that they will be evaluated on their success.

But such encouragement, at least by itself, is not enough. A good delegator needs to feel secure in his job. Insecure executives tend to delegate less. Do everything you reasonably can to help your people develop faith in themselves—though in this regard nothing is as important as the way you assign and preside over the responsibilities you've delegated.

Then emphasize that you expect mistakes will be made. When managers feel that no allowance is made for human error, they tend to make most decisions themselves in order to minimize mistakes. When the reverse is true, they feel freer to delegate. To help create a tolerance for minor errors, consider telling subordinates, as one president does, "If you have anybody reporting to you who hasn't made a mistake in the last sixty days, you better get rid of him because obviously he isn't doing anything."

Making Sure It Happens

Probably the best way to ensure that the delegation cascade is working is to insist that management by objectives be practiced at all levels. Clearly defined responsibilities and quantified performance standards encourage delegation. When your subordinates know what is expected of them and what they should expect from their employers, they are generally more willing to delegate. And so on down the line. It is management's responsibility, at each level, to make sure that the procedure is adopted by the echelon of management below it. The results: Managers on all levels must specify what they want their personnel to accomplish and also define the operating constraints. In this way delegation becomes an inherent part of the corporate system.

14

A Look Back and a Look Ahead

A typical reaction at the close of seminars where this approach is discussed is: "It makes a great deal of sense." The reason for this reaction is that we already do the general process intuitively: We decide where we want to go, consider strengths and weaknesses, simultaneously develop strategic and operational plans, and think about what we'll do when things go wrong. The major benefit of these seminars—and this book—is that they show how to formalize, in a shirt-sleeve way, what we do instinctively. The value of the formal approach is readily apparent: It enables involvement and communication among the firm's top executives. Then, too, the formal approach causes top management to be more rigorous in their thinking, and it ensures that planning will be done and with a certain degree of thoroughness.

Key to the process is the shirt-sleeve approach, which enables operating managers to be planners in a way that does not interfere with their operating responsibilities. To begin with, setting objectives, mission, and policies can be done in two or three meetings.

The situation analysis will take more time, but you don't need to (and you certainly don't want to) cover everything all at once. Besides, operating managers can delegate some of the data collection. All in all, this may take four to five days of their time. But look at the benefits. Operating managers will have a much better understanding of their own functional areas. Besides providing a better foundation for long-range plans, this better understanding will probably pay off in the first year by pointing to deficiencies that should be corrected (and conversely, opportunities that can be capitalized on) immediately. Moreover, the operating managers will have a much better grasp of the company as a whole. That's what you want, because they'll be better able to understand the problems of other areas, and that will lead to more constructive problem solving.

Strategy formulation will take another four to five days of operating managers' time. Naturally the entire process of strategy development will take longer, but you can use task forces to develop forecasts, make special studies, and the like.

Normally you would use such task forces anyway. But because your top managers will have been involved every step along the way, change will be more understandable, results more acceptable, and deep personal commitments more likely.

As far as developing operating plans, this you do anyway.

All in all, the time required is small compared to possible benefits. And also keep in mind that the next time around, the process will be easier, take less time, and even be more fun to do.

Sometimes presidents are reluctant to start formal long-range planning. They're afraid that it might not work out, and they don't want to be involved in a failure of any kind. The fear is justified. Regardless of how solid a president's position is, he or she cannot afford failures, particularly those which will be obvious to top executives of the firm and members of the board.

Here's three basic pointers on how to keep comprehensive planning from failing. First, don't overpromise. Remember that even with hard work it takes time to develop a sophisticated planning system within a company. Some experts have placed this time at five years. Accept the fact that the first plans are going to be rather rudimentary. Make sure that no one expects more. Emphasize that what you are doing is involving the top people within your organization, utilizing their talents to help decide upon the proper course of action for the firm.

Second, be sure to keep the planning process simple. This will not be easy to do. You'll always see how the process could be done a little bit better. But accept the fact that planning is not a natural activity, and that people tend to fight it. Again, if you structure the planning process so that your executives can get involved in it without taking too much time from their operating duties, you'll meet with less resistance. Keep it simple enough that the pressure for more detailed methods of planning comes from members of the planning team (a pull variety) instead of having it come from the president (a push variety). Try to make planning fun to do. The planning team should look forward to the meetings. Treat members of the planning team like top executives (which they are). When possible, hold meetings at special places. Get away from the plant. Try to vary the spots. Consider inviting wives to join the team for a wrap-up dinner.

Finally, you must make sure that you go through all of the steps. Set up, and adhere to, timetables. And insist that members of the planning team do their assigned tasks, and thoroughly.

Remember, you have a leg up on making it work. You're involving people, and people like to become involved in important activities. And certainly deciding upon the future of the firm is important work. When things arise—like the multitude of daily fires—that make formal planning hardly seem worth the while, keep in mind this question: "What are the costs of not doing comprehensive planning?"

Notes

PREFACE

1. Kenneth Boulding, "The Prospects of Economic Abundance," a lecture at the Nobel Conference, Gustavus Adolphus College, 1966, as quoted in Alvin Toffler, *Future Shock* (New York: Bantam, 1970), p. 13.

CHAPTER 1

1. Stanley S. Thune and Robert J. House, "Where Long-Range Planning Pays Off," *Business Horizons,* 8 (August 1970), pp. 81–87.
2. H. Igor Ansoff, J. Avener, R. G. Brandenberg, F. E. Portner, and R. Radosevich, "Does Planning Pay? The Effect of Planning on Success of Acquisitions in American Firms," *Long-Range Planning,* 3 (December 1970), 2–7; H. Igor Ansoff, R. C. Brandenberg, F. E. Portner, and R. Radosevich, *Acquisition Behavior of U.S. Manufacturing Firms 1946–1965* (Nashville, Tenn.: Vanderbilt University, 1971); D. M. Herold, "Long-Range Planning and Organizational Performance," *Academy of Management Journal,* 15 (March 1972), 91–102.
3. "Amcord: A Cautious Second Try at Diversifying Beyond Cement," *Business Week,* March 13, 1978, pp. 104–6.
4. "Leesona: The Accelerating Move Away From Textile Machinery," *Business Week,* April 17, 1978, p. 98.

CHAPTER 3

1. George A. Steiner, *Top Management Planning* (New York: Macmillan, 1969), pp. 126–32.

CHAPTER 4

1. Rochelle O'Connor, *Corporate Guides to Long-Range Planning* (New York: The Conference Board, 1976), p. 67.
2. "Focus on Balance Sheet Reform," *Business Week,* June 7, 1976, p. 56.
3. F. Kappel, *Vitality in a Business Enterprise* (New York: McGraw-Hill, 1960), pp. 37–38.
4. Charles H. Kepner and Benjamin B. Tregoe, *The Rational Manager* (New York: McGraw-Hill, 1965), pp. 183–90.
5. Edmund P. Learned, C. Roland Christensen, Kenneth R. Andrews, and William D. Guth, *Business Policies Text and Cases,* original ed. (Homewood, Ill.: Richard D. Irwin, 1965), p. 229.
6. O'Connor, *Corporate Guides to Long-Range Planning,* p. 22.
7. Congressional Research Service, *Long-Range Planning,* prepared for the Subcommittee on the Environment and the Atmosphere of the Committee on Science and Technology, U.S. House of Representatives, Ninety-Fourth Congress (Washington, D.C.: Library of Congress Serial BB, May 1976), p. 294.
8. "Arcata: A Plan to Hang Tough in the Business It Knows Best," *Business Week,* May 1, 1978, p. 96.
9. William F. Christopher, "Marketing Planning that Gets Things Done," *Harvard Business Review,* 48 (September-October 1970), pp. 56–64.
10. Textron Inc., Annual Report, 1976, p. 4.
11. Textron Inc., Annual Report, 1976, p. 4.
12. Congressional Research Service, *Long-Range Planning,* pp. 269, 272. Reprinted with permission of Hewlett-Packard Company.

CHAPTER 6

1. "Two Poor Years for the Forecasters," *Business Week,* December 21, 1974, p. 51.
2. "Two Poor Years for the Forecasters," p. 51.
3. Frank L. Moreland, "Dialectic Methods in Forecasting," *The Futurist,* 5, No. 4 (August 1971), p. 169.
4. Robert E. Linneman and Harold E. Klein, "The Use of Multiple Scenarios by U.S. Industrial Companies," *Long-Range Planning,* 11 (February 1979), pp. 83–90.

CHAPTER 7

1. "Hallmark Now Stands for a Lot More Than Cards," *Business Week,* May 29, 1978, p. 57.
2. "Selling Business a Theory of Economics," *Business Week,* September 8, 1973, p. 85.
3. "Interpace: Zeroing In on a Single Product Line to Induce Growth," *Business Week,* July 17, 1978, p. 88.
4. "Corporate Strategies: Singer Company," *Business Week,* June 26, 1978.
5. Richard A. Smith, *Corporations in Crisis* (Garden City, N.Y.: Doubleday, 1963), p. 27.
6. Philip Kotler, *Marketing Management,* 2nd ed. (Englewood Cliffs, N.J.: Prentice-Hall, 1972), p. 237. *See* Kotler for other suggestions for generating ideas for marketing programs. Some of these have also been included in this section. Also see David J. Luck and Arthur E. Prell, *Marketing Strategy* (New York: Appleton-Century-Crofts), pp. 175–83.
7. This guideline (as well as some others which follow) is from Charles W. Hofer, "Toward a Contingency Theory of Business Strategy," *Academy of Management Journal,* 18, No. 4 (December 1975), 748–810; and Charles W. Hofer, "Research on Strategic Planning: A Survey on Past Studies and Suggestions for Future Efforts," *Journal of Economics and Business,* 28, No. 3 (Spring-Summer 1976), 261–86. Both are excellent articles, giving additional guidelines as well as containing excellent bibliographies.
8. Darryl J. Ellis and Peter P. Pekar, Jr., "Market Expansion Through Acquisition —A Planned Approach," *Industrial Marketing Management,* 6 (1977), 447–48; J. Kitching, "Why Do Mergers Miscarry?" *Harvard Business Review,* 45 (November-December 1967), 84–101.
9. Peter Drucker, *The New Enterprise* (New York: Harper & Row, 1968), p. 57.
10. "Basic Black," *Forbes,* December 15, 1977, p. 38.
11. *The Philadelphia Inquirer,* August 13, 1978, Sec. C, p. 8, Martin J. Sikora.
12. Herbert N. Woodward, "Management Strategies for Small Companies," *Harvard Business Review,* 54 (January-February 1976), pp. 113–121.
13. Donald K. Clifford, Jr., "Thriving in a Recession," *Harvard Business Review,* 55 (July-August 1977), 57–65.
14. William R. King and David I. Cleland, "Information for More Effective Strategic Planning," *Long-Range Planning,* 10 (February 1977), p. 59.
15. King and Cleland, "Information For More Effective Strategic Planning," p. 60.
16. "Piercing the Future Fog in the Executive Suite," *Business Week,* April 28, 1975, p. 49.

CHAPTER 8

1. Adapted by permission of the publisher from *Long-Range Planning for Your Business: An Operating Manual,* Merritt Kastens, © 1976 by AMACOM, a division of American Management Associations, pp. 68–69. All rights reserved. Kastens presents charts showing a different method of analyzing market growth, market penetration, and market share relationships which may provide additional clarity. Also, pages 64–85 offer a number of suggestions to "plug the gap," some of which have been incorporated in this chapter.
2. "Financial Controls Help a Valve Maker Expand," *Business Week,* August 1, 1977, p. 47.
3. Antony Jay, *Corporation Man* (New York: Random House, 1971), p. 175.
4. Max Gunther, *The Luck Factor* (New York: Macmillan, 1977).

CHAPTER 9

1. For a similar, yet more detailed approach, see Merritt Kastens, *Long-Range Planning for Your Business* (New York: AMACOM, 1976), Chaps. 8 and 9. Besides the more detailed approach, Kastens has many excellent down-to-earth ideas as to how to make planning work, some of which have been incorporated in this chapter.
2. "Simmons: A Turnaround Proves Hard to Bring Off," *Business Week,* June 5, 1978, p. 146.
3. Dennis Cooper-Jones, *Business Planning and Forecasting,* (New York-Toronto: John Wiley & Sons, A Halsted Press Book, 1974). Chapter 5, "Contingency Planning," contains a more detailed—and slightly different—explanation of how to implement variable budgeting. I am indebted to this source for several ideas.
4. "Emerson Electric's Rise as a Low-Cost Producer," *Business Week,* November 1, 1976, pp. 47–48.

CHAPTER 10

1. Many of the ideas expressed in this chapter are from Merritt Kastens, *Long-Range Planning for Your Business* (New York: AMACOM, 1976). For the reader who would like a more sophisticated approach to planning for implementation and control, it is highly recommended that you consult Kastens, especially Chaps. 10 and 11.

Index

A

B

C

D

E

F

G

N

O

P

Q

R

S

T